Development, Education, and Participatory Action Research to Empow Marginalized Groups

Drawing on a rich variety of participatory action research methods including ethnographic observation, artefact collection, focus groups, and interviews, this volume explores the transformational potential of development programs which actively involve marginalized groups. Foregrounding the experiences of women migrant workers in Beirut, the text reveals how direct participation in NGO-led, community programs and education empowers women to create counter-cultural communities and spaces for learning and activism. The text ultimately combines aspects of critical pedagogy, spatial analysis, and Third World feminisms to propose a critical subaltern praxis for research, development, and teaching. It will appeal to scholars and researchers with interests in research methods in education, migration, equality and human rights and the anthropology of education.

Shireen Keyl is Assistant Professor in the School of Teacher Education and Leadership at Utah State University, US.

Critical Ethnographic Research in Education

Series Editor: Julia Hall, D'Youville College, USA

Critical Ethnographic Research in Education is a unique blue book series grounded in explorations of the political economy and politics of education.

Today humanity is pushed to the brink by authoritative control, global extinction, urban implosion, rampant inequality; and state-sponsored violence and silencing for those who question and/or dare to live outside the norm. This series offers a place to disrupt and displace hierarchical, dominant discourses in education theory and policy. Multidisciplinary, theoretical perspectives and voices are investigated. The experiences of those on the margins of knowledge production are foregrounded. In pushing back against the forces that diminish critical thought, a wide range of immersive methods are featured.

The series includes authored and edited books featuring interviews/observations, oral histories, counter stories, multi-site, and multi-species approaches and looped field techniques. Also included are those positioned at the intersections of meaning across communication platforms, such as digital media, film, audio, and graphics. The goal is to decolonize, democratize, and think differently. This emphasis is more crucial than ever given life on the ground.

Books in this series include:

A Critical Ethnography of an Outdoor School
Reimagining the Relationship between Science Education and Climate Change Politics
Tristan Gleason

Development, Education, and Participatory Action Research to Empower Marginalized Groups
Critical Subaltern Ways of Knowing among Migrant Domestic Workers
Shireen Keyl

For more information about this series, please visit: https://www.routledge.com/Critical-Ethnographic-Research-in-Education/book-series/CERE

Development, Education, and Participatory Action Research to Empower Marginalized Groups

Critical Subaltern Ways of Knowing among Migrant Domestic Workers

Shireen Keyl

Routledge
Taylor & Francis Group
NEW YORK AND LONDON

First published 2022
by Routledge
605 Third Avenue, New York, NY 10158

and by Routledge
4 Park Square, Milton Park, Abingdon, Oxon OX14 4RN

Routledge is an imprint of the Taylor & Francis Group, an informa business

Library of Congress Cataloging-in-Publication Data
A catalog record for this title has been requested

ISBN: 978-0-367-76345-9 (hbk)
ISBN: 978-0-367-76348-0 (pbk)
ISBN: 978-1-003-16656-6 (ebk)

DOI: 10.4324/9781003166566

Typeset in Sabon
by KnowledgeWorks Global Ltd.

This book is dedicated to all the migrant domestic workers worldwide and the grassroots NGOs that work in partnership with them. This book is also dedicated to my daughter, Grace Sophia Keyl.

Contents

Acknowledgments

Many people helped me bring this work to fruition: to my Routledge editorial team, Elsbeth Wright and AnnaMary Goodall, whose helpful and constructive critiques made this work see publication: I cannot thank you enough. Certainly, any shortcomings are mine alone. I also thank the series editor Julia Hall for seeing this project through and believing in this work, thank you! To my friend and colleague, Nayel Badareen, I owe a special thank you for your help with the Arabic translations. To Farah Salka, my dear friend in Lebanon: your work inspires me daily – you are my mentor and teacher for always, رفيقم! My parents Joseph and Joyce have been very supportive every step of the way with editorial and emotional support. I thank the migrant domestic workers whose lived experiences are the foundation of this book. Lastly, I thank my daughter, Grace Sophia Keyl, and dedicate this work to her. None of this would have been possible without her love, understanding, and support.

Abbreviations

ARM	Anti-Racism Movement
AUB	American University Beirut
CBPR	Community-based Participatory Research
CCCoP	Counter-Cultural Communities of Practice
CLS	Critical Legal Studies
CRT	Critical Race Theory
DS	Development Studies
GAD	Gender and Development
GRO	Grassroots Organization
HRW	Human Rights Watch
ILO	International Labour Organization
ISIS	Islamic State of Iraq and Syria
LAU	Lebanese American University
MC	Migrant Center
MENA	Middle East and North Africa
MWEG	Migrant Workers Educational Group
NGO	Non-Governmental Organization
PAR	Participatory Action Research
SWANA	South West Asia and North Africa
TTE	Teaching and Teacher Education
ZPD	Zone of Proximal Development

Chapter 1

Introduction

The Intersection of Migrant Domestic Labor in Beirut, Lebanon, and the Development Sector

Women's Labor Migration

Subaltern populations, be they migrant workers, refugee populations, or asylum seekers, oftentimes flee economic despair, climate change-fueled natural disasters, sectarian and religious violence, and human rights atrocities in their home countries. Since 2010, it has been estimated that over 230 million people live outside of their countries of origin; this number accounts for about 3 percent of the world's population (Williams & Baláž, 2014). For those who migrate for economic reasons, this number continues to increase: In 2015, the number of international migrants reached 244 million, up from 173 million in 2000 (Gray, 2016). In the Global North, women migrants outnumber men migrants, with a high concentration of women migrants in Europe and Northern America (McAuliffe & Triandafyllidou, 2021). This trend can be seen in the Middle East/ South West Asia and North Africa (SWANA) region as well. In Lebanon, with a total population of over 6.7 million (World Population Review, 2022), migrant domestic workers comprise 300,000 of the total population (Kassamali, 2021) coming from African countries such as Ethiopia and Southeast Asian countries such as Sri Lanka, Nepal, and the Philippines (see Figure 1.1).

Migrant domestic workers are often the most vulnerable compared to other migratory groups for several reasons: First, domestic laborers are usually women, and they are forced to live in the homes of employers, which radically increases their vulnerable status. Additionally, domestic workers are required to enter their work country by way of the *kafala* system, which is the visa sponsorship system to legally work in many Middle East/ SWANA countries. Employers pay job agents upwards of 2,000–3,000 USD, and this payment instills within the employer a sense of ownership of the domestic worker: The employer or job agent confiscates her passport and her autonomy becomes non-existent, rendering them agentless and incapacitated.

DOI: 10.4324/9781003166566-1

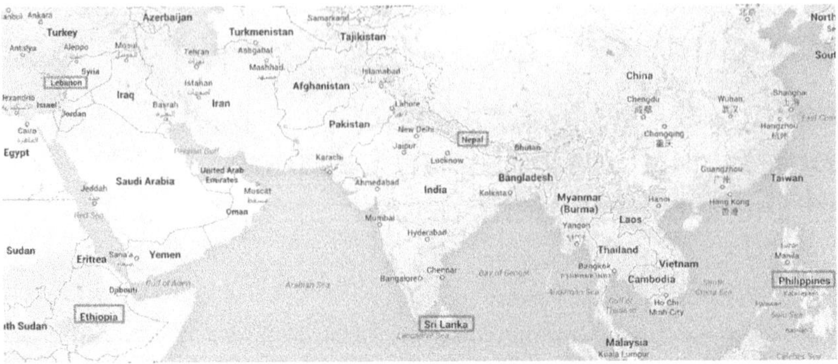

Figure I.1 Map showing home countries of migrant domestic workers and Lebanon

Source: Google Maps.

Throughout the decades, a gendered pattern in labor migration has emerged. According to the 2022 United Nations report on migration and women migrant workers, women comprise around 41.5% of the world's migrants (McAuliffe & Triandafyllidou, 2021, p. 37). Trends of women's international migration from the Global South to the Arab League States have increased rapidly since the 1960s. For example, according to a 2004 ILO report, in the United Arab Emirates, there was a 2,398% increase in women's migration from 1975 with 1,340 women migrants to 1985 with 32,134 women migrants (Sabban, 2004). Migratory patterns are referred to as the feminization of labor migration (Chammartin, 2002; Esim & Smith, 2004; Jureidini & Moukarbel, 2004; Manseau, 2007; Oishi, 2005). Several factors have influenced women's migration into the Middle East/SWANA region. In the 1970s, many Gulf countries experienced an oil boom, which provided their economies with the ability to pour money into the building of their infrastructures, resulting in an increase in male migrant labor (al-Najjar, 2004). Additionally, Arab women's participation in the labor force, especially within the white-collar sector, precipitated a need for domestic services (al-Najjar, 2004; Oishi, 2005). Oishi (2005) contends that the influx of oil wealth has increased conspicuous consumption; as a result, the ability to afford such a luxury as a domestic worker is the deciding factor in the employment of said worker (p. 47). Also noteworthy is the idea that employing domestic workers represents a measure of financial success, a "status symbol" of sorts, suggesting the family is of elite status within society (Jureidini, 2011; Oishi, 2005; Sabban, 2004).

Human Rights Issues of Migrant Workers

In the past two decades, awareness of the human rights abuses sustained by migrant workers in the Middle East/SWANA region has increased and drawn public scrutiny. For instance, Al Jazeera English documents these abuses regularly, such as the execution of a Sri Lankan housemaid, Rizana Nafeek, who was charged in the death of a child that was in her care in Saudi Arabia in 2007. She was sentenced to death and was beheaded in January 2013. Human rights groups questioned the fairness of her trial due to Ms. Nafeek's lack of access to adequate translation services and legal assistance ("Anger at Saudi Beheading of Sri Lankan Maid", para. 7). Human rights groups have taken a leadership role in bringing the plight of migrant domestic workers to the global forum.

Migration studies literature also focuses on the human rights atrocities endured by migrant workers and refugees and details the abject social and work conditions these groups suffer while in the host country (Esim & Smith, 2004; Jureidini, 2010, 2011; Manseau, 2007). Some of these studies are formal reports produced by governmental and non-governmental organizations (NGOs) such as the International Labour Organization (ILO) and Human Rights Watch (HRW) to document the abuse of migrant workers in host countries. A 2004 HRW report titled *Bad Dreams: Exploitation and Abuse of Migrant Workers in Saudi Arabia* details the wage exploitation, human rights atrocities in the criminal justice system, sexual, physical, and psychological abuse in employers' homes, and racism and xenophobia in Saudi society to name some of the exploitative and oppressive practices in Saudi Arabia perpetuated upon migrant workers. This HRW report was the first of its kind that focused specifically on the plight of migrant workers in Saudi Arabia (Sherry, 2004, p. 2).

According to a 2004 ILO report, migrant domestic workers residing in Lebanon suffer from similar human rights atrocities as the migrant workers in Saudi Arabia: They often have their wages withheld and suffer from verbal, physical, and sexual abuse. They are confined to the household and not provided days off; are given very little to eat while working a very labor-intensive job for often 12 or more hours a day; and are expected to work in the homes of their employers' relatives without pay (p. 70). This same report documents the case of Freda, a migrant domestic worker from the Philippines:

> Freda is an example of a woman from the Philippines who was given little food and not permitted to have any contact with the outside world. She was rationed to an egg, three spoons of rice and a small salad once per day. The employer's refrigerator had an alarm attached, which sounded throughout the house as soon as the door was opened. Madam[1] would personally take out the food for her. Freda slept in the laundry on a mattress on the floor, along with the washing machine and clothes dryer. Although her sister was also working in Lebanon, she was not allowed to contact her. Furthermore, she had been able to send one letter to her family in the Philippines. She later discovered that her family had sent letters every month to her. She had received only one. (Esim & Smith, 2004, p. 71)

Stories like this are unfortunately all too common and have been documented in several sources such as newspapers, published reports, scholarly research, and human rights organizations.

Racialization of Migrant Domestic Workers

In a 1998 essay, Lina Abu-Habib addresses the abuse and exploitation of migrant workers, especially women working in domestic service. She highlights the issue of the racialization that occurs in domestic employment. In one such example, Abu-Habib relays an experience of a politician speaking at a public rally where he complained to his constituents that some marginalized Arab minority groups were being treated in a deplorable condition "as if they were Sri Lankans" (p. 52). This statement highlights how the racialization of migrant workers has permeated the collective mind so much so that not only does the public domain understand these statements, but it is also completely acceptable to propagate such dehumanizing discourse within the public sphere. Jureidini (2004) also observes the racialization of domestic work in Lebanon – he notes that Arab women see domestic positions as degrading and unacceptable:

> Since the influx of foreign women from Africa and Asia particularly, the position of domestic maids has become one that carries with it a particularly low status...not only because of the servile nature of the tasks, the conditions of work and relatively low wages, but also because there is now a racial attachment to domestic employment. (pp. 65–66)

The common view that domestic labor is degrading and should be fulfilled by those who are "less than" runs parallel to the xenophobic and racist attitudes held by many Lebanese people toward foreign workers. Lebanese and non-Lebanese alike have argued the notion that "Lebanese are racist" (Jureidini, 2011, p. 10).

When a society at large holds such dehumanizing views, it is no wonder migrant workers experience degradation in the form of sexual, physical, and psychological abuse. For some domestic workers, suicide becomes a solution to escape such despair. According to a 2008 HRW report, on average, one foreign domestic worker per week commits suicide or dies in suspicious circumstances in Lebanon (para. 3). This reality reflects a dire human rights situation for many migrant workers, especially women; however, it does not stop women from migrating for employment opportunities in the face of great adversity, sometimes more than once. The tenuous political and economic conditions of their home countries compel women to take dangerous and often calculated risks in the hope of acquiring an income for the betterment of their families and themselves. Oftentimes, employment agencies lie to migrant domestic workers about the terms of their employment contract. For instance, they sign a one-year contract to work in the hotel industry but in actuality they are forced to work for three years as a domestic worker in a private home.

Current Situation in Lebanon: Instability of Lebanese Economy and Infrastructure

Because the initial fieldwork of this project was undertaken in Lebanon in 2012, it is important to note the changes that impact the lives of migrant domestic workers that have taken place since. The challenges migrant domestic workers faced and continue to face have been intensified by the 2019 financial collapse of Lebanon's economy. The economic collapse was the result of prolonged corruption and a depreciating currency: As of fall 2019, the Lebanese pound has lost almost 90% of its value, and consumer prices have increased 146% ("Lebanon Economic Collapse in Numbers", 2021). The Lebanese government cannot supply the most basic of utilities such as electricity. Food scarcity is at an all-time high while the poverty rate has skyrocketed to over 50% (Balkiz, Qiblawi, & Wedeman, 2020). A few months later in February 2020, COVID-19 appeared in Lebanon filling hospitals that were already hard hit by a lack of medical staff and supplies and unable to pay staff due to the economic crisis. As if the situation in Lebanon could not get worse, on August 4, 2020, an explosion in the Beirut port was detonated by the equivalent of 1.1 kilotons of TNT – so powerful was the blast it was heard in Cyprus ("Beirut Explosion Causes Strong Shock Waves", 2021), caused 15 billion USD worth of destruction (Hussain & Cohn, 2020), caused 300,000 to become homeless (Regencia, Alsaafin, & Allahoum, 2020), caused over 200 fatalities (Baloch, 2020), and added to the misery of an already tragedy-filled country.

This series of events became even more catastrophic for vulnerable groups like migrant domestic workers. COVID-19 exacerbated their already exploited status, as lockdowns increased the risk of abuse and overwork of migrant domestic workers at the hands of their employers. Amnesty International (2020) issued a statement declaring "The right to health, health care goods, facilities and services should be available and accessible to everyone without discrimination, especially to the most vulnerable or marginalized groups of society", especially migrant workers. In the aftermath of the economic crisis, COVID-19, and the explosion, some employers could no longer afford to uphold the job contract and keep migrant domestic workers in their employ. Several domestic workers were either kicked out of their employers' homes or dropped off at their job agencies or embassies without their paychecks and no access to food or shelter. Domestic workers sleeping on the streets with their suitcases with no way to return to their home countries became the norm in the aftermath of these multiple crises (Taleb, 2021).

Why this Book

At the intersections of women's migration, development studies (DS), critical theory, anthropology of education, and area studies, particularly the Middle East/SWANA region, this project hopes to contribute to a critical subaltern theory and practice for the benefit of those who cross borders in search of safety and who labor within an oppressive system – and for those who stand shoulder to shoulder with oppressed groups in an effort to empower them by amplifying and privileging the knowledge of the oppressed. In the international development sector, many NGOs do the "boots on the ground" work of advocacy, sustainability, and direction action. In the recent past, listening to the "voices of the knowers" (Wimpenny, 2010), that is, the populations receiving aid, was not a widely accepted course of action, as most NGOs were being managed by Western entities. However, it is more readily practiced to center subaltern voices and recognize their funds of knowledge as being a valuable source of knowledge to produce desired actions, especially within grassroots NGOs, which tend to function on community engagement. This book forwards a critical subaltern theory and practice for organizing and for educational initiatives.

What is a Critical Subaltern Theory and Practice?

Within post-DS, critical analyses of why and how we "do" development have contributed to a rich and thought-provoking body of scholarship that helps us to deconstruct the motivations and far reach of development; and, critical theory has clearly had its influence in the analyses put forth. In conjunction with a critical analysis of development is a critical analysis of how and why we teach the way we do; accordingly, critical pedagogy is its manifestation. Most educators in nonformal educational settings, such as NGOs in developing countries, tend to be volunteers with little teacher training; and most tend to be Western foreigners with little understanding of the lived experiences of border crossers like migrant workers, refugees, or asylum seekers. This book serves as a theoretical and practical justification for a critical subaltern praxis.

Focal Participants

As Wimpenny (2010) states, "[k]nowledge should be developed in collaboration with local experts; the voices of the 'knowers'" (p. 9). The knowledge produced in this project was the result of amplifying the "voices of the knowers" by centering their expertise, their leadership, and their insights. In 2011, the impetus for creating the NGO organization at the center of this study resulted from the activists' frustration with an existing system mired in bureaucracy and corruption that was not in alignment with their feminist, anti-racist, and decolonizing vision. Furthermore, they rejected the hierarchical structure of traditional NGOs in which power is concentrated at the top of the system, while the very communities they assist are viewed as receivers of services, not partners nor experts. As a result, the Lebanese activists partnered with migrant domestic workers to create an egalitarian system of shared knowledge, empowerment, and activism. Ten years later, this incredibly resilient NGO activist community continues to labor as migrant domestic workers, activists, volunteer teachers, and change-makers under unbelievable circumstances of duress. Below, I describe the people whose knowledge and action made this project come to fruition.

1 Fakira[2]: Fakira, a Lebanese woman who was 30 years old at the time of this project, is one of the key focal participants as one of the co-founders of Tamkin, the feminist NGO, and director of the Anti-Racism Movement, an initiative that existed under the umbrella of Tamkin. Fakira, in collaboration with fellow Lebanese activists, passionately endorsed a system of knowledge production and action not solely contingent on outsider/Western funding, unlike traditional NGOs in Lebanon that competed for financial assistance from Western-backed donors. Instead, she helped to create an organizational structure whose critical ideas truly inform its critical practice, as evidenced by the data collected in this study. For the past 10+ years, Fakira has labored hand in hand with migrant domestic workers, fighting the *kafala* system, organizing street protests, and helping to create spaces for formal and nonformal learning opportunities.
2 Suba: Suba is a Nepali 25-year-old former domestic worker who was hired as the coordinator of the Migrant Center (MC). She is married to Dakshi, and together they have a young toddler. Suba received a college education from Nepal. She was responsible for the day-to-day operations of the Center. She met with Fakira often to consult on financial matters, coordinate community leadership, and help in organizing activist activities. She identifies as an activist and advocate for migrant domestic worker rights.
3 Dakshi: As mentioned above, Dakshi is married to Suba and they share a young son. Dakshi assists Suba with coordination tasks of the Center. Like his wife, he is a community leader for the Nepali migrant workers in Lebanon. Dakshi followed up on the criminal investigations regarding the unnatural deaths of migrant workers collaborating with migrant advocacy agencies.
4 Faith: Faith is a domestic worker from Kenya. She has a bachelor's degree from her home country and at the time of this writing she was 29 years old. Back in her home country, her family was taking care of her five-year-old son. Faith was a victim of human trafficking: She was recruited by a job agency that lied to her about her job contract, telling

her she would work in customer service at a hotel; instead, she was tricked into working at a private home where she endured death threats from the madam. She eventually ran away from the employer's home, but was undocumented as the employer had confiscated her passport. Faith was living with other migrant workers living in fear of getting arrested. Undocumented workers face prison time when they run away from their abusive work situations. She and I met at the MC.

5 Felicity: Felicity is a 38-year-old domestic worker from Nigeria. She had attended a trade school in her home country and received training as a seamstress. She speaks five languages and has been in Beirut for five years as a domestic worker. Her employer was agreeable to Felicity working outside the home as a freelancer. Felicity states that her employer is respectful and kind. Felicity was also working as an independent fashion designer creating pieces from her own patterns that fuse African styles with more modern designs. She has a catalog to create custom order dresses. Felicity cannot read nor write yet has been a successful entrepreneur in her custom clothing business and freelancing in domestic labor. I met Felicity at the MC and she was my student.

6 Helena: Twenty-four-year-old Helena is from Ethiopia and has a high school diploma. I met her at the MC and she was in my EFL class at the MC. At this point, she had lived in Beirut for four years as a domestic worker.

7 Amara: Amara is also from Ethiopia and 25 years old. She has been living and working in Beirut for almost three years. Like most migrant domestic workers, she began to work as a domestic laborer because of the impoverished situation in her home country and her family was in great financial need. Her father died when she was young. She desired to attend university one day, as many migrant participants expressed.

8 Laurencia: Twenty-eight-year-old Laurencia is from Madagascar. She was attending the MC EFL classes. Laurencia and Suba became a close support system to each other because they both had young children and shared knowledge in how to navigate the racism and xenophobia prevalent in Lebanese society as mothers belonging to the migrant community.

9 Giftee: Thirty-year-old Giftee is from Ethiopia and has about two years of a high school education. She had been in Lebanon for almost 10 years when I came to know her. I met Giftee at the MC where she was taking EFL classes.

10 Antsa: Antsa is from the Ivory Coast and was 29 years old at the time of our interview. She has some college education. Antsa had what she described as a favorable employment situation as her employer encouraged her to attend the MC, honored the employment contract, and did

not overwork her. I met Antsa at the MC where she was my student in our EFL classes.

11 Naomi: Twenty-five-year-old Naomi is from Ethiopia with one year of a high school education. She is involved in the activist community activities such as Rakeb's theatre group and also attends *kafala* protests. Naomi attests to the power of shared knowledge production, as we will read in Chapter 5.

12 Rakeb: Rakeb is Ethiopian and 32 years old with a high school degree. She had been in Lebanon for 12 years at the time of this project. In her home country as a child, she attended theatre workshops. In Beirut, she has written, produced, and acted in her own plays that detail the lived experiences of domestic workers. Rakeb organizes and participates in *kafala* protests. She recently founded her own NGO that provides legal help, education, medical attention, and shelter for migrant domestic workers in need.

13 Thomas: Thomas is from Nigeria and was 34 years old at the time of this project. We met at the MC. Thomas came to Lebanon originally as a student but became a born-again Christian and decided to become a full-time pastor.

14 Maha: Maha is 30 years old and has her master's in social justice from a university in the United States. Maha is Lebanese and grew up in an African country because her father was employed overseas. Maha was the coordinator of volunteer teachers for the Migrant Workers Educational Group (MWEG). She was responsible for teacher recruitment, curriculum development, teacher meetings, and trainings. Maha's social justice background was apparent in her ideas about education of oppressed groups: She believes that education serves more than the purpose of formal learning, but rather the classroom acts as a counterspace, especially for marginalized groups in a hostile society to facilitate relationships, trust, and safety (Yosso & Lopez, 2010). Maha believes that an educator can simultaneously be an activist and an educator in their teaching practice.

15 Alim: Twenty-one-year-old Alim is Lebanese working toward a bachelor's in business and was volunteering at the MWEG as a teacher.

16 Omid: Omid is Lebanese and was 21 years old at the time of this project. He had been volunteering at MWEG as a teacher for almost two years. He was a pre-med student who had some previous experience as a health educator running reproductive and sexual health workshops. Currently, Omid is a physician-researcher at a well-known university on the U.S. east coast. He is identified as a teacher-activist.

17 Abe: Abe is Lebanese and was also 21 years old. He was finishing up his bachelor's in mechanical engineering, and is currently working on his Ph.D. in a European country. He had been volunteering at MWEG for almost one year as a teacher. He identified as a teacher-activist.

18 Sofia: Sofia was a 26-year-old Italian woman volunteering as a teacher at MWEG for four months. Sofia had some teaching experience volunteering as a tutor in her home country for refugee students who had sought asylum in Italy from Morocco. She also volunteered at an orphanage in Burundi, Africa, as a daycare worker. She was in Lebanon attending a master's program in Islamic studies and also taking Arabic language classes.
19 Ashraf: Ashraf is Lebanese-French and was 26 years old during this project. He was volunteering at MWEG as a French teacher. Suba had recruited him to teach French. He was currently finishing his graduate work in a Ph.D. program in France.

Context for this Study

In summer 2010, I conducted a two-month, Institutional Review Board (IRB)-approved study at a women's center in Tehran, Iran, where I taught an English language course and interviewed the center's administrators, social workers, teachers, and students. This center was an NGO with the goal of assisting young Iranian girls and women from backgrounds of abuse and neglect and Afghan refugees to attain social services, educational opportunities, and medical services. The emerging theme in my research that caused the most tension was the Center's feminist agenda of women's empowerment. Because a majority of the women who received services come from marginalized backgrounds, the Center believed it was essential to instill in the students a sense of empowerment, self-esteem, and self-awareness that is informed by Western or White feminist ideology (Grande, 2004). For example, one of the workshop leaders who was Iranian-American and educated in the United States cited the text *Women's Ways of Knowing* (Belenky et al., 1997) as the source of her ideas for feminism and empowerment. This work is well-respected by many Western feminist scholars and considered influential in terms of its ideas about feminist epistemology; however, the question that arose for me during this fieldwork was, Is it not problematic to "import" Western ideas about knowledge production informed by largely homogenous populations, such as the study conducted for *Women's Ways of Knowing* research, that draws from one nationality (American), one socioeconomic group (middle- to upper-middle class population), and largely from one ethnically homogenous group (White research participants) – to the neglect of other categories of analysis, such as ethnicity, class, religion, nationality, and sexual identity?

Also worthy of noting was the racialized dimension that was evident in this study. Half of the students at the Center were Afghan refugees; problematic at the Center was that some administrators and teachers gave Iranian students preferential treatment over Afghan students. Afghan students frequently told me they experienced xenophobia, racism, and structural discrimination within Iranian society. The Afghan students, at that time, had not reported that any positive steps had been undertaken to deal with the internal discrimination they frequently encountered from students and administrators alike.

Both Iranian and Afghan students commonly come from practicing religious households, so Western ideas of feminism that neglect Islamic values are not necessarily viewed favorably. As Sohrab, a social worker at the Center, stated, "Ideas of self-empowerment within these walls [of the Center] are fine, but how do we make that idea of empowerment meaningful for these girls within Iranian society so that it does not cause internal conflict? Why don't we contextualize their experiences so empowerment makes sense?" The internal conflict Iranian and Afghan students experienced and that Sohrab described is caused by an ideological disconnect, a lack of congruency between the NGO's feminist agenda, and the lived experiences of the women who seek the services of these organizations.

Decolonizing Research in the South West Asia and North Africa (SWANA) Region

I had read extensively during my graduate program about the problematics of Western researchers performing fieldwork in the "Third World" and "developing" countries. In my master's program in Near Eastern Studies at the University of Arizona, I had for the first time been exposed to the writings of Edward Said in his book, *Orientalism* (2014). His ideas resonated deeply with me as the daughter of an Iranian immigrant who grew up in the Chicagoland area in a predominantly White suburb – I was all too familiar with what it felt to be otherized, fetishized, objectified, and discriminated against, especially throughout my U.S. schooling. Then I began reading the scholarship of Lila Abu-Lughod, Chandra Mohanty, and Gyatri Spivak as I continued on my academic journey, which introduced me to the necessity of decolonizing my mind, and the continuous journey of reflexivity required of me as a woman, a mother, an educator, and researcher. And, if I were to continue to do any type of work in the Middle East/SWANA region, it was expedient to participate in this intellectual and emotional transformation.

At the women's center in Tehran, to see with my own eyes how Western-trained researchers, being of Iranian origin no less, attempt to "fix" the women at the Iranian center armed with Western feminism was a powerful learning experience for two reasons: First, those with heritage ties to the Middle East/SWANA region continuously must work to unlearn the fallacy that the Western canon of knowledge is superior to knowledges in the local context. Second, as an U.S.-trained researcher of Iranian heritage, I would be remiss not to acknowledge the power disparity that exists between myself as an U.S. American and the participants I interact with in the field, and actively work to not replicate the damage caused by preceding researchers. For this reason, I commit to decolonizing and participatory research paradigms.

The good news is that shifts in social science fieldwork are slowly taking place. In 2018–2019, I was a Fulbright Scholar in Amman, Jordan. I was heartened to see, during the first day-orientation in Amman, that a copy of Nayel's (2013) essay, "Palestinian Refugees Are Not at Your Service", was passed out to all U.S. scholars. Nayel shares his own experience as a translator working in refugee camps in Lebanon assisting U.S. researchers and their trainees from Ivy league institutions. He observes how the researchers demanded information from a woman refugee whose son had recently sustained head trauma from shrapnel while fleeing the civil conflict in Syria, with no concern for this mother's grief and anguish. While I am glad to see Fulbright administrators making efforts to disrupt the blatant exploitation committed by U.S. researchers in the fieldwork process, it is also distressing that, in the twenty-first century, such blatant exploitation still exists. I say all this for the reader, as they read this text, to enact reflexivity, exercise humility, and be teachable by the local experts and those they desire to partner with, help, and assist.

Based on the pilot study at the Tehran women's center, I learned that within the development and NGO sectors, therein potentially lie ideological disconnects that can affect the pedagogical theory and practice of an organization, which, in turn, can potentially impact the efficacy of program goals; I entered my research site in Beirut, Lebanon, which was also an NGO system that provided educational opportunities for marginalized groups, with this understanding. In this space, the NGO system assisted African and Southeast Asian migrant domestic workers, some of whom were victims of human trafficking. This system is comprised of three main entities: Tamkin, a feminist collective and NGO; the MC, a migrant community space managed by migrant workers in conjunction with Tamkin; and the MWEG, a grassroots collective of volunteers who teach language and computer classes to migrant workers.

Research Questions: Theory, Practice, and Knowledge Production

As I entered my site, and, learning what I had from the NGO in Iran, I wanted to learn about three main issues, mainly regarding the ideology and functionality of this NGO system and of their educational opportunities: 1. What are the theoretical and pedagogical constructs of this NGO system and are they congruent to the lived experiences of the women migrant workers? 2. How does migrant workers' knowledge production inform power and empowerment of their community? 3. What role does the MC play in the education and empowerment of migrant workers? As an authentic educator, critical scholar, and researcher, my main objective is to theorize practices to understand how to improve existing pedagogical functionality and encapsulate a praxis specifically for migrant workers, refugees, border crossers, the colonized, or any subaltern peoples. A pedagogical theory and practice could have ramifications for the way one "does" development and the way one "does" education for subaltern groups. Because most allocation of services for subaltern groups is provided under the auspices of NGO services, such a critical subaltern praxis is expedient for any local member (e.g., practitioners, volunteer teachers, coordinators, administrators, other community members, and the recipients of services themselves) who works with these populations, either directly or indirectly.

Why "Doing" Development Differently Matters

A paradigm shift in the development sector is necessary for two reasons: The first reason is that we live in an ever-increasing globalized world, where transnational and internal movement is on the rise. Such an influx in movement precipitates a theoretical shift in how we conceptualize the world around us, especially in terms of formal and nonformal education. For instance, the recent U.S. military withdrawal from Afghanistan and the subsequent government takeover by the Taliban have led to a mass exodus of Afghans fleeing to receiving countries. Since late summer 2021, the United States and other Western countries have been in the process of resettlement of Afghan refugees ("Waves of Afghan Refugees Are Arriving in the U.S.", 2021). Such a situation necessitates an urgency to provide these children the medical, social, and educational services they need. And, for the refugee agencies and educators, administrators, and caregivers who encounter these children in classrooms or other learning spaces, a critical subaltern theory and practice is advantageous to all involved in the learning process.

A paradigm shift in the development sector is necessary for an additional reason: DS tends not to be interested in knowledge generation for its own sake but more for its applied or instrumental value; the development industry is not inherently interested in the epistemological, ontological, or theorizing processes of its own discipline (Sumner & Tribe, 2008, p. 35). If the development sector does not value the knowledge production of its own field of study, and development is predicated upon notions of prescriptive action, how can development value the knowledge production of the populations and entities they want to assist? This study aims to theorize subaltern ways of knowing as valuable funds of knowledge that are not only advantageous in empowered spaces of learning, but to the efficacy of the development and NGO sector as well.

Prior to discussing the chapter overviews, it is important to identify the interdisciplinary nature of this study, as it draws from the critical theories as they relate to two main fields of study: education and DS. While the literature of the former speaks to the critical pedagogical theories and critical teaching and learning that occur in educational spaces, the DS literature review serves as a platform to examine the deficit nature of development's historical genesis, its prescriptive nature, and the lack of reflexivity of the field and its practitioners itself; as such, the analysis of the latter is informed by a post-development theoretical lens. Also worthy of mention is that the anthropologist's voice contributes to the field of DS (Gupta & Ferguson, 1997; Sharma, 2008); to be sure, the existence of the subfield of development anthropology demonstrates the significance of the anthropological lens to the field of DS.

The critical pedagogue and philosopher from whom I draw continuously throughout this study is Paulo Freire, who is considered one of the founding members of critical pedagogy and is responsible for bringing a critical and social consciousness to the study of teaching and learning. Freire's work is sparingly cited in the development literature, with some exceptions. Critical pedagogy, as an educational theory and philosophy, as a teaching practice, and as a research methodological approach (De Genova, 2005, pp. 23–25), has monumental implications for the researcher-practitioner in the development sector.

Chapter Divisions

In the current chapter, I have introduced the issues that surround labor migration for women, such as the feminization and racialization of women's migration and the human rights issues women who migrate encounter in the host country. I then provide a theoretical framework for this book, that being a critical subaltern theory and practice, and its significance in the current context of development and NGO work. Also within this chapter can be found a justification for decolonizing research in the Middle East/ SWANA region, and an explanation for why a paradigm shift in how we "do" development matters.

Chapter 2 focuses on critical theory. Because the fieldwork of this study was conducted in the Middle East/SWANA region where the United States has a long and complicated history, and the research participants of this study have been historically and socially subjugated, marginalized, and oppressed, not just in the host country but in their homelands as well, this study demands a critical theoretical approach situating it in its historical context. I then present a historical summary of development and the NGO sector, followed by a description of the DS literature, specifically the post-development theories that critically scrutinize development as a practice. The second part of the chapter closely examines feminist postcolonial thought, critical race theory, and critical pedagogy; I situate the discussion of critical race theory and anti-Blackness in the Middle East/SWANA region context. I close Chapter 2 with a discussion of the constructs that inform critical pedagogical theorizing.

In Chapter 3, I present this study's research methodology. I start the chapter providing an in-depth justification for the pilot study in Tehran, Iran, and the focal research project in Beirut, Lebanon, then segueing into a description of participatory action research and its use in this study. I then describe my positionality as a researcher with heritage ties to the Middle East region and how my lived experiences growing up in the United States as an Iranian-American shaped my own ideological framing and interpretation of social phenomena. I use a community-based participatory research approach and position myself within a social justice orientation. The last part of Chapter 3 describes my design of grounded theory, the tools for data analysis, my sampling method, a description of the participants, and an explanation of data analysis.

In Chapters 4–6, I employ an analysis of the data from my fieldwork. Chapter 4 analyses the narratives of the migrant domestic workers relaying their encounters with human trafficking, sexual abuse, xenophobia, and racism in Beirut and orients the discussion to the constructions of "power as domination" as situated in an analysis informed by the works of Foucault and Bourdieu to illustrate how oppressive forces attempt to disempower migrant workers. I utilize Foucault's (1984) conceptualization of disciplining the body by way of the panopticon and the ideas of Bourdieu's (1986) habitus, field, and capital. Chapter 5 examines migrant domestic workers' knowledge production in interstitial, subaltern spaces through narratives of empowerment and resistance. Chapter 6 provides an overview of the NGO system: the MC, the educational and cultural space for migrant domestic workers; Tamkin, the feminist collective who provides the scaffolding for the MC; and the MWEG, the group that provides volunteer teachers for the computer and language classes that are held at the MC. I approach the teaching and learning that occurs at the MC by presenting the pedagogical perspectives of volunteers who teach language and computer classes to migrant workers. In particular, I bring to the forefront their justifications for participating in the migrant-activist movements, their thoughts on Western development, and their on-the-ground experiences teaching migrant workers. This chapter illustrates the Freirean framework utilized in this NGO, grassroots system. In Chapter 7, I introduce the idea of a critical subaltern praxis, by drawing from spatial analysis (Soja, 2010), critical pedagogy (Freire, 1970), and postcolonial/Third World feminist thought (Abu-Lughod, 2002; Said, 1978; Spivak, 1988). Such a praxical turn is meant to heed the call for a paradigm shift in DS as asserted by post-development theorists (Escobar, 2000) and inform new ways of contributing to projects of development that utilize subaltern epistemological spaces for critical teaching and learning. I conclude this chapter by including the implications for a critical subaltern theory and practice, and ideas for future research.

Note

1 "Madam" and "Mister" are the conventional titles used by migrant domestic workers when addressing employers.
2 I use pseudonyms to protect the anonymity of this study's participants.

References

Abu-Habib, L. (1998). The use and abuse of female domestic workers from Sri Lanka in Lebanon. *Gender and Development*, *6*(1), 52–56. https://doi.org/10.1080/741922630

Abu-Lughod, L. (2002). Do Muslim women really need saving? Anthropological reflections on cultural relativism and its others. *American Anthropologist*, *104*(3), 783–790. https://doi.org/10.1525/aa.2002.104.3.783

al-Najjar, S. (2004). Women migrant domestic workers in Bahrain. In S. Esim & M. Smith (Eds.), *Gender and migration in Arab States: The case of domestic workers*. Beirut: International Labour Organisation.

Amnesty International. (2020, April 14). Lebanon: Migrant domestic workers must be protected during COVID-19 pandemic. Retrieved from https://www.amnesty.org/en/latest/news/2020/04/lebanon-migrant-domestic-workers-must-be-protected-during-covid19-pandemic/

Anger at Saudi beheading of Sri Lankan maid. (2013, January 10). Al Jazeera English. Retrieved from https://www.aljazeera.com/news/2013/1/10/anger-at-saudi-beheading-of-sri-lankan-maid

Balkiz, G., Qiblawi, T., & Wedeman, B. (2020, August 5). Beirut explosion shatters windows across Lebanese capital. CNN. Retrieved from https://www.cnn.com/2020/08/04/middleeast/beirut-explosion-port-intl/index.html

Baloch, B. (2020). Beirut blast death toll includes dozens of refugees, emergency response ramps up. UNHCR. Retrieved from https://www.unhcr.org/news/briefing/2020/8/5f32469f4/beirut-blast-death-toll-includes-dozens-refugees-emergency-response-ramps.html

Belenky, M. F., Clinchy, B. M., Goldberger, N. R., & Tarule, J. M. (1997). *Women's ways of knowing: The development of self, voice, and mind*. New York, NY: Basic books.

Bourdieu, P. (1986). The forms of capital. In J. Richardson (Ed.), *Handbook of theory and research for the sociology of education* (pp. 241–258). New York: Greenwood.

Bundesanstalt für Geowissenschaften und Rohstoffe. (2021, March 19). Beirut explosion causes strong shock waves. Retrieved from https://www.seismologie.bgr.de/sdac/erdbeben/big_quakes/beirut_200804_eng.html

Chammartin, G. M. F. (2002). The feminization of international migration. *International Migration Program*, 39–47. https://library.fes.de/pdf-files/gurn/00072.pdf

De Genova, N. (2005). *Working the boundaries: Race, space, and "illegality" in Mexican Chicago*. Durham, NC: Duke University Press. https://doi.org/10.2307/j.ctv120qt8g

Escobar, A. (2000). Beyond the search for a paradigm? Post-development and beyond. *Development*, *43*(4), 11–14. https://doi.org/10.1057/palgrave.development.1110188

Esim, S., & Smith, M. (2004). *Gender and migration in Arab States: The case of domestic workers*. Beirut: International Labour Organization.

Foucault, M. (1984). Panopticism. In P. Rabinow (Ed.), *The Foucault reader* (pp. 206–213). New York, NY: Pantheon Books.

Freire, P. (1970). *Pedagogy of the oppressed*. New York, NY: Herder and Herder.

Grande, S. (2004). *Red pedagogy: Native American social and political thought*. Oxford: Rowman and Littlefield Publishers, Inc.

Gray, A. (2016, December 19). At least one-fifth of people from these countries lives abroad. Retrieved from https://www.weforum.org/agenda/2016/12/fifth-of-people-from-these-countries-live-abroad/

Gupta, A., & Ferguson, J. (1997). *Culture, power, place: Explorations in critical anthropology*. Durham, NC: Duke University Press.

Human Rights Watch. (2008). Lebanon: Migrant domestic workers dying every week. Data File. Retrieved from https://www.hrw.org/news/2008/08/26/lebanon-migrant-domestic-workers-dying-every-week

Hussain, N. Z., & Cohn, C. (2020, August 7). Insured losses from Beirut blast seen around $3 billion: Sources. https://www.reuters.com/ Retrieved from https://www.reuters.com/article/us-lebanon-security-blast-insurance/insured-losses-from-beirut-blast-seen-around-3-billion-sources-idINKCN2532IF?edition-redirect=in

Jureidini, R. (2004). Women migrant domestic workers in Lebanon. In S. Esim & M. Smith (Eds.), *Gender and migration in Arab States* (pp. 64–85). Geneva: International Labour Organization.

Jureidini, R., & Moukarbel, N. (2004). Female Sri Lankan domestic workers in Lebanon: A case of "contract slavery"? *Journal of Ethnic and Migration Studies*, *30*(4), 581–607. https://doi.org/10.1080/13691830410001699478

Jureidini, R. (2010). Trafficking and contract migrant workers in the Middle East. *International Migration Special Issue: Special Issue on Human Trafficking*, *48*(4), 142–163. https://doi.org/10.1111/j.1468-2435.2010.00614.x

Jureidini, R. (2011). *An exploratory study of psychoanalytic and social factors in the abuse of migrant domestic workers by female employers in Lebanon*. Lebanon: Human Rights.

Kassamali, S. (2021). Understanding race and migrant domestic labor in Lebanon. *Middle East research and information project*. Retrieved from https://merip.org/2021/07/understanding-race-and-migrant-domestic-labor-in-lebanon/

Lebanon economic collapse in numbers. (2021, March 18). *Gulf Times*. Retrieved from https://m.gulf-times.com/story/686941/Lebanon-economic-collapse-in-numbers

Manseau, G. S. (2007). Contractual solutions for migrant labourers: The case of domestic workers in the Middle East. *Human Rights Law Commentary*, *3*, 25–47.

McAuliffe, M. & Triandafyllidou, A. (2021). *World Migration Report 2022*. Geneva: International Organization for Migration.

Nayel, M. A. (2013). Palestinian refugees are not at your service. Retrieved from https://electronicintifada.net/content/palestinian-refugees-are-not-your-service/12464

Oishi, N. (2005). *Women in motion: Globalization, state policies, and labor migration in Asia*. Stanford, CA: Stanford University Press.
Regencia, T., Alsaafin, L., & Allahoum, R. (2020, August 10). "Endemic corruption" caused Beirut blast, says Diab: Live updates. https://www.aljazeera.com/ Retrieved from https://www.aljazeera.com/news/2020/8/10/endemic-corruption-caused-beirut-blast-says-diab-live-updates
Sabban, R. (2004). Women migrant domestic workers in the United Arab Emirates. In S. Esim & M. Smith (Eds.), *Gender and migration in Arab states: The case of domestic workers*. Beirut, Lebanon: International Labour Organisation.
Said, E. W. (2014). *Orientalism*. United States: Knopf Doubleday Publishing Group.
Sharma, A. (2008). *Logics of empowerment: Development, gender, and governance inneoliberal India*. Minneapolis, MN: University of Minnesota Press.
Sherry, V. N. (2004). *Bad dreams: Exploitation and abuse of migrant workers in Saudi Arabia*. New York, NY: Human Rights Watch.
Soja, E. W. (2010). *Seeking spatial justice*. Minneapolis, MN: University of Minnesota Press. https://doi.org/10.5749/minnesota/9780816666676.003.0005
Spivak, G. C. (1988). Can the subaltern speak? In C. Nelson & L. Grossberg (Eds.), *Marxism and the interpretation of culture* (pp. 271–314). Champaign, IL: University of Illinois Press. https://doi.org/10.1007/978-1-349-19059-1
Sumner, A., & Tribe, M. (2008). *International development studies: Theories and methods in research and practice*. Thousand Oaks, CA: SAGE Publications. https://doi.org/10.4135/9781446279397
Taleb, W. (2021, March 31). Lebanese economic crisis imperils migrant domestic workers. https://www.al-monitor.com/ Retrieved from https://www.al-monitor.com/originals/2021/03/lebanese-economic-crisis-imperils-migrant-domestic-workers
Waves of Afghan refugees are arriving in the U.S. Here's some help they can expect. (2021, August 28). *National Public Radio*. https://www.npr.org/2021/08/28/1031854899/afghan-refugee-aid-resettlement
Williams, A., & Baláž, V. (2014). *International migration and knowledge*. New York, NY: Routledge. https://doi.org/10.4324/9780203894651
Wimpenny, K. (2010). Participatory action research: An integrated approach towards practice development. In M. Savin-Baden & C. Major (Eds.), *New approaches to qualitative research: Wisdom and uncertainty* (pp. 89–99). London: Francis and Taylor.
World Population Review (2022). World Population by Country. https://worldpopulationreview.com/
Yosso, T., & Lopez, C. B. (2010). Counterspaces in a hostile place. In L. Patton (Ed.), *Culture centers in higher education: Perspectives on identity, theory, and practice* (pp. 83–104). Sterling, VA: Stylus Publishing.

Chapter 2

Understanding Critical Theory and Its Frameworks as It Applies to the Development Sector and NGO Work

According to post-development scholars and critical pedagogues, globalization and transnational movement open up new avenues for theoretical frameworks and pedagogy for understanding how and why we "do" development; to be sure, some scholars assert the development sector is in need of a paradigm shift to accommodate "new forms of pedagogy" (Appadurai, 2000) while subaltern scholars call for "alternative pedagogies" (Kumar, 2015; Sherpa, 2014) for the theorizing and understanding of the "Subaltern School" within the educational realm. In the search for and transition to a critical subaltern development theory and pedagogy, it is necessary to tap into the very voices of those who comprise subaltern, marginalized groups, because, as Kelly and Lusis (2006) assert, "Researchers are frequently interested in understanding the experiences of 'the immigrant', as an objective analytical category, rather than the experiences of 'an immigrant'" (p. 831). To counter the positivist position some social scientists utilize conducting fieldwork in the "Global South" within the development sector, I call for bringing an understanding of critical theories to the realm of non-governmental organization (NGO) work, whether it is policy analysis, large-scale, quantitative research, performance reports, program evaluations, or educational endeavors.

I examine two closely related concerns in this chapter – the first being critical theory in its iterations as they relate to development as a field of study and as an action-oriented entity. Such an interrogation is needed, as it precipitates and informs the other topic of this chapter, which pertains to international development as a theory and practice – it is this sector that provides the humanitarian services to marginalized populations. Specifically, I will examine the theoretical frameworks that inform development studies (DS) as a discipline and practice. Because the end result of this research project is to forward a critical theoretical shift in how we think about and do on-the-ground development work in the NGO sector, it is important to provide a historical overview of development while also deconstructing the existing theoretical frameworks that inform development as a theory and practice so as to suggest new theoretical intersections. First, I will provide

DOI: 10.4324/9781003166566-2

the historical emergence and significance of critical theory and what we know today as development.

The Emergence of Critical Theory

The origins of critical theory start with a discussion about The Institute of Social Research, otherwise known as the Frankfurt School, and the critical theorists who comprised its early members: Max Horkheimer, Erich Fromm, Herbert Marcuse, and Theodor Adorno. The creation of the School was the result of the historical and political transformations taking place during the mid-twentieth century (Darder, Baltodano, & Torres, 2009, p. 2). According to Jay's (1973) historical overview of the Institute's formation and contributions, he states that the driving force behind the School's mission was concerned with "an analysis of bourgeois society's socio-economic substructure" and after 1930, its "prime interests lay in its cultural substructure" (p. 21). Jay (1973) recounts the lineage and beginnings of the Institute in addition to a review of the world-changing events occurring in Europe, from the Bolshevik Revolution to World War I, and the development of European Marxism; these events inevitably shaped the mission and social criticisms of the Frankfurt School, especially the occurrence of the First World War. It was the disruption of the War that led to the re-examination of "the very foundations of Marxist theory, which with the dual hope of explaining past errors and preparing for future action", lending to a "process that inevitably led back to the dimly lit regions of Marx's philosophical past" (Jay, 1973, p. 3). As Kincheloe (2008) asserts, due to the numerous devastating events of World War I, inflation and unemployment, and overall economic depression, "the world was in urgent need of reinterpretation" (p. 46). And, the Frankfurt School sought to provide "a social emancipation from the various economic, social, and cultural oppressive qualities, such as social prejudices and economic inequalities" (Kanpol, 1999, p. 29). It is within the School's interrogation of Marxist thought through which the members laid a foundation for their most critical writings and paved the intellectual space for a theory of consciousness. According to Giroux (2001), it is the early critiques of positivist thought that "represents the major theoretical impetus currently shaping educational theory and practice" (p. 13). In other words, what emerged from this critique of positivism has shaped our understanding and applications of critical social theory, which, in turn, has contributed to the formation of other iterations of critical theories founded upon critiques of society, culture, and power, such as feminism, critical race theory (CRT), and postcolonial theory.

Marcuse asserted that the Frankfurt School generally defined positivism as "the validation of cognitive thought by experience of facts; the orientation of cognitive thought to the physical science as a model of certainty and exactness; [and] the belief that progress in knowledge depends on this orientation" (as cited in Giroux, 2001, p. 14). The Frankfurt School members addressed several key concerns, such as "the suppression of ethics in positivist rationality precludes the possibility for self-criticism, or more specifically, for questioning its own normative structure" and the inability of positivist thought to assess the "complicated interaction of power, knowledge, and values and to reflect critically on the genesis and nature of its own ideological presuppositions" (Giroux, 2001, p. 16). In other words, "positivism produces a sterile form of thinking, or as Marcuse puts it, a one-dimensional man" (Kanpol, 1997, p. 9). Generally, positivists maintain that the rules that govern the study of the natural sciences can and should also govern the ways social scientists measure, interpret, and study society (Kincheloe, 2008). In essence, positivism's supposition that knowledge cannot be separated from facts, nor can we question the factors behind the facts, lent to a necessity for a paradigm shift in the theoretical processes that govern knowledge production in the social sciences.

The shared notion among the early theoreticians of the Frankfurt School of placing importance on the everyday lived experience and placing significance on historical context informed the ideological processes of critical theory; this, coupled with a desire for social justice, emancipation from oppressive forces, and human freedom as the impetus for the formation of critical theory, presented a liberatory philosophical tradition (Giroux, 2001). In so doing, the School did not negate the necessity of rational thought within the process of critical inquiry; instead, rational thought "became the nexus of thought and action in the interest of liberating the community or society as a whole" (Giroux, 2001, p. 22). The theoretical and philosophical reconstruction in the early years lent to the existing commitment of transforming societal conditions of oppressed peoples.

The Development Sector and Its Origins

In the same era that the Frankfurt School's theoreticians were contemplating the devastating economic and social impacts of World Wars I and II which led to their conception of critical theory, the government of U.S. President Harry S. Truman formulated a path to continue its political presence in developing countries. The genesis of the concept of international development work has its roots in Europe's colonization of the Global South[1] in the late nineteenth century and early twentieth century and paved the way for the technical assistance known today as "development" (Rist, 2008, p. 47). In the decades preceding World War II, the shift from colonialism to "development cooperation" is evident in the historiographies of the development literature; Kothari (2019) examines this shift in "From Colonial Administration to Development Studies: A Post-Colonial Critique of the History of Development Studies" and notes that it is essential to situate the United Kingdom's colonial past in a historical analysis "that identifies the particularities, and varied expressions, of the continuities between colonialism and development" (p. 63). The academic discipline of DS has its origins in the institutions of the United Kingdom, which parallels the colonial legacy of that region (Kothari, 2019). Because of its colonialist roots, the philosophical and theoretical foundations in development studies have received much attention in the past two decades; this comprises a main theme in the development literature. In order to situate that critique, a historical overview of development as a "doctrine of intervention" (Rist, 2008, p. 49) and an academic discipline follows.

Historical Overview of Development

The formation of this discipline can be traced to the devastation of World War II's effects on the world economies. U.S. foreign policy in the post-World War II era called for preemptive measures to counter the threat of Communism in Europe. According to Rist (2008), the reification of U.S. development work can be traced to President Harry S. Truman's inaugural address on January 20, 1949, in which he describes the Point Four Program. It is the fourth point in his speech that outlines the plan of the U.S. government, in partnership with other developed nations, in alleviating poverty and disease and bringing prosperity and democracy to under developed countries:

> Fourth, we must embark on a bold new program for making the benefits of our scientific advances and industrial progress available for the improvement and growth of underdeveloped areas. More than half the people of the world are living in conditions approaching misery. Their food is inadequate. They are victims of disease. Their economic life is primitive and stagnant. Their poverty is a handicap and a threat both to them and to more prosperous areas. For the first time in history, humanity possesses the knowledge and the skill to relieve the suffering of these people. The United States is pre-eminent among nations in the development of industrial and scientific techniques. The material resources which we can afford to use for the assistance of other peoples are limited. But our imponderable resources in technical knowledge are constantly growing and are inexhaustible. I believe that we should make available to peace-loving peoples the benefits of our store of technical knowledge in order to help them realize their aspirations for a better life. And, in cooperation with other nations, we should foster capital investment in areas needing development. Our aim should be to help the free peoples of the world, through their own efforts, to produce more food, more clothing, more materials for housing, and more mechanical power to lighten their burdens. We invite other countries

> to pool their technological resources in this undertaking. Their contributions will be warmly welcomed. This should be a cooperative enterprise in which all nations work together through the United Nations and its specialized agencies wherever practicable. It must be a worldwide effort for the achievement of peace, plenty, and freedom. ("Harry S. Truman Inaugural Address", 2014)

As evidenced by the above iteration, Truman's Point Four is an attempt to justify future U.S. presence in economically depressed countries while simultaneously asserting the United States as a mecca of industrialization and modernization. The idea of the Point Four Program emerged from the Truman Administration's reactions to the Cold War and the Soviet bloc's threat of the spread of Communism, in addition to the priority of post-World War II reconstruction in Europe (Arndt, 1987). In order to block the "Soviet threat", the Truman administration manufactured a reason for U.S. presence. Another reason for implementing the Point Four Program was to "win the hearts and minds" of the people in developing countries (Kinkela, p. 80). It is upon this goal and Truman's grandiose Point Four program on which hinge the mission and future operations of U.S. development in the "Third World" countries.

By 1950, the Technical Assistance Group was established within the U.S. Department of State and substantial funding was allotted to the economic development program for the improvement of agricultural output in countries with which the United States had bilateral agreements. The first region to receive assistance from the Point Four Program was the Middle East (Butterfield, 2004). By 1962, the U.S. government, the United Nations, the Ford Foundation, and other donors had given financial support in the amount of $50 million for community development in 25 countries (Butterfield, 2004). It is also around this time, in the 1960s, that DS as an academic discipline commenced in the United Kingdom (Sumner & Tribe, 2008). One could surmise that these two entities, development as an outreach activity and DS as a field of study, are closely connected to each other; this is important to note as both of these entities have colonialist roots. Kothari (2019) states, "Development studies emerged out of colonial studies but that DS rarely acknowledges it colonial roots...and the variety of ways in which the West produces knowledge about people in other places" (as cited in Sumner and Tribe, p. 33).

Definition of Development and Non-Governmental Organizations

As mentioned earlier, for migrant workers in host countries, their quality of life can be abysmal due to all forms of abuse, abject employment conditions, and the racialized and social stigmas attached to domestic work. For these reasons, humanitarian groups and NGOs provide the social, medical, legal, and educational support migrant workers need. Because this study was conducted at an NGO and within the auspices of the development sector, and because this study ultimately examines "how" the West "does" development, I will provide in the following an overview of NGO work, its historical origins in the West, its definition, and critique of its theoretical underpinnings.

Non-Governmental Organizations

The NGO academic literature can be divided into roughly two groups: the literature that defines and describes the ways in which NGOs are organized and how they function, which is found within the development and organizational studies and the study of economics; and the literature that critiques the systems of the delivery of the goods and services of these NGOs from theoretical and philosophical perspectives. This discussion will begin with a brief overview of NGOs. The phrase "non-governmental organization" is a post-World War II expression coined in 1950 by the United Nations (Martens, 2002, p. 271). The United Nations defines NGOs as

> any non-profit, voluntary citizens' group which is organized on a local, national or international level. Task-oriented and driven by people with a common interest, NGOs perform a variety of services and humanitarian functions, bring citizens' concerns to governments, monitor policies and encourage political participation at the community level. ("NGOs and Corporations: Conflict and Collaboration", p. 4)

Variations of the above definition exist, depending on the agenda and role of the NGO itself. According to the bylaws of an NGO in Bangladesh, they define their NGO in simple terms as "organizations committed to the development of the underprivileged and underserved" and they define their purpose as ensuring "sustainable development of the poor in Bangladesh through poverty-alleviation, building capacity and institutions among poor people, and increasing their participation in productive activities" (Edwards & Hulme, 1995, p. 113). These two definitions of NGOs have in common the task of providing humanitarian functions.

NGOs look to various sources for funding, such as private donations, governmental and intergovernmental organizations, and national and international corporations. A mechanism for securing NGO funding is called "contracting", where the donor calls upon the NGO to carry out specific tasks in projects or programs of the donor's choice; the most common method for securing funding is the grant model in which the NGO proposes to the donor agency a project or program in need of funding (Lewis & Kanji, 2009). Acquisition of funding may or may not be a complex process – it is the connection between the funding source and the NGO that can be fraught with complexities. In an ethnographic study of an NGO in the Philippines, the author details this fragile relationship, noting the "politics of partnership" that can be a "main source of conflict and calls into question the generalized complaints about efficiency and accountability that... dominate the discussions regarding local development NGOs" (Hilhorst & Hilhorst, 2003, p. 26). According to Yaziji and Doh (2009), NGOs are also referred to as "non-profits" and "third sectors" which act as an extension of civil society, or beyond the public and the private sectors (p. 3).

Within the development literature, NGOs can be categorized and broadly divided in several different ways. Yaziji and Doh (2009) describe NGOs by what they do and who receives the benefits of NGOs; for instance, there are NGOs whose sole purpose is advocacy, such as Amnesty International, while others whose aim is service, such as Salvation Army.

The term NGO is often used interchangeably with grassroots organizations (GROs), although there is a distinct difference. GROs are located in communities and have a local membership (Green & Haines, 2016). They develop at the micro level, driven by a political and/or social commonality in goals among the "on the ground" individuals. NGOs are typically international organizations under obligation to the agendas of trustees or board members, not local members (Sutton & Arnove, 2004).

The academic literature discussing NGOs, GSOs, and their various types, activities, structures, and theoretical foundations are replete with unclear and undefined ideas as to what exactly constitutes an NGO or differentiates it from other organizations (Martens, 2002). These complexities become more actualized vis-à-vis the discursive practices informing DS; according to Hilhorst and Hilhorst (2003), "the question of what is *non-governmental* about NGOs has been extensively debated, whereas the more essential one of what is *organizational* about them has largely been ignored" (p. 2). The multifarious and hierarchical relationships of the various NGOs, GROs, and myriad other organizations that surround the international development landscape make for a complex interconnected network, especially in terms of funds and services. In the following, I will discuss the theoretical and practical debates that surround the development sector.

Development and Its Critiques

Development literature is informed by many conceptualizations, fields of study, ideological orientations, and so on. According to Sumner and Tribe (2008), three main and overlapping conceptualizations of development prevail and serve as a reifying model of development: The first definition views development as historical and transformative; the second definition places value on measurable outcomes; and the last perspective encapsulates the view that development and the motives that support it are extensions of the hegemonic, Western-centric discourse that surrounds and informs development studies. Other scholars use a typology to differentiate between "development" and "DS", with the former being viewed as a measurable action, or "deliberate actions of progress", or "historical change process" while the latter is understood from the perspective of what development is "about" and "for" which can be understood through different fields of study, such as economics, anthropology, political science, and organization studies (Thomas, 2004, as cited by Kothari, 2019, p. 5). These comprehensive and practical models for understanding development are useful for those who work in the development sector.

Depending on several variables, such as the researcher-practitioner's training particular to their field of study, the scholar's ideological positionality regarding development, and/or the theoretical frameworks they employ in their projects, she/he/they may approach fieldwork in ways that are indicative of their orientation toward the "subject" of their work. Clearly, understanding development as an academic field of study and as an action-oriented practice is a complex endeavor that requires those who practice research in the development sector to have a very thorough understanding of development from the perspective of local members who are embedded in the everyday realities of "doing development" and the very populations the development sector serves.

The metanarratives that drive DS and are central to its scope and meaning as an action-oriented field of study emerge from economics and policy studies. Because these fields of study are viewed as positivist, more focused on measurable and immediate outcomes and more driven by applied research, the field of DS has been and presently still is rife with criticism. Varying aspects of development generate contentions within the literature. The field of DS has been referred to as an "uneasy discipline" (Schuurman, 2009, p. 831); the term "development" in and of itself is problematic, as it refers to "both the ideal of improvement in people's well-being and to a far more dystopian reality on the ground" (Bhavnani, Foran, Kurian, & Munshi, 2009, p. 1); it has been referred to as the "contested nature of development" (Sumner & Tribe, 2008, p. 5) and the "interrelationships between theories, ideas and histories of development policy and practice which makes the identity of development as a subject of study so complicated and contested" (Kothari, 2019, p. 5). These iterations convey "contestedness", a commonality among many development detractors.

Another concern is the use of a deficit lens by the Global North researchers, practitioners, government workers, and volunteers when conducting and participating in NGO projects and other development work. The dominant discourse of "development studies", according to critical development scholars, is self-serving and perpetuates the deficit lens (Bhavnani, Foran, Kurian, & Munshi, 2009; Escobar, 1992; Rahnema, 1997; Rist, 2008). To reference back to Truman's Point Four speech, the former U.S.

president constructs a justification of a development agenda by juxtaposing the United States as an economic and agricultural savior of sorts who needs to "save" the "lesser than" regions of the world. Escobar (2011) also describes the "reformer's zeal" of Harvard economist, Lauchlin Currie, a former official of the Roosevelt administration, who was commissioned by the World Bank in 1949 to conduct an economic studies "mission" in Colombia; Escobar also cites Currie (1967), who stated, "No economic subject more quickly captured the attention of so many as the rescue of the poor countries from their poverty...To be involved with the poor countries provided the scholar with a foothold in the field of study that would assuredly expand and endure" (as cited by Escobar, 2011, p. 57). As Escobar notes, Currie's epistemological base is informed by Keynesian economics, a theoretical frame produced in a British context and within a developed/industrialized society. The discourse of universal economics, whether in the classical, capitalist, or neoliberal strain, contributes to the reproduction of social, political, and cultural domination of the Global North (Escobar, 2011), thereby shaping the Global South's position of subservience, acquiescence, and accommodation to the Global North as power brokers.

By virtue of attempting to amend the problems of poverty, the development industry and major actors of this entity superimpose Western-influenced, prescriptive ideas to produce change in the Global South. The very notions of "development" and "poverty" are social constructs, from a post-structuralist perspective, not existing outside of its objective realm (Sumner & Tribe, 2008). The scholarship of some Western social scientists and historians, for instance, Butterfield (2004), Eelens, Schampers, and Speckmann (1992), and Oishi (2005), is evidence of the Western-centric and orientalist lens from which these academicians produce knowledge. Oishi (2005) cites Weberian thought as a justification for applying the notion of "fixed types" in her causal analysis of international women's migration in Asia, as if women migrant workers are two-dimensional and easily categorized (pp. 112–124), and Eelens et al. (1992) posited that migration for women was a means for liberation (p. 227), which is a simplistic notion by not taking into account the physical, sexual, and emotional abuse migrant women suffer at the hands of their employers. Butterfield (2004), in his historical account of U.S development in the Global South, lauds the trajectory of outreach and involvement while omitting the flaws of development policy or their true intentions. These bodies of work operate on assumptions and pre-conceived notions of the "other" as archetypes, simplistic reductions of cultures and peoples, which perpetuate and produce distorted bodies of knowledge, further replicating the narrow and binary-like scholarship; because, if a woman does not fit the label of "dutiful daughter", as Oishi (2005) portends, would she fall into the converse, or binary category? One would conclude she is disobedient, insolent, and discourteous, all labels which are problematic.

One of the central assertions of scholars within the development literature is an agreement that a lack of a unifying, cohesive, and functioning theoretical framework is utilized within DS (Desai & Potter, 2014; Martinussen, 1997). Pieterse (1999) asserts, "Development theory is now being torn between paradigms – mainstream, alternative and post-development...or between 'internal' and 'external' critiques of development" (p. 84) while Sumner and Tribe (2008) state, "Theory has been, and remains, a major area of controversy for DS" (p. 82). Since the late 1980s onward, a trend in the DS literature is to critique the prescriptive theoretical frameworks emerging from the fields of economics and policy studies. The crisis of development theory is referred to in the literature as having "reached an impasse" in the mid-1980s (Munck & O'Hearn, 1999; Schuurman, 1993; Sumner & Tribe, 2008), due to the flurry of development theories contesting the structuralist and modernist views that were informing development theory since the 1950s. A 1989 article, titled "The Irrelevance of Development Studies" by Michael Edwards, sparked much debate within DS, and provoked an introspective glance by the practitioners, academics, and policy makers within the field to question its motives, its methodologies, and institutional, professional, and personal positionalities. For instance, Edwards (1993) calls for more transparency on the part of the researcher, openly declaring the goals and objectives of the project, and allowing for the NGO or research participants to reject the researcher's proposal and positionality (p. 81); in this way, the work of empowerment within development may be achieved.

In *Critical Development Theory* (Munck & O'Hearn, 1999), the ongoing discussions about theory and practice in development were extensively written. This compilation of essays proposed a merging of critical theory with development theory, so as to move beyond the hegemony of development and seeks a plurality of discourses, to contribute to a much-needed paradigm shift in the theoretical applications that scaffold international development. In post-development discourse, Fagan's (1999) essay proposes a theoretical shift to cultural politics from the starting point of material struggle, integrating the voices and situatedness of those receiving assistance from the development sector (p. 178). In order to move beyond the criticisms of the development enterprise, she suggests that cultural politics transcend the power of the local, or the integration of cultural analysis alone; it is the political schema in addition to the cultural prospect that holds the potential for power and liberation for the social actors on the receiving end of development work. She goes on to suggest that "...[I]f development is to have a real value at the local level it requires a qualitative understanding of the complexities and dynamics of everyday lives" and "development must be an integral part of existing cultural and social relations" (p. 186).

It is my position that at the intersections of DS, education, area studies, and migration studies lies the paradigm shift toward a new theoretical paradigm the above post-development scholars call for; this praxical supposition is informed by Third World feminisms, postcolonial theory, and a critical pedagogical orientation within a larger critical theoretical framework. In the following, I will examine these discourses from historical and contextual lenses, examining them against the backdrop of development and their situatedness in the Middle East/South West Asia and North Africa (SWANA) context, starting with a discussion of feminism.

The Feminist Lens

In the late 1980s and early 1990s, from the perspective of Women's Studies discursive practices, the noticeably absent discussion of the feminist voice within the realm of critical theory and how it applied to critical pedagogical thought was taken on by the leading feminist writers. According to Weiler (1995), this era represented a time of serious challenges for the feminist project in the field of education: "One of the strengths of the feminist vision of education…was its challenge to the fundamental assumptions and power arrangements of academic disciplines" (p. xiii). Darder et al. (2009) suggests that "critical pedagogy has often been accused of challenging structures and practices of patriarchy in society, solely from a myopic and superficial lens" (p. 14). The confrontations of the use of dominant rationality against a confluence of new epistemological terrain in the academic arena presented new realms for interdisciplinary endeavors, as it related to several branches of feminist scholarship: socialist, radical, Marxist, and liberal, among others.

Concurrently, within the feminist discourse of the late 1980s and early 1990s, the internal tensions of the third-wave feminist movement furthered a lack of academic and political cohesiveness within the developments of feminism itself; Fisher (2001) states that "Feminism as a movement also has had to contend with the especially problematic character of the group it claims to represent" (p. 28). Early critiques asserted that feminist pedagogy was intellectually irresponsible and politically biased; moreover, feminist pedagogy "rejected the time-tested academic standards of careful reasoning and objectivity" (Fisher, 2001, p. 15).

Perhaps as a reaction, other feminist pedagogical texts attempted to employ frameworks of objectivity and impartiality as a means for instigating reflexive thought for the feminist teacher; one such example is the text *Gender and Teaching* (Maher & Ward, 2002), which offers four case studies of classroom scenarios involving issues of race, class, gender, and sexuality, and provides reflexive questions to process one's positionality from a positivist standpoint in relation to these scenarios. Inherent to these feminist works, such as *Gender and Teaching* and many others, is the use of the post-structuralist feminist framework.

Feminism as a theoretical platform and as a political and social movement draws on the discursive traditions of early critical theorists as well as drawing on the disciplines that work in conjunction against inequity, discrimination, and oppression (Villaverde, 2008). Weedon (1987) asserts,

> Feminism is a politics. It is a politics directed at changing existing power relations between women and men in society. These power relations structure all areas of life, the family, education and welfare, the worlds of work and politics, culture and leisure. They determine who does what for whom, what we are and what we might become. (p. 1)

Villaverde (2008) posits that feminist theory and feminism have been viewed myopically, as "singular, monolithic entities that mean one thing, stand for one thing, and speak to one group: women"; focusing on the dichotomies of gender can cause one to set aside or ignore issues of class, race/ethnicity, culture, sexual identity, and language (pp. 1–2). This singular view does not serve the overarching goal of a liberatory theory of feminism, and as a result, feminist scholars have employed a post-structuralist theoretical framework, which serves to understand issues of power inherent to the construction of knowledge (Yates, 1993).

The early feminist pedagogical texts of the 1990s are replete with the use of post-structuralism intertwined within feminist theory, which, according to Weedon (1987), does not carry one fixed meaning and can be applied to a range of theoretical positions. Villaverde (2008) asserts that a post-structuralist framework helped instill within the feminist view a "more clear analysis of power and representation to alter monolithic interpretations of gender and identity" (p. 49). It is the influence of post-structuralism's principles on feminist scholarship that gives it space to be complex, fragmented, plural, and multidimensional (Holland & Ramazanoglu, 1995, p. 288). Certain post-structural concepts are applied to the feminist framework, such as subjectivity, social organization, and power as discourse as they relate to knowledge production and self as producer of knowledge; according to Weedon (1987),

> "Subjectivity" is used to refer to the conscious and unconscious thoughts and emotions of the individual, her sense of herself and her ways of understanding her relation to the world...post-structuralism proposes a subjectivity which is precarious, contradictory and in process, constantly being reconstituted in discourse each time we think or speak. (pp. 32–33)

St. Pierre's (2000) analysis of the constructed subject is that the subject "exhibits agency as it constructs itself by taking up available discourses and cultural practices and a subject that, at the same time, is subjected, forced into subjectivity by those same discourses and practices" (St. Pierre, as cited by Suspitsyna, 2010, p. 65). In other words, power is enacted via an exercise of agency. Foucault (1978) defines power as

> the multiplicity of force relations immanent in the sphere in which they operate and which constitute their own organization; as the process which, through ceaseless struggles and confrontations, transforms, strengthens or reverses them; as the support which these force relations find in one another, thus forming a chain or a system, or on the contrary, the disjunctions and contractions which isolate them from one another; and lastly, as the strategies in which they take effect, whose general design or institutional crystallization is embodied in the state apparatus, in the formation of the law, in the various social hegemonies. (p. 92)

A post-structuralist perspective recognizes power as entity in shaping reality. For women, an understanding of power as a socially and culturally constructed concept vis-à-vis the post-structuralist lens provides a theorizing of women's oppression within the feminist pedagogical model. By utilizing approaches of resistance, opposition, and deconstruction, post-structuralist feminist pedagogy challenges the dominant discourse of the masculine.

Just as early critical pedagogy is fraught with criticisms for its lack of inclusion of the feminist voice, feminist theory itself has come under fire for various reasons. One issue, according to feminist critics, is the heavy reliance of the post-discourses as theoretical models for framing the feminist stance. Some scholars assert a fetishizing of post-modernist/post-structuralist thought is prominent within feminist pedagogy. Grande (2003) asserts that "mainstream" feminism includes "a heavy dependence on post-modern/post-structuralist theories, a privileging of 'academic feminism' over the feminist political project, and an undertheorizing of patriarchy as the universal oppression of all women—all features that have been critiqued by feminists of color and other radical scholars" (p. 330). She maintains that the discursive approaches of the post-discourses as appropriated by Anglo feminists allows for them to "distort the material significance of their privileged position"; this is evident in the Anglo feminist discussions of the power concept, which rely on overly abstract verbiage, instead of framing power as something that is "historically and materially determined" (p. 331). Such discussions simultaneously absolve Anglo feminists of any wrongdoing of the colonialist project (Grande, 2003). Chela Sandoval's (2009) theoretical analysis describes a third-wave feminist movement that endorses a dominant, Anglo-hegemonic model, one that excludes cultural, racial, class, and gender differences and fails to include an examination of power relations, beyond an analysis of gender; Sandoval states, "Hegemonic feminist theoreticians and activists are trapped within the rationality of this structure, which sublimates or disperses the theoretical specificity of U.S. third world feminism" (p. 344).

Another key issue focuses on the inaccessible language use of feminist theorists and the academy as a whole and how it prescribes an intellectual class hierarchy; Black feminist scholar bell hooks (1994) suggests it is ironic

> that a certain kind of theoretical performance which only a small cadre of people can possibly understand has come to be seen as representative of any production of critical thought that will be given recognition within many academic circles as "theory". It is especially ironic when this is the case with feminist theory. (p. 64)

The irony is, within the proverbial ivory towers of academia exists a body of scholarship whose language is cloaked in highly abstract and jargonistic terms, making it difficult to read, and containing obscure references, making it inaccessible to the very population which it claims to speak for and represent: the communities of color that have been oppressed, and the socioeconomically disenfranchised and marginalized.

Also problematic among some White feminists is a tendency to otherize or exoticize the lived experiences of women in the Middle East/SWANA region; in so doing, a replication of the colonizer/colonized dichotomy perpetuates as the Anglo-bourgeois feminist advances her own academic currency capitalizing on real women's lived experiences (Grande, 2003). By reducing the lived experiences of women from communities of color and other minoritized groups as the fetishized object, such post-modern/post-structuralist discourses only serve to promulgate a hegemonic class rule, thereby forwarding the capitalist agenda (McLaren, 1998). hooks (1994) states that patriarchal resistance as a common goal within White feminism takes precedence over actions against racial resistance and other forms of domination.

White feminism is organized along a gender binary that ultimately negates other categories of class, culture, sexual orientation, and especially race within the United States; Sandoval (2000) cites Toni Morrison: "There is something inside [U.S. women of color] that makes us different from other people. It is not like men and it is not like white women" (p. 46). The "something" of which Morrison speaks is neglected by the hegemonic, White feminist discourse and which intersectionality theory addresses. Theoretical frameworks utilized within contemporary critical pedagogy speak to both the interdisciplinary approach by the theorists of the past two decades and the foregrounding of race, gender, and socioeconomic status as salient themes when discussing goals of emancipation and empowerment, especially for women from historically marginalized backgrounds. Intersectionality theory defined is when the categories of race, class, and gender converge, and they are recognized as being crucial to the understanding of one's position in the social world; how they intersect is referred to as the "race-class-gender matrix" and those utilizing the intersectional approach "will socially locate individuals in the context of their 'real lives'" (Berger & Guidroz, 2009, p. 1).

This perspective on post-structuralist feminism and intersectional feminism serves to segue into the following discussion in which feminism is foregrounded by postcolonial thought and DS, and then provide an overview of CRT in the theory and practice of development.

Feminism, Postcolonial Thought, and Development

How does feminism as an ideology and practice intersect with the development sector and NGO practices? The study of gender as an analytic category within the field of DS began in the 1970s and has since been integrated into governance and economic policy studies over the past 50 years. Recent publications, such as the edited volume *The Routledge Handbook of Gender and Development* (Coles, Gray, & Momsen, 2015) provides a comprehensive analysis utilizing empirical data that examines the Gender and Development (GAD) agenda within the international development sector. Other edited anthologies, such as Kothari's (2019) *A Radical History of Development Studies: Individuals, Institutions and Ideologies*, explores the genealogy of development discourses from critical perspectives. One such essay by Ruth Pearson, a noted researcher and scholar on gender and work in the global economy, examines the historical relevance of gender in the study of development in her essay, *The Rise and Rise of Gender and Development* (2005). She notes that, while gendered discourses such as women's empowerment are now embedded in most unilateral and multilateral agencies' mission statements, that "radical gender analysis has yet to be acknowledged in key sites of development analysis and policy within the global context of development, in spite of its apparent success in terms of institutional development practice" (2005, p. 158); this notion suggests that, while gender is an accepted tool for understanding development analysis and planning, it has not been fully embraced for possible reasons such as "academic machismo" (p. 170). Kothari, a postcolonial scholar, has written extensively on the intersection of feminism, racism, and DS. Kothari (2019) critiques the Western corpus of feminist and postcolonial approaches to development as failing to deal with issues of race and racism and neglects to challenge orientalist and Eurocentric discourses in the literature. More recent scholarship evaluates the nexus of feminist thought in the study of development. Wendy Harcourt's comprehensive anthology examines development discourses within the GAD agenda which include critiques of Northern feminism, and "the contemporary crisis of feminism" (Connell,

2016, p. xvii). Several chapters of this anthology (Harcourt, 2016) focus on the intersectionality of feminism and issues of race and racism against the backdrop of development theory and practice (de Lima Costa, 2016, p. 48; Petchesky, 2016, p. 145; Yuval-Davis, 2016, p. 367; Paulson, 2016, p. 395). This rich scholarship offers a necessary theoretical framing for on-the-ground fieldwork in the broader development spectrum of praxis. In the next section, I will provide a more focused discussion on the theorizing of racism in the Middle East/SWANA context within the development literature.

Critical Race Theory and Its Significance in the World of Development

Critical Race Theory Defined

Critical race theory examines racism and notions of race by drawing on legal scholarship, critical social theory, and narrative inquiry within the U.S. context (Ladson-Billings, 2006, p. viii). CRT originates from the Critical Legal Studies (CLS) discourse in the United States, which criticizes the "mainstream legal ideology for its portrayal of U.S. society as a meritocracy but failed to include racism in its critique" (Ladson-Billings, 1998, p. 11). CLS emerged from the critical theory of the Frankfurt School and argued "legal language is a discourse that continues to perpetuate hierarchies – male over female, rich over poor, Whites over Blacks and other people of color" (Ladson-Billings, 2009, p. 88). According to Ladson-Billings and Tate IV (2006), they define racism as "Culturally sanctioned beliefs which, regardless of the intentions involved, defend the advantages Whites have because of the subordinated positions of racial minorities" (p. 19). Race is defined as a socially constructed concept, one with no scientific basis (although linked to phenotypic characteristics); it is a racial categorization that "foregrounds social structure and action" while the ideology surrounding notions of race are steeped in cultural and social determinants (Darder, Baltodano, & Torres, 2009, pp. 152–153).

Particular to CRT are six common themes, the first being the assertion that racism is considered normal and not aberrant to American society, and is an "ingrained feature" of the American landscape and is seen as normal or natural in American culture (Delgado, 1995, p. xiv). Second, CRT recognizes the experiential knowledge of communities of color in the analysis of society (Ladson-Billings, 2006, p. 4) and employs notions of "voice" and storytelling (which departs from traditional legal scholarship) to illustrate that "Engaging stories can help us understand what life is like for others, and invite the reader into a new and unfamiliar world" (Delgado & Stefancic, 2001, p. 41). An important reason for inserting the personal narrative within the CRT framework is because "[personal narrative] add necessary contextual contours to the seeming 'objectivity' of positivist perspectives" (Ladson-Billings, 1998, p. 11).

The third theme centers on challenging the positivist notions of "objectivity, neutrality, colorblindness, and merit" (Ladson-Billings, 2006, p. 4) and that liberalism, as shaping the legal discourse, is failing the civil rights movement; CRT argues that liberalism "fails to understand the limits of current legal paradigms to serve as catalysts for social change and its emphasis on incrementalism" (Ladson-Billings, 1998, p. 12). Gillborn (2006) asserts that criticisms of liberalism stems from the inability of traditional legal discourse to address the more complex and hidden forms of racism, while only addressing the most obvious and crude forms (p. 253).

The fourth theme asserts that CRT is an interdisciplinary theoretical framework that "borrows from numerous traditions and is frequently characterized by a readiness to cross epistemological boundaries" (Gillborn, 2006, p. 253). CRT, as a fifth theme, "challenges ahistoricism and insists on a contextual/historical analysis to the law" (Ladson-Billings, 2006, p. 4). Lastly, the ultimate goal of CRT is to eradicate all forms of racism, oppression, and inequality. CRT argues Anglo-Americans have generally been the beneficiaries of civil rights laws; according to a comparative study of African-American and Anglo-American women's salaries and employment statistics, Anglo-American women consistently outpace their African-American women counterparts in terms of employment and wages earned (Wise, 1998, p. 5).

In the Western context, critical pedagogues agree that it is necessary to dismantle racism within the educational and social sphere and is the topic of much debate among social actors in how to achieve this goal. Most educators are uninformed about how to critically engage Black students (or students from any minoritized group) in a dominantly homogeneous setting, which can bring about feelings of alienation for the Black student. Carter (2008) addresses how "racial framing" in the classroom can impede academic engagement; the issue of racial spotlighting and racial ignoring is a phenomenon that occurs when a Black student perceives that he/she is being positioned as racially hypervisible or invisible, particularly by a White teacher or White students (pp. 231–232). Pollock (2004) refers to this notion of refusing to discuss racial disparities in school as "colormuteness" which can have harmful consequences. To substantiate this point, Pollock (2004) states, "Trying to achieve racial equality—or demonstrate improvements toward it—with a largely colormute discourse often seemed like trying to have a group fix a machine without discussing where it was broken" (p. 108).

Issues of "culture" and how teachers appropriate culture as ideology or a fixed, concrete notion are also problematic for students from communities of color. Ladson-Billings (2006) talks about the "culture of poverty" and believes one of the shortcomings within some teacher education programs is the result of novice teachers who reduce teaching challenges with Black students to being one of "culture" or "self-esteem"; she states, "I do not believe my teacher education students are unusual in their tendency to suture race to culture and then struggle to disentangle the two. Culture is regularly used as a code word for difference and perhaps deviance in the world of teacher education" (p. 107). González (2010) also discusses the "culture of poverty" model as being ineffective and reductionist:

> Perhaps the most infamous example of how the centripetal forces of reductionism came to affect quality education is the "culture-of-poverty" model. Although critiques of the culture-of-poverty model have excoriated the inadvertent promulgations that have resulted from policy enactments that embraced this concept, it maintains currency in circulating discourses concerning the poor and the disenfranchised. (p. S251)

Students from disenfranchised backgrounds, be they Black students from urban settings, refugee students in the Middle East/SWANA region, or domestic workers attending EFL classes at a Beirut NGO, are often viewed through a deficit lens, "substandard in their socialization practices, language practices, and orientation toward scholastic achievement" (González, 2005, p. 34). The reductionist model of codifying of culture fits the dominant discourse and only serves a privileged few, yet perpetuates subjugation and oppression of minoritized students. For a teacher to be compelled to utilize such a lens necessitates training from educators who engage in anti-racist work and continue to unlearn their own harmful tropes so as to dismantle the inherent deficit views that not only prospective teachers hold, but all humans.

As stated earlier, one of the tenets of CRT is recognizing that racism and racialized discourse is an inherent characteristic of American society. However, there are ways to combat its prevalence in the space of the classroom in nonformal and formal educational spaces, such as public school classrooms and NGO settings. Anti-racist discourse and praxis can be foregrounded in the everyday moments of school and student interactions; several educators offer real-life classroom experience in *Everyday Antiracism: Getting Real about Race in Schools* (Pollock, 2008), a text providing "in the trenches", real-life classroom experiences from anti-racist educators. According to Chang and Conrad (2008), "Children's attempts to make sense of racial categories are often revealed through spontaneous questions and remarks that emerge in the contexts of everyday conversations and activities" (p. 34). Pollock (2008) provides suggestions for making classroom discussions about equal/unequal opportunities between minoritized groups more meaningful; she states that educators should "take great care to consider whether their own actions offer students optimal opportunity" as some teachers tend to remove themselves from the analysis (p. 26).

Now that I have outlined CRT in the U.S. context from an educator's perspective, I will discuss CRT and anti-Black racism in the Middle East/SWANA context and call for a critical race understanding that is particular to this region, as CRT is a framework that is largely informed by the Black American experience with racism.

Critical Race Theory and Anti-Black Racism in the Middle East/SWANA Context

As described above, CRT is an idea particular to the U.S. context, informed by an understanding of its flawed legal system and the Black American experience with racism. Indeed, the study of racism and anti-Blackness, including racial ideologies, systemic and structural racism, ethnic identification, and intersecting oppression, has often been understood in the Western context, primarily the United States, due to its long and sustained history of racial oppression. As noted, Black scholars, writers, theorists, and activists have documented their own experiences with racism utilizing a critical race theoretical framework (hooks, 1994; Kendi, 2019; Ladson-Billings, 1998; Saad, 2020). Non-Black scholars also have contributed to the study of racial discrimination and anti-Blackness (DiAngelo, 2018; Matias, 2016). The social phenomena of the school-to-prison pipeline, racial discipline gap, redlining, police brutality, and other forms of institutional racism have been well documented in empirically driven research in the United States (Glantz & Martinez, 2018; Nelson & Lind, 2015; School Climate and Discipline, 2016; Sinyangwe & McKesson, 2020) and recent scholarship explores the idea of a global CRT (Christian, 2019; Macedo & Gounari, 2015; Weiner, 2012).

African postcolonial scholars like Nardal (1929), Césaire (1955), and Fanon (1961) and activists such as South African Bantu Stephen Biko, the founder of the Black Consciousness Movement, have established a Black intellectual movement writing about and speaking against the colonial racism of its time. In the Middle East/SWANA region, Afro-Arab racism, xenophobia, colorism, and tribalism also persist and manifest in laws like the *kafala* system, which is akin to human trafficking. These topics have historically been met with denial in much of the Arab and Persian world (Eltahawy, 2008; Whitaker, 2006), even though some Middle East/SWANA scholars have documented xenophobia and racism from a historical perspective (Powell, 2003) and within the field of social sciences against vulnerable groups in the region (Ahmed, 2017; Jureidini, 2005, 2010; 2011; Macedo & Gounari, 2015). As of late, scholarly and public discourse about anti-Black racism and race relations in the Middle East region have been a focus in Western academia as a result of the May 25, 2020, death of George Floyd – his murder has had reverberations throughout the region (Malekian, 2020; Salloum, 2020). In the United Arab Emirates, for instance, it was noted, "Floyd's tragic death has also sparked a conversation about racism in the Middle East creating space for black Arabs to give voice to their own experiences" ("George Floyd: Honouring his legacy one month on", 2020). To be sure, higher education institutions such as The Watson Institute for International and Public Affairs at Brown University held a speaker series titled Racialization & Racism in the Middle East: Historical Perspectives, a series that aims to explore the intersectional struggle of anti-Black racism and forms of racialization in the Middle East and also its diasporas. Dr. Nadje Al-Ali, director of The Center for Middle East Studies, states that "this is a long overdue initiative…we were particularly inspired and moved by the events of the summer [protests regarding the murder of George Floyd] and our solidarity with the Black Lives Matter movement" (Watson Institute for International and Public Affairs, 2020, 0:57).

There are on-the-ground organizations in the Middle East region doing the anti-racism work necessary for bringing awareness to anti-Black racism such as the Anti-Racism Movement in Lebanon, Sawiyan for Community Development in Jordan, and other GROs that identify as LGBTQIA+ allies – they have been doing local community organizing for years. Ahmed's (2017) critical race analysis of Jordanian law concludes that said law does not address race in a more concrete way, nor does Jordanian law "even deliberately criminalize discrimination on the basis of race" (p. 25). This scholarship speaks to the urgency in understanding anti-Blackness in the Middle East/SWANA context, especially in educational settings, where bullying of Afro-Arab children and other vulnerable groups persists. The application of CRT that is particular to the Middle East/SWANA context within education in civil society and public/private schools is vital for examining the relationship between race and achievement as it places race in the center of the discussion in terms of educational disparities and the dismantling of racism in the educational sphere (Howard, 2010, pp. 98–99).

CRT in the Development Sector

Critical race theory has salience within the study of the development sector and NGOs, especially those that include an educational component. As Ladson-Billings(1998) explains, by examining the ways that public education currently works, "CRT can be a powerful explanatory tool for the sustained inequity that people of color experience" (p. 18). This can also be applied to systems of education in the Middle East/ SWANA context as well, both public and nonformal. As noted above, CRT has its roots in Western discourses based on the experiences of racism in the United States. However, wherever racism exists and persists necessitates a theoretical understanding for its existence that should be particular to that context and can be applied in the fields of education, DS, social sciences, humanities, STEM fields, and so on. As mentioned previously, Harcourt's (2016) edited volume, *The Palgrave Handbook of Gender and Development: Critical Engagements in Feminist Theory and Practice* includes several chapters that discuss feminist theorizing on systems of discrimination relating to racism, domestic violence, and the patriarchy as a human rights violation and to combat exclusion in development.

The above mentioned scholars write extensively on issues of race and race relations as related to the GAD agenda, a much-needed mission and focus within the field of development as a study and as a practice. I contend that a theoretical construct particular to racism in the Middle East/SWANA region is also necessary, especially as we witness social movements fueled by anti-racist advocates and activists. If CRT, which is scaffolded by critical legal scholarship, is a way to theorize the systemic prejudices and discrimination against people of color, specifically Black Americans in the United States, then an understanding of the social processes that allow and act as currency for racism to continue to proliferate unabated in the Middle East/SWANA region is very much needed in order to allow for a blueprint in combating racism – that is to say, we need to understand how and why the political, social, religious, and educational systems allow for and accommodate racism, colorism, tribalism, and xenophobia to sustain and flourish in a region, place, and space in order to combat those systems. To enact a practice, it must be propelled by an understanding of why we do what we do, or we risk engaging in ungrounded or blind activism. For this reason, I strongly encourage regional Middle East/SWANA scholars in development and education who actively participate as researchers-practitioners utilizing humanizing research methods to forward a theorizing of racism specific to the Middle East/SWANA context, much like in the vein of Edward Said's orientalism, a theorizing of the West's xenophobic imagination of the Middle East/SWANA cultures and peoples; whereas orientalism provides a framework for understanding the xenophobia and objectification in the West toward the "other", what of the anti-Black racism that is endemic to the Middle East/SWANA region?

Next, I will transition to a discussion about critical pedagogical frameworks as they relate to dialogism, the dialectic, and praxis.

Critical Pedagogy: Dialogism, the Dialectic, and Praxis

The ideology of critical pedagogy emerged from several different academic disciplines, from the humanities and the social sciences. The interdisciplinary tradition of the field of education and its theoretical components are noted by the early critical pedagogues. According to Kincheloe and Steinberg (1997), critical pedagogy is that discourse which emerged when "critical theory encountered education" (p. 24). Pedagogy defined is the study of teaching as a theoretical concept; when adding criticality to that, we examine how the platform of teaching, in formal and nonformal spaces, can be utilized for creating awareness of social, gendered, economic, and race-based disparity – in essence, as educators, we commit to creating critical consciousness and awareness within ourselves as human beings and into our teaching practices (Freire, 1970). Paulo Freire's most recognizable and influential work is *Pedagogy of the Oppressed*, a Marxist class analysis that objects to a traditional model of education, one that includes the banking concept, a teacher-centered, authoritarian method of teaching and learning. According to Freire,

> Education thus becomes an act of depositing, in which the students are the depositories and the teacher is the depositor. Instead of communicating, the teacher issues communiqués and makes deposits, which the students patiently receive, memorize, and repeat. This is the "banking" concept of education, in which the scope of action allowed to the students extends only as far as receiving, filing, and storing the deposits. (1970, p. 72)

Other indicators of a banking system of education are teacher-centered teaching practices, such as indicating that the teacher holds all the knowledge and should not be challenged; emphasis is on right answers and assessments; only the student is framed as a learner, never the teacher; and a culture of competition is encouraged and celebrated (Huba & Freed, 2000). This way of being and teaching is the antithesis of a critical pedagogical stance; in fact, it forwards an authoritarian positionality.

The second reason why critical pedagogy and its underlying theoretical constructs such as the dialogic approach and praxis are expedient to international development and NGOs is due to their potential for impacting the organizational features of development practices. Freire's ideas on dialogic action were informed by the literary theorist Mikhail Bakhtin's notion of dialogism. According to Freire (1970), it is the act of dialoguing in a shared learning space about a common social struggle that is the essence of dialogic learning. He asserts that "dialogue" is

> [T]he encounter between men, mediated by the world, in order to name the world....Dialogue is thus an existential necessity. And since dialogue is the encounter in which the united reflection and action of the dialoguers are addressed to the world which is to be transformed and humanized, this dialogue cannot be reduced to the act of one person's "depositing" ideas in another, nor can it become a simple exchange of ideas to be "consumed" by the discussants. (Freire, 1970, pp. 88–89)

The dialogic approach recognizes that all voices at the table have worth. Power structures are horizontal in that no one person has all the authority, it is shared, and dialogic action is key to achieving such a structure. As an organizational feature in an NGO system, dialogic learning and action facilitate an egalitarian organizational style that recognizes input and insights as valuable to the function of the overall group and its objectives. Dialogic action creates and fosters a community of practice, which has the potential to lend to a social movement.

The other underlying construct of critical pedagogy is praxis, which is the result of theory plus practice. The early critical theorists proposed a paradigm shift in how critical social scientists, educators, and intellectuals could perform an interaction of theory and practice. What is the interplay between these two constructs? It is no easy task to define praxis; notions of praxis in terms of its application within the field of education and the critical theory/critical pedagogy literature are defined by Freire (1970) as purposeful action (p. 87); according to Grande (2009), the Freirean idea of praxis can be described as "best understood as action and reflection upon the world in order to change it or simply as intentional action" (p. 206). McLaren (2009) argues for informed action, or praxis, to be guided by the "disposition to act truly and rightly" (p. 74), while Darder et al. (2009) assert that question-posing as a practice is key within the educational process (p. 13). However one wants to shape notions of praxis, the commonality in the discussion is that praxis ultimately intends to provide the theoretical constructs as an explanation for the motives of human behavior and activity (whether as the oppressed or oppressor) while performing the ongoing interaction of self-reflection, purposeful action, and dialogue (Darder, Baltodano, & Torres, 2009, p. 13). Darder et al. (2009) capture the essence of critical praxis by stating, "Cut off from practice, theory becomes abstraction or 'simple verbalism'. Separated from theory, practice becomes ungrounded activity or 'blind activism'" (p. 13). It is the criticality of praxis that sets the tone for a critical pedagogy in the learning space. According to Grande (2004), "it is not surprising that critical pedagogy has emerged, in more recent years, as a kind of umbrella for a variety of educators and scholars working toward social justice and greater equity" (pp. 20–21); we can also apply Grande's words to how an NGO system organizes and functions. An NGO's local members should have an intimate understanding and endorsement of the very notions and ideologies that propel them to act, to function, to work, and to create social change.

As mentioned in the beginning of this chapter, Appadurai (2000) calls for "new forms of pedagogy" in the vein of Freire within a "grassroots globalization" movement (p. 17). A handful of post-development scholars acknowledged the breadth of knowledge that Freire contributes to the field of DS (Desai & Potter, 2014; Escobar, 2000, 2011; Tucker, 1999), and Freire's work is cited in anthropological studies of NGOs (Sharma, 2008). Critical pedagogy and its underlying theoretical constructs are salient in development practices for two reasons, the first being the teaching and learning experience. Many NGOs have educational initiatives for both adults and children. Typically, students who attend NGOs for their educational initiatives come from disenfranchised backgrounds, such as refugees and migrant workers. In their everyday lived experiences, they often contend with sexism, racism, classism, xenophobia, misogyny, and homophobia if they belong to an LGBTQIA+ group. While having the opportunity to attend educational activities such as EFL and computer classes, or craft and cooking classes, or any kind of learning activity is important in and of itself, how much more consequential is it to be taught by an educator who embraces an empowering and transformational way of teaching? A critical stance positively impacts an educator's pedagogy, curriculum choices, and teaching space – in sum, the whole of the teaching and learning encounter in a revolutionary way.

Note

1 In Development literature, the term "Global South" refers to the developing countries in Southeast Asia and the African continent in which the "Global North" intends to provide assistance.

References

Ahmed, A. K. (2017). #RhodesMustFall: Decolonization, praxis and disruption. *Journal of Comparative & International Higher Education*, 9(Fall), 8–13.

Appadurai, A. (2000). Grassroots globalization and the research imagination. *Public Culture*, *12*(1), 1–19. DOI: 10.1215/08992363-12-1-1.

Arndt, H. W. (1987). *Economic development: The history of an idea*. Chicago, IL: University of Chicago Press.

Berger, M. T., & Guidroz, K. (2009). Introduction. In M. T. Berger & K. Guidroz (Eds.), *The intersectional approach: Transforming the academy through race, class, and gender*. Chapel Hill NC: The University of North Carolina Press.

Bhavnani, K., Foran, J., Kurian, P., & Munshi, D. (2009). *On the edges of development: Cultural interventions*. New York, NY: Routledge. DOI: 10.4324/9780203880449

Butterfield, S. H. (2004). *U.S. development aid – An historic first: Achievements and failures in the twentieth century*. Westport, CT: Praeger.

Carter, D. J. (2008). On spotlighting and ignoring racial group members in the classroom. In M. Pollock (Ed.), *Everyday antiracism: Getting real about race in school* (pp. 230–234). New York, NY: The New Press.

Césaire, A. (1955). *Discours sur le colonialisme*. Paris: Présence Africaine.

Chang, K., & Conrad, R. (2008). Following children's leads in conversations about race. In M. Pollock (Ed.), *Everyday antiracism: Getting real about race in schools* (pp. 34–38). New York, NY: The New Press.

Christian, M. (2019). A global critical race and racism framework: Racial entanglements and deep and malleable whiteness. *Sociology of Race and Ethnicity*, *5*(2), 169–185. DOI: 10.1177/2332649218783220

Coles, A., Gray, L., & Momsen, J. (2015). *The Routledge handbook of gender and development*. New York, NY: Routledge. DOI: 10.4324/9780203383117

Connell, R. (2016). Foreword. In W. Harcourt (Ed.), *The Palgrave handbook of gender and development: Critical engagements in feminist theory and practice*. London: Palgrave MacMillian.

Currie, L. (1967). *Obstacles to development*. East Lansing MI: Michigan State University Press.

Darder, A., Baltodano, M. P., & Torres, R. D. (2009). Critical pedagogy: An introduction. In A. Darder, M. Baltodano, & R. Torres (Eds.), *The critical pedagogy reader* (pp. 1–20). New York, NY: Routledge.

Delgado, R. (1995). *Critical race theory: The cutting edge*. Philadelphia, PA: Temple University Press.

Delgado, R., & Stefancic, J. (2001). *Critical race theory*. New York NY: New York University Press.

de Lima Costa, C. (2016). Gender and equivocation: Notes on decolonial feminist translations. In W. Harcourt (Ed.), *The Palgrave handbook of gender and development: Critical engagements in feminist theory and practice* (pp. 48–61). London: Palgrave Macmillan.

Desai, V., & Potter, R. (2014). *The companion to development studies* (3rd ed.). New York, NY: Routledge. DOI: 10.4324/9780203528983

DiAngelo, R. (2018). *White fragility: Why it's so hard for white people to talk about racism*. Boston, MA: Beacon Press.

Edwards, M. (1989). The irrelevance of development studies. *Third World Quarterly, 11*(1), 116–135.

Edwards, M. (1993). How relevant is development studies? In F. J. Schuurman (Ed.), *Beyond the impasse: New directions in development theory* (pp. 71–92). London: Zed books.

Edwards, M., & Hulme, D. (1995). Beyond the magic bullet? Lessons and conclusions. In M. Edwards & D. Hulme (Eds.), *Non-governmental organisations – performance and accountability: Beyond the magic bullet* (pp. 219–228). London: Earthscan Publications.

Eelens, F., Schampers, T., & Speckmann, J. D. (1992). *Labour migration to the Middle East: From Sri Lanka to the Gulf*. London: K. Paul International, Ltd.

Eltahawy, M. (2008, November 10). The Arab world's dirty secret. *The New York Times*. Retrieved from https://www.nytimes.com/2008/12/10/opinion/10iht-edeltahawy.1.18556273.html

Escobar, A. (1992). Planning. In W. Sachs (Ed.), *The development dictionary: A guide to knowledge as power* (pp. 132–145). London: Zed Books.

Escobar, A. (2000). Beyond the search for a paradigm? Post-development and beyond. *Development, 43*(4), 11–14. DOI: 10.1057/palgrave.development.1110188

Escobar, A. (2011). *Encountering development: The making and unmaking of the Third World*. Princeton, NJ: Princeton University Press. DOI: 10.1515/9781400839926

Fagan, G. H. (1999). Cultural politics and (post) development paradigms(s). In R. Munck & D. O'Hearn (Eds.), *Critical development theory* (pp. 178–195). London: Zed Books.

Fanon, F. (1961). *Les damnés de la terre*. Paris: François Maspero.

Fisher, B. M. (2001). *No angel in the classroom: Teaching through feminist discourse*. Lanham, ML: Rowman & Littlefield Publishers, Inc.

Foucault, M. (1978). *The history of sexuality: Volume I: An introduction*. New York, NY: Random House.
Freire, P. (1970). *Pedagogy of the oppressed*. New York, NY: Herder and Herder.
Gillborn, D. (2006). Critical race theory beyond North America. In A. D. Dixson & D. K. Rousseau (Eds.), *Critical race theory in education*. New York, NY: Routledge.
Giroux, H. A. (2001). *Theory and resistance in education*. Westport, CT: Bergin and Garvey.
Glantz, A., & Martinez, E. (2018, February 15). For people of color, banks are shutting the door to homeownership. Reveal: From the Center for Investigative Reporting. Retrieved from https://www.revealnews.org/article/for-people-of-color-banks-are-shutting-the-door-to-homeownership/
González, N. (2005). Beyond culture: The hybridity of funds of knowledge. In N. González, L. C. Moll, & C. Amanti (Eds.), *Funds of knowledge: Theorizing practices in households, communities, and classrooms* (pp. 29–46). Mahwah, NJ: Lawrence Earlbaum and Associates.
González, N. (2010). Advocacy anthropology and education: Working through the binaries. *Current Anthropology*, *51*(2), S249–S258. DOI: https://doi.org/10.1086/653128
Grande, S. (2003). Whitestream feminism and the colonialist project: A review of contemporary feminist pedagogy and praxis. *Educational Theory*, *53*(3), 329–346. DOI: 10.1111/j.1741-5446.2003.00329.x
Grande, S. (2004). *Red pedagogy: Native American social and political thought*. Oxford: Rowman and Littlefield Publishers, Inc.
Grande, S. (2009). American Indian geographies of identity and power. In A. Darder, M. Baltodano, & R. Torres (Eds.), *The critical pedagogy reader* (pp. 1–20). New York, NY: Routledge Falmer.
Green, G. P., & Haines, A. (2016). *Asset building & community development*. Thousand Oaks, CA: SAGE publications.
Harcourt, W. (Ed.). (2016). *The Palgrave handbook of gender and development: Critical engagements in feminist theory and practice*. London: Palgrave Macmillan.
Hilhorst, D., & Hilhorst, T. (2003). *The real world of NGOs: Discourses, diversity, and development*. London: Zed Books.
Holland, J., & Ramazanoglu, C. (1995). Accounting for sexuality, living sexual politics: Can feminist research be valid? In J. Holland & M. Blair (Eds.), *Debates and issues in feminist research and pedagogy* (pp. 273–291). Bristol: The Open University.
hooks, b. (1994). *Teaching to transgress: Education as the practice of freedom*. New York, NY: Routledge. DOI: 10.4324/9780203700280
Howard, T. C. (2010). *Why race and culture matters in schools: Closing the achievement gap in America's classrooms*. New York, NY: Teachers College Press.
Huba, M. E., & Freed, J. E. (2000). *Learner-centered assessment on college campuses: Shifting the focus from teaching to learning*. Boston, MA: Allyn and Bacon.
Jay, M. (1973). *The dialectical imagination: A history of the Frankfurt School and the Institute of Social Research 1923–1950*. Boston, MA: Little, Brown.
Jureidini, R. (2005). Migrant workers and xenophobia in the Middle East. In *Racism and public policy* (pp. 48–71). London: Palgrave Macmillan.

Jureidini, R. (2010). Trafficking and contract migrant workers in the Middle East. *International Migration Special Issue: Special Issue on Human Trafficking*, *48*(4), 142–163.

Jureidini, R. (2011). *An exploratory study of psychoanalytic and social factors in the abuse of migrant domestic workers by female employers in Lebanon*. Beirut: Kafa (enough) Violence & Exploitation Organization.

Kanpol, B. (1997). *Issues and trends in critical pedagogy*. Cresskill, NJ: Hampton Press.

Kanpol, B. (1999). *Critical pedagogy: An introduction*. Westport, CT: Greenwood Publishing Group.

Kelly, P., & Lusis, T. (2006). Migration and the transnational habitus: Evidence from Canada and the Philippines. *Environment and Planning A*, *38*(5), 831–847.

Kendi, I. X. (2019). *How to be an antiracist*. New York, NY: One world.

Kincheloe, J. L. (2008). *The critical pedagogy primer*. New York. NY: Peter Lang Publishing.

Kincheloe, J., & Steinberg, S. (1997). *Changing multiculturalism*. Bristol: Open University Press.

Kinkela, D. (2011). *DDT and the American century: Global health, environmental politics, and the pesticide that changed the world*. Chapel Hill CA: The University of North Carolina Press.

Kothari, U. (2019). *A radical history of development studies: Individuals, institutions and ideologies*. London: Zed Books.

Kumar, R. (Ed.). (2015). *Neoliberalism, critical pedagogy and education*. New York: Routledge. DOI: 10.4324/9781315659817

Ladson-Billings, G. (1998). Just what is critical race theory and what's it doing in a nice field like education? *Qualitative Studies in Education*, *11*(1), 7–24.

Ladson-Billings, G. (2006). They're trying to wash us away: The adolescence of critical race theory in education. In A. D. Dixson & D. K. Rousseau (Eds.), *Critical race theory in education*. New York, NY: Routledge.

Ladson-Billings, G. (2009). "Who you callin' nappy-headed?" A critical race theory look at the construction of black women. *Race Ethnicity and Education*, *12*(1), 87–99.

Ladson-Billings, G., & Tate IV, W. F. (2006). Toward a critical race theory of education. In A. D. Dixson & D. K. Rousseau (Eds.), *Critical race theory in education*. New York, NY: Routledge.

Lewis, D., & Kanji, N. (2009). NGOs and the aid system. In D. Lewis & N. Kanji (Eds.), *Non-governmental organisations and development*. New York, NY: Routledge.

Macedo, D., & Gounari, P. (2015). *Globalization of racism*. New York, NY: Routledge. DOI: 10.4324/9781315634388

Maher, F. A., & Ward, J. V. (2002). *Gender and teaching*. Mahwah, NJ: Lawrence Erlbaum Associates, Inc.

Malekian, S. (2020, June 2). George Floyd vigil in Iran leads to online backlash. *ABC News*. Retrieved from https://abcnews.go.com/International/george-floyd-vigil-iran-leads-online-backlash/story?id=71011654

Martens, K. (2002). Mission impossible? Defining nongovernmental organizations. *Voluntas: International Journal of Voluntary and Nonprofit Organizations*, *13*(3), 271–285.

Martinussen, J. (1997). *Society, state, and market: A guide to competing theories of development*. London: Zed Books.

Matias, C. E. (2016). *Feeling white: Whiteness, emotionality, and education*. Boston, MA: Sense. DOI: 10.1007/978-94-6300-450-3

McLaren, P. (1998). Revolutionary pedagogy in post-revolutionary times. *Educational Theory*, *48*(4), 431–463. DOI: 10.1111/j.1741-5446.1998.00431.x

McLaren, P. (2009). Critical pedagogy: A look at the major concepts. In A. Darder, M. Baltodano, & R. Torres (Eds.), *The critical pedagogy reader* (pp. 61–83). New York, NY: Routledge Falmer.

Munck, R., & O'Hearn, D. (1999). *Critical development theory: Contributions to a new paradigm*. London: Zed Books.

Nardal, J. (1928). Internationalisme noir. *La Dépêche Africaine*, *1*(1), 5.

Nelson, L., & Lind, D. (2015, February 24). The school to prison pipeline, explained. Justice Policy Institute. Retrieved from http://www.justicepolicy.org/news/8775

Oishi, N. (2005). *Women in motion: Globalization, state policies, and labor migration in Asia*. Stanford, CA: Stanford University Press.

Paulson, S. (2016). Towards a broader scope and more critical frame for intersectional analysis. In W. Harcourt (Ed.), *The Palgrave handbook of gender and development: Critical engagements in feminist theory and practice* (pp. 395–412). London: Palgrave Macmillan.

Pearson, R. (2005). The rise and rise of gender and development. In U. Kothari (Ed.), *A radical history of development studies: Individuals, institutions and ideologies* (pp. 157–179). London: Zed Books.

Petchesky, R. P. (2016). Gendered well-being, globalization, women's health and economic justice: Reflections post-September 11. In W. Harcourt (Ed.), *The Palgrave handbook of gender and development: Critical engagements in feminist theory and practice* (pp. 145–172). London: Palgrave Macmillan.

Pieterse, J. N. (1999). Critical holism and the Tao of development. *The European Journal of Development Research*, *11*(1), 75–100.

Pollock, M. (2004). *Colormute: Race talk dilemmas in an American school*. Princeton, NJ: Princeton University Press. DOI: 10.1515/9781400826124

Pollock, M. (2008). *Everyday antiracism: Getting real about race in school*. New York, NY: The New Press.

Powell, E. T. (2003). *A different shade of colonialism*. Los Angeles CA: University of California Press. DOI: 10.1525/9780520928466

Rahnema, M. (1997). Towards post-development: Searching for signposts, a new language and a new paradigm. In M. Rahnema & V. Bawtree (Eds.), *The post-development reader* (pp. 377–404). London: Zed Books.

Rist, G. (2008). *The history of development: From Western origins to global faith*. London: Zed Books.

Saad, L. F. (2020). *Me and White supremacy: Combat racism, change the world, and become a good ancestor*. Naperville, IL: Sourcebooks, Inc.

Salloum, S. (2020, June 9). The killing of George Floyd sparks controversy over African-Iraqi rights. *Al-Monitor*. Retrieved from https://www.al-monitor.com/pulse/originals/2020/06/iraq-minorities-afropiraqis-us-protests-george-floyd.html

Sandoval, C. (2000). *Methodology of the oppressed*. Minneapolis: The University of Minnesota Press.

Sandoval, C. (2009). U.S. Third World Feminism: The theory and method of oppositional consciousness in the postmodern world. In G. Henderson & M. Waterstone (Eds.), *Geographic thought: A praxis perspective* (pp. 338–354). New York, NY: Routledge.

Schuurman, F. J. (Ed.). (1993). *Beyond the impasse: New directions in development theory*. London: Zed books.

Schuurman, F. J. (2009). Critical development theory: Moving out of the Twilight Zone. *Third World Quarterly*, *30*(5), 831–848. DOI: 10.1080/01436590902959024

Sharma, A. (2008). *Logics of empowerment: Development, gender, and governance in Neoliberal India*. Minneapolis MN: University of Minnesota Press.

Sherpa, C. (2014). *Countering the hegemony of "hegemony" in social science: A Marxist critique of "subaltern" pedagogy in Indian academia*. Paper presented at International Conference on Educational Transformation and Transformative Education: Possibilities and Alternatives to the Educational Crisis. Abstract retrieved from http://sau.ac.in/~mlta/soc/abstracts.html

Sinyangwe, S., & McKesson, D. (2020, June 23). Police have killed 576 people in 2020. Mapping Police Violence. Retrieved from https://mappingpoliceviolence.org/

St. Pierre, E. A. (2000). Poststructural feminism in education: An overview. *International Journal of Qualitative Studies in Education*, *13*(5), 477–515. DOI: h10.1080/09518390050156422

Sumner, A., & Tribe, M. (2008). *International development studies: Theories and methods in research and practice*. Thousand Oaks, CA: SAGE Publications. DOI: 10.4135/9781446279397

Suspitsyna, T. (2010). Purposes of higher education and visions of the nation in the writings of the department of education. In E. J. Allen, S. V. D. Iverson, & R. Ropers-Huilman (Eds.), *Reconstructing policy in higher education: Feminist poststructural perspectives*. New York, NY: Routledge. DOI: 10.4324/9780203870037

Sutton, M., & Arnove, R. F. (2004). *Civil society or shadow state?: State/NGO relations in education*. Charlotte, NC: Information Age Publishing.

The American Presidency Project. (2014). Harry S. Truman Inaugural Address. Data file. Retrieved from https://www.presidency.ucsb.edu/documents/inaugural-address-4

The National Editorial (2020, June 25). *George Floyd: Honouring his legacy one month on*. Retrieved June 28, 2021, from https://www.thenational.ae/opinion/editorial/george-floyd-honouring-his-legacy-one-month-on-1.1038672

Thomas, A. (2004, November). *The study of development*. Paper presented at DSA Annual Conference (Vol. 6).

Tucker, V. (1999). The myth of development: A critique of Eurocentric discourse. In R. Munck & D. O'Hearn (Eds.), *Critical development theory: Contributions to a new paradigm* (pp. 1–26). London: Zed Books.

U.S. Department of Education (2016, July 11). *School climate and discipline: Know the data*. Retrieved June 22 2020, from https://www2.ed.gov/policy/gen/guid/school-discipline/data.html

Villaverde, L. (2008). *Feminist theories and education*. New York, NY: Peter Lang Publishing.

Watson Institute for International and Public Affairs. (2020, November 17). Racialization & Racism in the Middle East: Historical Perspectives [Video file]. Retrieved from https://www.youtube.com/watch?v=YItbkQ_l5IM

Weedon, C. (1987). *Feminist practice and poststructuralist theory*. Oxford: Blackwell Publishing.

Whitaker, B. (2006, September 8). The race taboo. *The Guardian*. Retrieved from https://www.theguardian.com/commentisfree/2006/sep/08/racisminthemiddleeast

Weiler, K. (1995). Foreword. In J. Jipson, P. Munro, S. Victor, K. F. Jones, & G. Freed-Rowland (Eds.), *Repositioning feminism in education: Perspectives on educating for social change* (pp. xiii–xvii). Westport, CT: Bergin & Garvey.

Weiner, M. F. (2012). Towards a critical global race theory. *Sociology Compass*, *6*(4), 332–350. DOI: 10.1111/j.1751-9020.2012.00457.x

Wise, T. (1998). Is sisterhood conditional? White women and the rollback of affirmative action. *NWSA Journal*, *10*(3), 1–26. DOI: 10.2979/nws.1998.10.3.1

Yates, L. (1993). Feminism and Australian state policy: some questions for the 1990s. In M. Aront & K. Weiler (Eds.), *Feminism and social justice in education: International perspectives* (pp. 167–185). London: The Falmer Press.

Yaziji, M., & Doh, J. (2009). *NGOs and corporations: Conflict and collaboration*. Cambridge: Cambridge University Press. DOI: 10.1017/cbo9780511626708

Yuval-Davis, N. (2016). Power, intersectionality, and the power of belonging. In W. Harcourt (Ed.), *The Palgrave handbook of gender and development: Critical engagements in feminist theory and practice* (pp. 367–381). London: Palgrave Macmillan.

Chapter 3

Participatory Action Research at the Migrant Center

The Migrant Center (MC) is located in the ethnically diverse and low-income eastern Beirut suburb of Naba'a. Naba'a is a complex place, home to Sunni and Shi'i Muslims, Armenian Christians, and other religious, ethnic, and political groups. This suburb is densely populated, with an estimated population of 12,000 in an area of three square kilometers. Naba'a is situated within meters of a highway running literally over the top of the interconnecting neighborhoods. Directly under this stretch of highway run several lanes of traffic; on the one side is Naba'a, and on the other is the suburb of Borj Hammoud, the Armenian Christian district. Along this centralized thoroughfare of commerce, street vendors, and heavy traffic, one finds the busyness and chaos of urban life. The narrow side street to the MC is lined with two- and three-story buildings that function as commercial and residential spaces.

On weekday mornings, coffee and friendly conversation are available from the Armenian Christian metal shopkeeper whose shop is steps from the Center. Nighttime brings the scent of *shisha* [flavored tobacco] bubbling from the *nargile* [water pipe] as friends and family gather to sit around the pipe while the business day winds down. The narrow alleys off the busy side streets are wide enough for one car to slowly creep through, although motorcycles commonly use these narrow passageways to avoid traffic. A zigzag pattern of miniature political and religious flags hang from top-story balconies and spot the blue sky. This particular alleyway of the MC is home to Shi'i Muslims and Armenian Christians. Along the maze of intertwining back alleyways and ubiquitous residential entrances, the shiny red door of the MC with its red metal shutters stands out amongst the faded brick.

Naba'a can be an unsafe place for migrant workers. Several of the domestic workers described being sexually and/or verbally harassed in close proximity to the MC. Suba, the coordinator of the Center, reports: "Every single day, I go five meters from here to there, there is someone who teases you, who asks you, 'What's your price?' Very stupid, you feel so angry.

DOI: 10.4324/9781003166566-3

This is very, very non-human". I too have witnessed many occasions of the harassment described by the migrant workers. On one particular day at the Center, someone had lit fireworks and had thrown them up against the window, and we heard an extremely loud blast. According to Dakshi, Suba's husband, these were not isolated incidents, and occurred often. The Center had also been vandalized.

In recent years, non-governmental organizations (NGOs) in Lebanon have been recognizing the plight of migrant workers, especially women migrant workers, and have been filling the void of legal and social assistance, as evidenced by the pioneering work of such organizations as Amel and Caritas. A recent development within Lebanon's migrant NGO and grassroots network is the offering of educational opportunities, such as English classes, French classes, and computer classes for adult migrant workers. It is within this educational context, in the space of the MC, this study performs: I seek to learn about the pedagogical and ideological frameworks from which the NGOs operate to meet the needs of the populations they serve. This ethnographic, participatory action research (PAR) study also sought to examine the life and educational trajectories of the migrant women who receive services at the MC and juxtapose their lived experiences against the agendas of these NGOs.

It is within this context of the MC that this PAR project takes place, and I seek to examine the following research questions: 1. What are the theoretical and pedagogical constructs of this NGO system and are they congruent to the lived experiences of the women migrant workers? 2. How does migrant workers' knowledge production inform power and empowerment of their community? 3. What role does the MC play in the education and empowerment of migrant workers? I will provide the story behind this project, describe my positionality, discuss the iterations of PAR, and outline my research methodology in the following pages.

Why This Study? The Pilot

In summer 2010, I conducted a pilot study in Tehran, Iran, at an NGO women's center that provided social, legal, and educational services for Afghan refugees and Iranian women who had suffered abuse and neglect. I volunteered as an English teacher at the center. At that time, Afghan refugees were not allowed to attend the public schools in Iran[1] so classes at this NGO and others like it[2] were their only option for educational opportunities. According to Sohrab, a social worker who works closely with the students, and whom I interviewed for the pilot study, he is dismayed by the way empowerment is taught and appropriated at the center, as if empowerment in and of itself is a cure-all to all of these women's problems. The use of self-esteem workshops and their ideology work well in the space of the center, but, according to Sohrab, those ideas lose all meaning once the women step outside of the center into Tehran's streets. Sohrab feels that the women were becoming more acutely aware of the intensity of their captivity and, according to Sohrab, "What is so empowering about that?" The appropriation of the term "empowerment" associated with the center and its empowerment workshops invokes a "magic bullet" quality, or a feminist "cure-all" to the women who attend the center; McLaren and Giarelli (1995) assert that "if educational research is to have emancipatory force it must contribute to the empowerment of stakeholders whose emancipatory interest is compromised under existing educational arrangements" (p. 301). The "empowerment" ideology of the center does not address the existing power disparity between nationalities within Iranian society nor within the center itself, perpetuated by the political and educational institutions. Sohrab asserts that it is necessary to contextualize "empowerment" to fit the lived experiences of these women's lives.[3]

From the pilot study at the Tehran women's center, I learned a lack of alignment exists between the feminist ideology that drives the center's mission statement and curriculum of its empowerment workshops and the lived experiences of the women who attend the center, as recognized by some staff members. From observations at the women's center, I also learned that Afghan students experienced pervasive racism and xenophobia at the center. These racialized tensions were also present in our classroom space. As a teacher-researcher, the aim of this participatory research was to bring a contextualized lens for improving the social services and educational experiences for the Iranian and Afghan students by recognizing that, as McCarty (2002) noted, "learning is participation in the social world-involvement in communities of social practice...." (p. 32).

Why This Study? The Focal Research Project

My aim was to return to Iran and continue my research project at the women's center; however, in March 2012, I was told by the Institutional Review Board's (IRB) Export Control council at the University of Arizona that I would no longer be able to return to Iran for further research due the Obama Administration's ongoing cooperation with the United Nation's sanctions being placed on Iran. These restrictions required that I seek another research site to complete my research project. A colleague and friend of mine who had lived in Beirut for several years and had worked with some NGOs regarding public health initiatives facilitated my acquaintance with the research site in Beirut. Four parameters needed to be in place when I was considering a research site: First, I wanted the site to be in the Middle East/South West Asia and North Africa (SWANA) region; second, I wanted to continue to teach English; third, I wanted the core of my students to be adult women from marginalized backgrounds; and, fourth, I wanted the space of the learning to occur in a nonformal learning environment, one whose educational opportunities were not governed by an institutional or governmental oversight committee, reminiscent of public schooling in the United States. It was important to me, as an educator, for the students to want to be there, to exercise agency in participating in their learning, and to have the freedom to leave the class at any time. I was fortunate to find a research site within a short amount of time that fulfilled my research parameters.

I began corresponding with Maha via email, the volunteer coordinator and teacher for the Migrant Workers Educational Group (MWEG), prior to entering the field in Beirut. I introduced myself as a volunteer English teacher who has had past experience teaching Afghan refugees at a women's center in Tehran. I discussed my interest in conducting a research project which included student interviews in Beirut with the objective of learning about my future students' educational and life trajectories. I relayed to Maha that I would like to contribute to curriculum development and teacher training in the time I would be in Beirut; so, not only would I volunteer as an English teacher, but I would be interested in being a part of other educational aspects as well. Reciprocity ties into my belief that as an authentic educator, it is my responsibility to give back to the communities who allow me to conduct research and who share with me their life stories.

As a scholar who seeks to learn about the educational processes of groups who have been historically marginalized, oppressed, and dispossessed; as a teacher-researcher who seeks to access those groups' funds of knowledge for understanding issues of agency and power as related to educational access; and as an activist who seeks to "channel" this knowledge by way of contextualized curriculum development and teacher training at my research site, I chose a community-based participatory research (CBPR) methodology.

Community-Based Participatory Research

This research project employs a participatory research approach that takes into account the political, social, and historical situatedness of the macro, meso, and micro contexts of the research site, and also engages the community in the research process. Since the advent of action research, several variances exist in reference to its core ideas and principles, such as community-based action research, participatory research, community-based research, and so on (Hunter, Emerald, & Martin, 2013; Kindon, Pain, & Kesby, 2007; Minkler & Wallerstein, 2008). According to Kindon et al. (2007), the term "participatory" is added to "action research" to indicate a "political commitment, collaborative processes and participatory worldview" while to some other activist-researchers the use of the term "action" is redundant as the emancipation project is part of and parcel to the participatory research process (p. 11). The commonality among these different variances is the strong sense of social justice that motivates the researcher in conducting the research in the first place (Creswell, 2009; Minkler & Wallerstein, 2008; Teddlie & Tashakkori, 2010). Distinguishing features of PAR from other research approaches is the "systematic form of praxis that begins from what you learn from the reconnaissance phase of your research" and understanding that the participants are key in "identifying problems, collecting and analyzing data and implementing solutions" (Hunter et al., 2013, p. 7). For this research project, my pilot study was crucial in understanding the core issues subaltern groups encounter in their everyday lives, such as racism, oppression, and systemic abuse, so as to be a more effective and compassionate researcher and educator. First, I discuss the epistemological position of participatory research and then discuss the qualitative approaches of this research project.

Epistemological and Philosophical Assumptions of Participatory Research

PAR and CBPR have historical roots grounded in the work of psychologist Kurt Lewin, who, in 1944, first coined the term "action research"; he rejected the positivist claim that the researcher should apply the laws that govern the natural scientific realm should also govern the social realm (Minkler & Wallerstein, 2008, p. 27), a view also held by the early critical theorists of the Frankfurt School. The sociologist Talcott Parsons' action theory, a theoretical statement which takes into account the subjective stance of the human condition while acknowledging the scientific rigor of positivism (Parsons, 1978), also contributes to the foundational ideas that inform CBPR.

As social scientists, we assume a position on the epistemological spectrum as it relates to social science research (Kanbur & Shaffer, 2007). On one end of the spectrum is the positivist position; the positivist rejects the *a posteriori* position and asserts the necessity to remain as objective as humanly possible, to mitigate all extenuating variables, and to maintain a neutral place so as to not taint data. The epistemological assumptions of positivism are such that "there is one reality, which is observable; the aim of knowledge inquiry is to acquire a single truth, in the form of a general law; the researcher aims to maintain an objective position, remaining independent of the researched" (Sumner & Tribe, 2008, p. 59).[4] The problematic of the positivist/postpositivist turn for the social constructivist lies in the refusal to forego the idea of objectivity that there is some reachable "truth" out there to be got (Cousin, 2010, p. 9), whereas the participatory worldview endorses a more subjective view, as will be discussed.

In the middle of this characterization of epistemology falls realism, a position that asserts that reality exists independently of the researcher and is describable; that the aim of inquiry is to describe reality, and it is not possible to establish the truth about a reality; and that the researcher, a dependent observer, is part of reality (Sumner & Tribe, 2008). On the other end of the spectrum, a relativist standpoint (often used interchangeably with constructivism, Sumner & Tribe, 2008) is such that "there are multiple realities which can be experienced"; knowledge inquiry is an "informed construction of understanding"; and, most pivotal, the researcher is subjective within the research process (Sumner & Tribe, 2008, p. 59). According to Creswell (2014), the goal of the relativist/social constructivist researcher "is to rely as much as possible on the participants' views of the situation being studied" (p. 8); in this way, the researcher recognizes the importance of the participants' funds of knowledge (González, Moll, & Amanti, 2005) by privileging a multi-perspective stance.

The Social Justice Orientation of Participatory Research: Goals and Aims

In the 1980s, researchers recognized that existing methodologies were informed by positivist/postpositivist philosophical assumptions which did not take into account the social, lived realities of populations which had experienced marginalization and oppression. Participatory research emerged from the philosophical assumptions of the transformative worldview, which holds that the aim of the research inquiry is enmeshed with and motivated by the researcher's agenda to "confront social oppression at whatever level it occurs" (Mertens, 2010, as cited by Creswell, 2014). According to Creswell (2009), researchers who advocate for a participatory orientation assert that

> the postpositivist assumptions imposed structural laws and theories that did not fit marginalized individuals in our society or issues of social justice that needed to be addressed...An advocacy/participatory worldview holds that research inquiry needs to be intertwined with politics and a political agenda. Thus, the research contains an action agenda for reform that may change the lives of the participant, the institutions in which individuals work or live and the researcher's life. Moreover, specific issues need to be addressed that speak to important social issues of the day, issues such as empowerment, inequality, oppression, domination, suppression, and alienation. (p. 9)

Several scholars have contributed to the merging of research methodologies and social justice initiatives. The educational outreach of Brazilian educator and philosopher Paulo Freire is considered to have laid the groundwork of participatory research and is largely cited by several leading critical scholars and PAR studies as being a transformative educational approach (Creswell, 2014; Denzin & Lincoln, 2011; Duncan-Andrade & Morrell, 2008; Kapoor & Jordan, 2009; Minkler & Wallerstein, 2008).

To be sure, like any research paradigm, PAR has its share of critics, who consider PAR to be biased, not "pure" in terms of its methodology, and as such, it is "rarely taught in our leading postsecondary institutions" (Duncan-Andrade & Morrell, 2008); however, if its greater objective is to meld a theory with practice and to produce results of which are not solely for the benefit of the researcher, but on the contrary, are meant to be empowering *for the participants' communities*, then a "purist", positivist/postpositivist position holds little place in a researcher's motivation. In fact, PAR is working against the failure of the institution (be it educational, health care, social work, and so on) "to decolonise the underlying ideological impulse that administers our professional imaginations" which have the tendency to "(re) produce a narrowly individualistic and pragmatic paradigm…PAR is an open and interconnected approach, one that is unashamed of its political and ideological foundations and is constructed through relationships to the 'other' as defined by shared place-based interests" (Hunter et al., 2013, p. 8). Budd Hall (1992), a leading Participatory Action (PA) researcher, asserts that participatory research is "a practice that attempted to put the less powerful at the center of the knowledge process; to move people and their daily lived experiences of struggle and survival from the margins of epistemology to the center" (pp. 15–16).

In sum, my aim as a researcher and as a critically conscious human being is to contribute to a body of knowledge which first and foremost honors the voices and lives of those who share their stories with me. As an educator, I aim to continue to serve those groups who desire educational opportunities, and I will continue to practice a liberatory pedagogy with all groups, especially the marginalized and oppressed. It is my hope to bring front and center the epistemologies of the oppressed and contribute to a critical subaltern pedagogy that takes into account the traversing of physical and metaphysical borders of those who inhabit the margins and borders of new and old spaces.

The Subjective Voice: A Plurality of Lenses

My epistemological position affects the ways in which I conduct and collect data, and the very research projects I choose (or choose me). Denzin and Lincoln (2011) note, "All approaches to knowledge production or inquiry are shaped by the historical contexts in which they emerge" (p. 388). As a social scientist and critical constructivist, I assert the problematic of the positivist standpoint is that it positions human beings in such a way as to deny them of their human agency, as being unfree; positivist research paradigms "consider knowledge creation to be a neutral and value-free activity" (Minkler & Wallerstein, 2008, p. 28). It is my belief that knowledge creation is not a neutral action. Researchers, like any member of the human species, are influenced by their experiential knowledge. We, as human beings first and social scientists second, are not capable of being independent of the observations we encounter in our daily lives and in the field. My own lived experiences compel me to work with dispossessed and marginalized groups.

Vygotskian theory holds that the learner's cognition is embedded in his/her social and cultural worlds (Moll, 2014). In social constructivist fashion, as I reflect on the circumstances that have shaped my life trajectory, my own background shapes my interpretation, and I position myself in the research to acknowledge how my interpretation "flows from [my] personal, cultural, and historical experiences" (Creswell, 2014, p. 8). Like most people, several experiences in my youth have inevitably shaped my worldview and my claims of knowledge. My father is Iranian and my mother is Anglo-American. Being of mixed heritage, I encountered my Iranian-ness in the U.S. context. In the space of some months, the Iranian Revolution (popularly known as the 1979 Revolution or Islamic Revolution) occurred, followed by the U.S. embassy takeover and hostage crisis. These events happened when I was seven years old, and I remember clearly the images of the blindfolded men on TV, causing my father great concern, as a xenophobic haze and racist hatred plagued the United States: Popular at the time was the song, "Bomb Iran" (pronounced, "eye-ran"), a parody of The Regents' 1961 hit, "Barbara Ann". Derogatory bumper stickers and t-shirts about Iran and Iranians still sit in my seven-year-old mind. I remember my father's stories of disgruntled co-workers and the hateful comments he endured.

My father instructed us to never reveal his national identity – if ever we were asked, we were to say he was from Iraq, not Iran, a convenient cover for a fearful father. My sister and I were often asked this question in our predominantly White, middle-class Chicagoland suburban neighborhood. I can still vividly recall that awful sinking feeling of shame and fear when my sister and I were drilled with questions from a neighbor girl's father: "Where is your father from? How long has he been here? When is he going back? Why is he here?" Overnight, he had turned into an angry man taking out his prejudice and anger on children. I remember the awful names being flung our way and the constant façade of keeping up that "front" of my father's fictitious homeland. My father's fears led him to change our last name from the Middle Eastern-sounding "Yousefkheyl" to the more ubiquitous-sounding "Keyl" when I was ten years old. As I got older, that shame turned into indignation. I no longer pretended my father was from Iraq. I still encountered the prejudice and ignorance and outright racism, but I stuck my Iranianness out there like a flag flying in the wind, a resilient attitude that would protect me in coming years.

When I was 22, I gave birth to my daughter, Grace. I became an unwed mother, a single mom. This label is fraught with many socioeconomic, racialized, politicized, and sexualized implications, of which I learned quite quickly. Not only did the Muslim-Iranian community condemn me, but my American friends as well, in addition to Christian socioreligious circles to which I belonged. Every facet of my life was impacted in myriad ways.

Except for one close friend, all others abandoned me, even family. What could and should have been a joyous event was filled with sorrow, criticism, and rejection. However, just like my resilience had carried me through the torrent of racism of my younger years, I once again gathered my strength. I was truly blessed in my motherhood with a beautiful, intelligent, wise, and kind daughter. And, during her growing-up years, we had a wonderful support network of friends and family who helped me so I could attend graduate school.

Binaries seem to define me: I am educated, but experienced relative poverty; I am both American and Iranian, national identities that seem to be diametrically opposed by power entities; my single parent status, a point of contention not only in Iranian society, but American society as well, tends to "color" or distort the perception of whoever is in a position to draw assessments, usually causing one to conclude stereotypical judgments found in popular media about single moms. The ensuing years put me in places of a constant juggling of margins and borders, physically and mentally inhabiting those liminal spaces of the "in-between", usually finding myself in opposition to whatever hegemonic power structures were in place. Just as Sandoval (2000) asserts a fresh mapping of new epistemologies is needed for understanding "new sets of alterities" (p. 195, fn 42), I assert this mapping of the "third space" can navigate for the dispossessed and disempowered new ways of learning, especially when combined with the act of "civic courage" (Giroux, 1989), the idea of one (and in this case, the researcher) committing to redefining one's "identity and practice with compassion for the plight of 'others'" (Hunter et al., 2013, p. 6). This research project requires a "counterhegemonic approach to knowledge production" (Kindon et al., 2007, p. 9), as it is a navigation of those in-between epistemological spaces, and, as McDermott argues, resists "traditional models of knowledge construction which privilege expert knowledge" (as cited by Denzin & Lincoln, 2011, p. 388).

The characteristics that make my study a participatory project is an understanding that a disconnect between research and practice exists (Pine, 2009) and I deeply believe that my educational research should endorse a research agenda involving a liberatory pedagogy (Freire, 1970), especially when working in a classroom of historically oppressed and marginalized groups, like the Southeast Asian and African migrant workers in Beirut and Afghan refugees in Iran, both populations which have experienced incredible systemic racism and oppression.

I also discussed with Maha my experiences in the field and the observations I had been making to get her input. For example, she told me how an activist with whom she is acquainted questioned the whole point of providing educational opportunities for migrant workers; because, after all, don't they have more pressing needs, such as medical care and food? Her friend also debated whether or not Maha's participation in the Migrant Worker's

Education Group as a volunteer coordinator and teacher "really counts as activism". As a result of this discussion with Maha, I incorporated this dialogue into my interview questions with migrant workers so as to gain an understanding about what exactly they want and/or expect from these service and activist groups.

Other key characteristics of this research's being action-oriented and participatory in nature is are the process of sharing what I have learned vis-à-vis my participants' shared knowledge, or, the "voices of the knowers" (Wimpenny, 2010, p. 91). I volunteered to provide a teacher-training workshop for the volunteer teachers to share with them ideas about critical pedagogy and what that "looked" like in a classroom setting. I shared with them about using a place-based, culturally relevant curriculum; about forging relationships with their students; and learning about their own funds of knowledge so as to incorporate them into the learning space.

Reflexivity in (and out of) the Field

In the 2013 essay, "Palestinian Refugees Are Not at Your Service", Moe Ali Nayel relays his experiences working as a translator for a Harvard researcher and with her trainees who are gathering survey data in Lebanon regarding refugee migration from Syria (Nayel, 2013). As the Harvard trainee peppers the refugee participant, Um Muhammad, with rapid fire questions in a cold and brusque manner, she attempts to share her agonizing story about her son who was in desperate need of medical attention due to a head wound from a Syrian regime bomb – she was hoping the researchers would be able to offer some assistance. The head researcher abruptly informs her that they were there to collect data, not to discuss her son. As if to console her, the researcher included again that she was from Harvard, a "very important" university, and the information they collect from her will be included in a published report.

I include this anecdote because it precisely captures Linda Tuhiwai Smith's sentiments in her seminal work, *Decolonizing Methodologies: Research and Indigenous Peoples* (1999): "In a very real sense research has been an encounter between the West and the Other" (p. 8), and in this instance, the West dictates that the Other, or, "the researched", serves the former's needs, in the most egregious and patronizing of ways, without any reciprocity, concern, or compassion for Um Muhammad's son. Like Nayel, I too have observed Westerners, namely, U.S. Americans, in the region who condescendingly engage with local peoples, who treat volunteering with oppressed groups as a pastime or as something to include as a byline in their CV, who exoticize, objectify, and otherize in orientalist fashion (Said, 1978), and who regard refugees as props for their social media posts. Anyone who is in a position of privilege to work with oppressed groups must undergo the rigorous undertaking of checking their privilege, questioning power dynamics (namely, theirs), and examining their own savior complex and/or inherent orientalist views. Nayel's essay is also a stark reminder that I, too, am an outsider, even if I do have heritage ties to the region, and I must always critique my own motivations for doing work in the region. I must be transparent with research participants and be constantly holding up myself to the light, engaging in reflexivity, to investigate my own positionality as a researcher, a teacher, an activist, and a critical scholar.

This is not to say that outsiders should not be conducting research in the region; rather, it is a call for researchers to engage in the necessary task of academic rigor, such as attaining an area studies degree and partake in language training, pursue rigorous research methods courses, commit to a decolonizing mindset, foster an attitude of humility, and engage in reflexivity, which is the act of being in "a continual internal dialogue and critical self-evaluation of the researcher's positionality… which leaves the researcher changed in its wake" (Finefter-Rosenbluh, 2017, p. 2). It should also be normalized for local development and NGO workers to expect outsiders to demonstrate the above benchmarks in addition to having a say in what kinds of research is allowed to occur in their space. Within such parameters, research collaboration would indeed flourish and create the conditions for new knowledge production; to be sure, according to Dr. Seteny Shami, Director-General at the Arab Council for the Social Sciences in Beirut, Lebanon, there are "inadequate linkages to global knowledge production between the knowledge production that takes place in the [Middle East] region and to global circulations of knowledge", which suggests that it is important for researchers in the region to "engage with scholars who are studying a particular topic, or a particular place to enhance transregional connections" for the sake of new knowledge production (The American Center of Research, 2021).

Transparency of Positionality

In my description to Maha about my research interests with MWEG, I explained to her that I had conducted a pilot study at a women's center in Iran as an English teacher and researcher with the interest of understanding the gendered and cultural narratives of the Afghan refugees who seek out educational opportunities at the women's center. I also shared that I was interested in how an NGO functions as a place of women's empowerment in the Islamic Republic of Iran. I wanted to continue to learn about the educational opportunities available to other marginalized groups, such as migrant workers, particularly in the Arab Middle East region.

Maha and I had several email exchanges over the course of a few weeks. I explained to her that I would like to interview the women migrant workers about their past educational experiences in their home countries, the detailed accounts of their migration to Beirut, and descriptions of their lived experiences in Lebanese society, paying particular attention to the discourses that surround their experiences with racism, power, and social justice. I also described how the Freirean thought informs my own positionality as a teacher-researcher.[5] While Maha was not an educator by training, she did have a graduate degree in social justice, so my description of dialogism in the classroom space was well received. I learned from Maha in those first initial emails that the teaching opportunities with MWEG would be a promising fit, as this organization provided English classes and computer classes to women migrant workers, and she was open to me conducting fieldwork. However, one of her stipulations of being allowed access to the teaching space for the purposes of conducting fieldwork was that I "give back" to the students as a teacher-researcher. Maha's conditions aligned with my own participatory research orientation and critical pedagogical objectives, so I readily agreed to her terms.

Strategy of Inquiry/Research Design

This qualitative study is informed by grounded theory methods, consisting of "...[S]ystematic, yet flexible guidelines for collecting and analyzing qualitative data to construct theories 'grounded' in the data themselves", also consisting of

> heuristic devices rather than formulaic rules...Thus, data form the foundation of our theory and our analysis of these data generates the concepts we construct. Grounded theorists collect data to develop theoretical analyses from the beginning of a project. We try to learn what occurs in the research settings we join and what our research participants' lives are like. We study how they explain their statements and actions, and ask what analytic sense we can make of them. (Charmaz, 2006, pp. 2–3)

What distinguishes a grounded theory approach from a positivist research approach is the former values a *posteriori* knowledge, or knowledge dependent on experience while the latter privileges *a priori* knowledge, or knowledge independent of experience; therefore, positivists deduce "testable hypotheses from existing theories", while grounded theorists advocate for "*developing* theories from research grounded in data" (p. 4). As one who advocates for the utilization of grounded theory, I adopt *a posteriori* justification when entering the research field and conducting fieldwork.

Grounded theory does not aim to make generalizable claims "abstracted from empirical realities"; rather, the strength of grounded theory situates "grounded theories in their social, historical, local and interactional contexts", which strengthens theorizing claims that emerge and allows for "making nuanced comparisons between studies" (Charmaz, 2006, p. 180). This study aims to contribute an emergent theory and practice of subaltern groups to explain how knowledge production and power are intertwined and create liberatory and resistance frameworks that function in educational and community spaces.

This study also utilizes a case study research design, which is defined as "a detailed examination of one setting, or a single subject, a single depository of documents, or one particular event" (Bogdan & Biklen, 2007, p. 59). The Center operates under the direction of Tamkin and the Anti-Racism Movement. While I do draw from my fieldwork at the women's center in Tehran to help me ground my initial research questions, this is not a comparative study. Comparative studies tend to engage in binary-type, causal thinking, a "better than/worse than" reductionism, which is not the aim of this study. A case study design, according to Creswell (2014), is a design of inquiry "in which the researcher develops an in-depth analysis of a case, often of a program, event, activity, [or] process...Cases are bound by time and activity, and researchers collect detailed information using a variety of data collection tools over a sustained period of time" (p. 14).

This research project, including the time spent in Tehran at the women's center, was a total of five months: The pilot study was two months in summer 2010, while the study at the Beirut site was three months in summer 2012. Several data collection tools were used, which will be discussed in detail in the coming pages. The case study research design is compatible with and is utilized in other participatory research projects as well. Many PAR studies conducted in K-12 schools use a singular case study design or a multiple case study design. One such example is teacher-researchers Duncan-Andrade and Morrell's (2008) PAR project in an Oakland, California, high school and in summer research seminars. They utilize a "cycle of critical praxis", which channels their research in a way that addresses the very problems they and their student-researchers discovered (p. 12). In terms of action research taking place in educational spaces primarily for migrants, refugees, or other marginalized groups in an international context, Seenarine's (2004) research regarding education and empowerment of Dalit, or "untouchable" women in India, does not name action research as the methodology in use, which is more of a phenomenological research design, but his study is telling in that it reveals how systemic racism, or "caste-ism", is perpetuated in the schools by teachers as well.

Sampling

The main participants in my study were adult migrant women between the ages of 23 and 38 from Nepal and the African countries of Ethiopia, Senegal, Kenya, Madagascar, Nigeria, and the Ivory Coast. They were enrolled in classes being offered at the MC through MWEG that took place at the MC from June 2012 through September 2012. Other migrant women interviewed for this study were taking classes at MWEG's sister site in central Beirut or attending rehearsal for play practice. In total, I interviewed 14 women migrant workers who worked in the domestic sector, 8 teachers, 5 coordinators, and 1 male migrant worker. As noted in other studies involving migrant workers, this is a very difficult population from which to recruit participants due to their daily structural limitations, such as the demand from their employers to often work 15+ hours per day; therefore, random sampling is not a viable option for this study (Ireland, 2011; Oishi, 2005).

I utilized the non-probability sampling technique called purposive sampling, a sampling technique "in which particular settings, persons, or events are deliberately selected for the important information they can provide that cannot be gotten as well from other choices" (Maxwell, 1997, p. 87). I used two specific purposive sampling strategies in order to achieve maximum "representativeness" within my sample: snowball sampling, which is the technique that "involves using [participants] to identify additional cases who may be included in the study" (Teddlie & Tashakkori, 2010, p. 175). An example of this is when participants would suggest a student in another class who they believed would be interested in talking to me. The other purposive sampling strategy I used was sampling of politically important cases, which "involves selecting...politically significant or sensitive cases for study" (Teddlie & Tashakkori, 2010, p. 175). As mentioned previously, many women migrant workers have experienced and/or continue to experience many human rights atrocities which have been the subject of international news coverage from media outlets such as Al Jazeera English, CNN International, and BBC News.[6]

Languages and Interviews

Because the center in which I conducted this project is a community center for migrant workers, it was common to hear several different languages in the course of one day: Filipino, the Nepali language, French, Arabic, English, and the languages spoken in African countries, such as Amharic, the official language of Ethiopia, or Wolof, the language of Senegal. Migrant-student participants' native languages were French, Amharic, Wolof, or English. One of my students is fluent in English, in addition to other languages, as she is from Nigeria and English is the official language; however, she cannot read or write, so she became my student that way. Additionally, another participant from Nigeria was not a student but frequented the Center to use the internet, and he was fluent in English as well.

I conducted the interviews in English. I used a Lebanese translator[7] who was fluent in French, English, and Arabic to conduct the interviews. The translator was a teacher for MWEG who had been a volunteer for a year, so he had already established trust and a rapport with the students I interviewed. After interviews, he and I would discuss the interviews so I was able to get his perspective as well. He provided insight in terms of the salient points made during the interviews. He also told me that being involved in the interview process helped him to get to know his students in a more personal way; thus, these interviews acted as a dialogic form of inquiry for him as a teacher.

The Research Site

The research project was conducted at the MC in Beirut, a center that provides a cultural and community space for migrant workers. The center also provides an educational space for other NGOs to teach migrant workers. The MC was chosen as the primary site of this study for a number of reasons. First, the site fulfilled the parameters for this study, as mentioned above. I was interested in learning about nonformal educational opportunities for women from marginalized groups in the Middle East/SWANA region, which was the catalyst for undertaking my pilot study at the women's center in Tehran, Iran. Lebanon was a first choice for seeking out a site because Tamkin, an internationally known NGO, is located there, and I wanted to work with women migrant workers, a marginalized group that experiences similar types of racism, xenophobia, and other structural inequalities as the Afghan refugees in Tehran. Tamkin forwarded my email to the MWEG who holds classes at the MC. The volunteer coordinator with MWEG, Maha, took me on as a volunteer teacher and researcher. The second reason I wanted to work with the MC is because the NGO network to which it is interconnected endorses a Third World feminist and anti-racism ideology. Lastly, the MC either directly runs or indirectly supports educational opportunities, such as English classes and computer classes for migrant workers.

While the pilot study was a catalyst for the focal research project in Beirut, I am not employing a collective or multiple case study design nor am I employing a comparative framework that seeks to compare and contrast the data from each site (Bogdan & Biklen, 2007, p. 69); as stated previously, I assert that drawing comparisons suggests two terms or binary divisions with the aim of creating a "better than/worse than" dichotomy. The data of this study will be viewed within a dialectical framework, seeing the worth of all units that comprise the whole of this study. By viewing this research study in an informative, descriptive, and dialectical perspective, the data collected at the primary research site, the MC, and its interconnected parts

(Tamkin and MWEG) are all viewed in their wholeness, all units informing each other in reciprocal ways.

Data Collection

In-Depth Interview

The in-depth interviews took place throughout the three months I was collecting fieldwork. I wanted participants to experience a sense of control in that they could "steer" or "monitor" the direction of the interview. The student interviews took place in the MC after classes or at the students' Sunday theatre practice location. Teachers and coordinators were interviewed at a restaurant, on the Lebanese American University campus, at the MC, or at their own homes. As a starting point, I used a list of questions to start the interview. However, the in-depth interview does not work off of a script of questions; on the contrary, the interview process is an organic process, one in which the interview becomes a dialogue, a space where the participant feels safe to share her lived experiences and her reflections on those experiences.

Sample interview questions fell within three broad categories: questions that engaged in their social memory (background/family questions), questions that examined their ideas about education, and questions that explore the women's opinions about empowerment and their ideas about the NGOs from which they receive services. One of the questions this project seeks to answer is learning if and how the ideological agenda of the NGO system aligns with the women's lived experiences. The in-depth interview is an excellent data collection tool for gathering information, as I aimed to capture the more nuanced meanings of these women's lived experiences that a survey or Likert-type scale cannot capture; according to Seidman (2006), "The in-depth interview is not to get answers to questions, nor to test hypotheses, and not to 'evaluate' as the term is normally used. At the root of in-depth interviewing is an interest in understanding the lived experience of other people and the meaning they make of that experience" (p. 9). While the goal of this interview process is to elicit information about the migrant worker's educational experiences in the NGO space, questions were not asked in any set order. The interviewee steered and contributed to the interview process as much as the interviewer did.

Participants in the In-Depth Interviews

The following is a list of the participants who agreed to be interviewed to support this study. In my IRB proposal, I did not include a signed disclaimer form, so at the beginning of every interview, I asked permission to record their voice and to use the interview to inform my research project. All the interviewees agreed to both items.

Migrant-Students and Patrons	*Teachers*	*Coordinators*
Felicity Woman, 38yrs, Nigerian In Beirut: 15 years Trade school: Sewing	*Alim* Male, 21 yrs, Lebanese teacher 1 year undergrad: Business	*Maha* Woman, 30 yrs, Lebanese volunteer 1 year MA: Social Justice
Faith Woman, 29 yrs, Kenyan In Beirut: N/A Some college: Development	*Omid* Male, 21 yrs, Lebanese teacher 1.5 years MD in training	*Fakira* Woman, 30 yrs, Lebanese paid coordinator MA
Eden Woman, 24 yrs, Ethiopian In Beirut: 1 year High school diploma	*Abe* Male, 21 yrs, Lebanese teacher 11 months Mechanical Engineer	*Suba* Woman, 25 yrs, Nepali paid coordinator high school diploma
Ady Woman, 27 yrs, Senegalese In Beirut: 8 years Middle school	*Zaid* Male, 17, Leb.-Palest. teacher 3 months High school student	*Dina* Woman, Lebanese Alt-City Coordinator PhD, media
Laurencia Woman, 28 yrs, Malagasy In Beirut: 16 years Some college	*Sofia* Woman, 26 yrs, Italian teacher 4 months MA student	*Jenny* Woman, Chinese–American Coordinator 1 year BA degree, Business
Thomas Man, 34 yrs, Nigerian In Beirut: 8 years College degree: Agriculture	*Ashraf* Male, 26 yrs, Lebanese–French teacher 12 months PhD student	
Beza Woman, 29 yrs, Ethiopian In Beirut: 14 years Left school at 15	*Roby* Male, 26 yrs, Syrian teacher 2 months BS: Pharmacist	
Makeda Woman, 28 yrs, Ethiopian In Beirut: 5.5 years High School diploma + professional degree (food prep)	*Cheraq* Male, 22 yrs, Lebanese teacher 10 months BA student	
Helena Woman, 24 yrs, Ethiopian In Beirut: 6 years High school diploma		
Naomi Woman, 25 yrs, Ethiopian In Beirut: 10 years 1 year of high school		
Antsa Woman, 29 yrs, Ivorian In Beirut: N/A Some college		
Rakab Woman, 32 yrs, Ethiopian In Beirut: 12 years		

(Continued)

Migrant-Students and Patrons	*Teachers*	*Coordinators*
High school diploma		
Giftee		
Woman, 30 yrs, Ethiopian		
In Beirut: 10 years		
2 years of high school		
Amara		
Woman, 25 yrs, Ethiopian		
In Beirut: 2.5 years		
N/A		
Abaynesh		
Woman, 29yrs, Ethiopian		
In Beirut: 12 years		
N/A		

In the Classroom: Participant Observation and the Focus Group

A majority of this research project took place in the space of the MC, at which I spent time every day, and in my classroom space on Sundays where I taught English. It is within these spaces that I utilized the anthropological research methods of ethnography, participant observation, and the focus group, which I will now discuss.

Ethnography, according to Brice-Heath and Street (2008), "forces us to think consciously about ways to enter into the life of the individual, group, or institutional life of the 'other'" (p. 31). By applying an ethnographic lens as a researcher in the classroom, my aim was to (with the permission of my participants) become aware of the attitudes, opinions, and ideas of the students in my class. The template I used for my ethnographic field notes is provided by Brian Street in *On Ethnography* (2008). In Street's field study on mathematics practiced in the home environment, he recorded details of his observations in one column, such as date, time, and other straight data, and in the opposite column he wrote his reflections of these recorded events (pp. 77–78). In my daily field notes, while I recorded the daily observations, I also utilized a journal-type data entry form, in which I recorded the situatedness of the classroom; the location of desks; how students interact; and how they answer questions and dialogue with each other, taking care to record their non-verbal cues (as these cannot be audio-recorded). Participant observation helped me understand how the students drew conclusions about knowledge and what informs their knowledge base (e.g., how do their lived experiences inform the ways they interpret the world? How do they use the advice given to them by friends and family? How do they use their formal, nonformal, and/or informal educational experiences?). The students in the classroom formed the focus group. Because I desired to create a healthy dialogic space in which an exchange of ideas, opinions, questions, and contributions could occur, my critical pedagogical stance as an authentic educator encouraged this dialogic space and the building of trust and relationships.

Social Media and Documents

In addition to the in-depth interviews, ethnography, participant observation, and focus groups, I also collected documents for data purposes as well. For example, the MWEG has a listserv, to which I subscribe, so I frequently received emails which discuss teaching issues, testing and assessment issues, ideas about curriculum, and teacher meetings. Social media like Facebook also contribute to this study's data in impactful ways (Creswell, 2014). The MC and the Anti-Racism Movement post updates on their Facebook accounts regarding events like upcoming protests, cultural events at the MC, and the sociocultural endeavors of migrant workers. These groups also post migrant workers' entrepreneurial endeavors such as promoting their catering businesses. I will now discuss the ways this data has been interpreted.

Data Analysis

Grounded theory calls for the use of coding as an analytic tool as we gather data: "Qualitative codes take segments of data apart, name them in concise terms, and propose an analytic handle to develop abstract ideas for interpreting each segment of data. As we code, we ask: which theoretical categories might these statements indicate?" (Charmaz, 2006, p. 45). For this study, I utilized coding for analyzing and interpreting the data, which will consist of two phases: initial and focused coding (Charmaz, 2006, p. 42). The initial phase of coding involves studying "fragments of data" and the focused coding phase calls for selecting the most useful codes and then testing them against the broader data (Charmaz, 2006, p. 42). The use of coding as an analytic tool applied to both the interview data and the ethnographic data I gathered.

The "focused" codes of these interviews are three: the ideological disconnect between how the West frames ideas of empowerment within the educational space, which ends up being a disempowering venture; the ways in which migrant domestic workers are creating their own economic opportunities by utilizing their existing funds of knowledge (González, Moll, & Amanti, 2005), thereby being agentive in their own right; and lastly, the ways that transformative education grounded in culturally relevant, place-based pedagogy can counter a disempowering and ineffective Western-centric ideology. Other initial codes or "subthemes" surrounded issues of empowerment and disempowerment; educational themes that stem from social memory, such as a lack of educational experiences in their youth, or memorable experiences with other teachers; how they view themselves as learners within a global context; how they would like to situate themselves within the broader context of society; issues regarding social networks and knowledge production; and the specter of sexual and physical violence in the work space and public space.

Notes

1 Iran now provides free education for the children of refugees and immigrants; see "Iran provides free education", 2021.
2 I had the opportunity to visit an NGO located in southern Tehran that serves Afghan children and some adolescents. The manager of the center was a kindly older man who donated much of his meager paycheck to keep the center open and functioning. The Afghan children's center was located in a decrepit building, with crumbling stairs, holes in the wall, and large cockroaches seen frequently; this center stood in stark contrast to the northern Tehran women's center, which was very well-funded from international sources.
3 Sohrab, the social worker, stressed the importance of utilizing Freirean pedagogy in the classroom space and the need for contextualizing the empowerment ideology.
4 The post-positivist perspective, often used interchangeably with positivism (Creswell, 2014, p. 7), is a worldview reacting to the criticisms of the absolutist notions of positivism while taking into account those criticisms to reconcile positivism with the more subjective stance of realism and relativism; even still, post-positivists maintain objectivity is necessary to mitigate the effects of bias (Cousin, 2010; Robson, 2011).
5 The Freirean frameworks that inform critical pedagogy as an educational theory and philosophy, as a teaching practice, and as a research methodological approach have monumental implications for an anthropologist of education working as a teacher-researcher, especially as it applies to ethnographic practice; yet, according to De Genova (2005), author of *Working the Boundaries: Race, Space, and "Illegality" in Mexican Chicago*, "Freire's *Pedagogy of the Oppressed*...is an extremely provocative, wildly influential, and seminal work that holds very little currency (indeed, is almost entirely neglected) in anthropological theory and practice" (p. 23).
6 CNN International visited the MC to do a story on migrant workers who were seeking out educational experiences; see Damon (2013, February 11).
7 In Lebanon, it is common for students from middle-class and upper middle-class families to attend French and English-speaking schools; many of my Lebanese contacts were fluent in all three languages.

References

The American Center of Research. (2021, May 17). *The landscape of research in Jordan and in the Arab region: Challenges, Ttansformations, prospects by Seteny Shami, Ph.D.* [Video]. YouTube. Retrieved from https://www.youtube.com/watch?v=Opxg32sKfz8

Bogdan, R. C., & Biklen, S. K. (2007). *Qualitative research for education: An introduction to theories and methods.* Boston, MA: Pearson Education.

Brice Heath, S., & Street, B. V. (2008). *On ethnography: Approaches to language and literacy research*. New York, NY: Teachers College Press.
Charmaz, K. (2006). *Constructing grounded theory: A practical guide through qualitative analysis*. London: SAGE Publications.
Cousin, G. (2010). Neither teacher-centred nor student-centred: Threshold concepts and research partnerships. *Journal of Learning Development in Higher Education, 2*, 1–9. DOI: 10.47408/jldhe.v0i2.64
Creswell, J. W. (2009). *Research design: Qualitative, quantitative, and mixed methods approaches* (3rd ed.). Thousand Oaks, CA: SAGE Publications.
Creswell, J. W. (2014). *Research design: Qualitative, quantitative, and mixed methods approaches* (4th ed.). Thousand Oaks, CA: SAGE Publications.
Damon, A. (2013, February 11). Not all colors welcomed in Lebanon's cultural tapestry. CNN.com. Retrieved from https://edition.cnn.com/2013/02/10/world/meast/lebanon-racism-migrants-sting/
De Genova, N. (2005). *Working the boundaries: Race, space, and "illegality" in Mexican Chicago*. Durham, NC: Duke University Press. https://doi.org/10.1215/9780822387091
Denzin, K., & Lincoln, Y. S. (2011). *The SAGE handbook of qualitative research*. Thousand Oaks, CA: SAGE Publications.
Duncan-Andrade, J. M. R., & Morrell, E. (2008). *The art of critical pedagogy: Possibilities for moving from theory to practice*. New York, NY: Peter Lang Publishing, Inc. DOI: 10.3726/b12771
Finefter-Rosenbluh, I. (2017). Incorporating perspective taking in reflexivity: A method to enhance insider qualitative research processes. *International Journal of Qualitative Methods, 16*(1). DOI: 10.1177/1609406917703539
Freire, P. (1970). *Pedagogy of the oppressed*. New York, NY: Herder and Herder.
Giroux, H. A. (1989). Schooling as a form of cultural politics: Toward a pedagogy of and for difference. In H. A. Giroux & P. McLaren (Eds.), *Critical pedagogy, the state, and cultural struggle* (pp. 125–151). Albany, NY: State University of New York Press.
González, N., Moll, L. C., & Amanti, C. (Eds.). (2005). *Funds of knowledge: Theorizing practices in households, communities, and classrooms*. Mahwah, NJ: Lawrence Earlbaum and Associates. DOI: 10.4324/9781410613462
Hall, B. L. (1992). From margins to center? The development and purpose of participatory research. *The American Sociologist, 23*(4), 15–28.
Hunter, L., Emerald, E., & Martin, G. (2013). *Participatory activist research in the globalised world: Social change through the cultural professions*. New York, NY: Springer. DOI: 10.1007/978-94-007-4426-4
Ireland, P. R. (2011). Female migrant domestic workers in Southern Europe and the Levant: Towards an expanded Mediterranean model? *Mediterranean Politics, 16*(3), 343–363. DOI: 10.1080/13629395.2011.613669
Kanbur, S. M. R., & Shaffer, P. (2007). Epistemology, normative theory and poverty analysis: Implications for Q-squared in practice. *World Development, 35*(2), 183–196. DOI: 10.1016/j.worlddev.2005.10.016
Kapoor, D., & Jordan, S. (2009). *Education, participatory action research, and social change: International perspectives*. New York, NY: Palgrave Macmillan. DOI: 10.1057/9780230100640

Kindon, S., Pain, R., & Kesby, M. (2007). *Participatory action research approaches and methods: Connecting people, participation, and place*. New York, NY: Routledge. DOI: 10.4324/9780203933671

Maxwell, J. A. (1997). *Qualitative research design: An interactive approach*. Thousand Oaks, CA: SAGE Publications.

McCarty, T. L. (2002). *A place to be Navajo: Rough rock and the struggle for self-determination in Indigenous schooling*. Mahwah, NJ: Lawrence Erlbaum Associates, Inc. DOI: 10.4324/9781410602503

McLaren, P. L., & Giarelli, J. M. (1995). *Critical theory and educational research*. Albany, NY: State University of New York Press.

Mertens, D. M. (2010). *Research and evaluation in education and psychology: Integrating diversity with quantitative, qualitative, and mixed methods* (3rd ed.). Thousand Oaks, CA: SAGE Publications.

Minkler, M., & Wallerstein, N. (2008). *Community-based participatory research for health: From process to outcomes*. San Francisco, CA: John Wiley and Sons.

Moll, L. C. (2014). *L.S. Vygotsky and education*. New York, NY: Routledge. DOI: 10.4324/9780203156773

Nayel, M. A. (2013). Palestinian refugees are not at your service. Retrieved from https://electronicintifada.net/content/palestinian-refugees-are-not-your-service/12464

Oishi, N. (2005). *Women in motion: Globalization, state policies, and labor migration in Asia*. Stanford, CA: Stanford University Press.

Parsons, T. (1978). *Action theory and the human condition*. New York, NY: The Free Press.

Pine, G. J. (2009). *Teacher action research: Building knowledge democracies*. Thousand Oaks, CA: SAGE Publications. DOI: 10.4135/9781452275079

PressTV. (2021, June 30). *Iran provides free education to thousands of illegal migrant kids*. Retrieved from https://www.presstv.ir/Detail/2021/06/30/661202/Iran-Afghan-migrants-education

Robson, C. (2011). *Real world research*. San Francisco, CA: John Wiley and Sons.

Said, E. (1978). *Orientalism: Western Concepts of the orient*. New York, NY: Pantheon.

Sandoval, C. (2000). *Methodology of the oppressed*. Minneapolis, MN: The University of Minnesota Press.

Seenarine, M. (2004). *Education and empowerment among Dalit (Untouchable) women in India: Voices from the Subaltern*. Lewiston, NY: The Edwin Mellen Press.

Seidman, I. (2006). *Interviewing as qualitative research: A guide for researchers in education and the social sciences*. New York, NY: Teachers College Press.

Smith, L. T. (1999). *Decolonizing methodologies: Research and Indigenous peoples*. London: Zed Books.

Sumner, A., & Tribe, M. (2008). *International development studies: Theories and methods in research and practice*. Thousand Oaks, CA: SAGE Publications. DOI: 10.4135/9781446279397

Teddlie, C., & Tashakkori, A. (2010). *Foundations of mixed methods research: Integrating quantitative and qualitative approaches in the social and behavioral sciences*. Thousand Oaks, CA: SAGE Publications. DOI: 10.4135/9781506335193

Wimpenny, K. (2010). Participatory action research: An integrated approach towards practice development. In M. Savin-Baden & C. Major (Eds.), *New approaches to qualitative research: Wisdom and uncertainty* (pp. 89–99). London: Taylor and Francis.

Chapter 4

Subalternt Epistemologies, Part I: Stories of Oppression and Resistance

The lived experiences of women who migrate are the narratives of hope, resilience, resistance (González, 2006; Scott, 1985), oppression, subjugation, and oftentimes violence (Jureidini, 2010; Jureidini & Moukarbel, 2004); the narratives of African and Southeast Asian women migrant workers who labor in domestic servitude in Beirut, Lebanon, encapsulate and epitomize all these categories. In this chapter, I provide the accounts of migrant laborers' experiences working as domestic laborers as they encounter the ebb and flow of abuses of power, agency, empowerment, and resistance in their lived experiences as migrant domestic workers. The narratives that follow are from my in-depth interviews with migrant domestic workers and archival data from news sources and social media sites that highlight and document women's struggles as domestic laborers.

Power as Discussed in Early Migration Studies Literature

Some early women's migration studies were predicated upon the notion that labor migration for women had an empowering effect. One such study suggested that migration would act as a vehicle for "liberation" or "emancipation" by virtue of the migrant worker's being autonomous of the predominant patriarchy of their home countries (Eelens, Schampers, & Speckmann, 1992, p. 227). Additionally, women's migration would bring about "stronger economic potential" for herself and her family (Eelens et al., 1992, p. 227). However, these same scholars readily admit that the discussion surrounding the "liberating" effects of international migration could potentially have on their sense of agency, stronger economic independence, and women's social status in their country of origin

> ...is difficult both conceptually and empirically. Apart from its philosophical bearing it is extremely hard to "measure" or grasp it concretely. Nevertheless it has been a central preoccupation as a perspective when

DOI: 10.4324/9781003166566-4

> women's status in various societies has been analyzed. To avoid the pitfall of structuralism, the possibility of improvement should be kept open. (p. 227)

They conclude that a series of anthropological studies are necessary to gauge the "transformation of social norms" on gender in addition to incorporating other categories of analysis "into the gender issue" (p. 227).

The Eelens et al. sociological study indicated most research examining migration neglected to analyze along the categories of ethnicity, race, and/or class, which may have provided valuable insight into the pervasive racism and xenophobia these women often encounter when working outside of their home countries, and an understanding of how the intersectionality of these categories informs the interplay between agency, power, resistance, and activism. However, one such study does examine the implications of labor migration among Sri Lankan women in the Gulf region, with an emphasis on a gendered analysis in terms of how migration affects the woman's social status as a laborer and wage-earner in her home country (Brochmann, 1993). In Sri Lanka, the causes and consequences of women's migration likely affect gender roles and relations (Brochmann, 1993, p. 3). Brochmann's biggest criticism of past studies of women Sri Lankan migrant workers surrounds social scientists' use of the terms "liberation" and "emancipation" for describing a woman migrant's experience. She finds these terms to be "pretentious", regardless of the space and place being described, "be it in the Third-or First-World" (Brochmann, 1993, p. 42). However, she describes a woman's migration in similar terms: "It is the woman who transcends the boundaries of her community, challenging structural and traditional limitations attached to sex and class" (1993, p. 2). Whether the author perceives it as an intentional transcendence of boundaries and a deliberate challenge of structural and traditional limitations on the part of women migrant workers is unclear, though she does find that women migrant workers return to their home country "more exhausted than liberated" (1993, p. 164). Even still, she finds examples of women who return from their two-year contract with "a new confidence" and "show a firmness that was not there before":

> They have gained personal strength by conquering a new world by themselves, enduring pressure and completing the set task in favour of their families back home. These examples are very few, indeed, but they nevertheless reflect that a possibility is there, if the working conditions are good or acceptable and the woman is mentally prepared for the job. (Brochmann, 1993, p. 165)

These two early quantitative studies (Brochmann, 1993; Eelens, et al., 1992) investigating women's migrant labor demonstrate that a positivist approach to the study of migration does not wholly allow for nuanced and complex understandings of the on-the-ground realities of migrant domestic workers; and that migration in and of itself is not a "liberating" practice when the migration is predicated upon economic necessity, nor do the majority of women migrant workers experience "emancipation" resulting from being unfettered by the patriarchal constraints of their households of origin. Rather, the women are bound by economic constraints within their families of origin that do not loosen by virtue of being a housemaid in the Arab Gulf region – if anything, migrant women laborers often enter dangerous private spaces of their employers' homes. These studies also reveal that a quantitative, macro perspective on the socioeconomic effects of migration neglected to bring to light the everyday, lived realities of migrant workers. Largely absent from these studies is viewing the construct of power through a plurality of discourses and theoretical understandings (Constable, 2007).

Later qualitative studies have also explored women's migration and domestic work and the idea of agency and power (Constable, 2007; Gamburd, 2011; Truong, Gasper, Handmaker, & Bergh, 2014). One study (Oishi, 2005) presents a typology of the women who migrate seeking employment, categorizing them in five types based on the additional reasons for migrating besides the economic motivation: "adventurous women": women who decide to work overseas to seek some adventure in life; "dutiful daughters": women who are motivated by filial piety and family obligations; "good wives and mothers": women motivated by a strong desire to give their children a better future; "distressed women": women who choose to emigrate to escape domestic abuse, such as an alcoholic husband and/or bullying in-laws; and "destitute women": women who choose to emigrate to escape extreme poverty (Oishi, 2005, pp. 112–124).

While the use of a typology in and of itself is not problematic, the labels used here are essentializing and distract from the overall idea presented. The choice of labels is indicative of a broader epistemological issue. "Types" and "typologies" in the social sciences, much like we see here in this example, are an attempt to capture meaning in a singular, monolithic assignment of persona, which confines and reduces the person being assigned a "type". Such a use of types, labels, and typologies in the social sciences can be viewed as positivist and reductionist. The above-cited studies emerge from the field of sociology, which often utilizes quantitative methodologies and applies a macro perspective in its analyses which lacks the humanizing factor and relies on categorization models, disempowering labels, and ascribed meanings (e.g., "adventurous women", "distressed women", "dutiful daughters", and so on). These practices suggest the researcher relies upon a deficit model of thinking in her framing of women. Such language serves to perpetuate an egocentric, "us-them" mentality within the social sciences. This problematic framing warrants a more nuanced understanding of the construct of power, agency, and/or autonomy and the migrant domestic worker's decision to traverse borders in seeking employment and economic opportunities.

When considering the narratives of African migrant domestic workers, one should be primarily concerned with "the multiplicity of power and the various forms of discipline, pleasure, resistance, and accommodation among domestic workers" (Constable, 2007, p. viii); Constable asserts,

> Power is viewed too unidimensionally [in the literature]. It is understood as emanating from the employer's superior class position, sometimes reinforced by issues of race or ethnicity, gender, or other factors. The worker is simply cast as a victim.... Such an approach neglects and even conceals other coexisting and competing forms of power and agency. (2007, p. 10)

True to point, some quantitative studies have maintained a binary tension in the discussion of power and agency of women migrants – migration is either framed as a "liberating experience" (Eelens et al., 1992) or as a disempowering experience (Jureidini, 2011). Rarely is migration framed in a more multidimensional, nuanced view.

Also problematic is the use of "fixed types" as categories of analysis because of its reductionist assertions. Constable states, "The tendencies and attitudes [domestic workers] expressed were complex and contradictory. Their views might fluctuate in the course of a day, or shift over the years with their work conditions and experiences" (2007, p. xviii). As mentioned previously, in employing a typology (Oishi, 2005), it reduces women who migrate as static, two-dimensional beings and reproduces tired, orientalist stereotypes, such as the labels mentioned above.

In the recounting of these women's stories, I do not attempt to fetishize the trauma many migrant domestic workers encounter nor "romantacize" the resistance (Abu-Lughod, 1990, p. 42),[1] empowerment, or activism of the migrant worker women at the center of this study, but rather the purpose is to illustrate the realities of women who encounter tremendous obstacles in their quest for economic opportunities and employment. In order to understand their ability to act independently and engage with their own innate agency, I include the following powerful excerpts from the in-depth interviews that provide meaning, depth, and substance of their lived experiences – a nuanced view of how they have dealt with oppressive forces and resisted oppression in the midst of terrible hardship. As Kelly and Lusis (2006) note,

> Immigrants have been extensively studied, but the ways in which immigrants themselves make sense of their lifeworlds has not always been at the top of the agenda. Researchers are frequently interested in understanding the experiences of "the immigrant", as an objective

> analytical category, rather than the experiences of "an immigrant". (p. 831)

I desire to honor the narratives they have shared with me, and, at their request,[2] I have highlighted their struggles to draw attention to the human rights issues they have experienced and continue to experience. These stories of resilience and perseverance speak to the construction of epistemological spaces that reconfigure learning and teaching (González, 2006) while also developing tools to help navigate a social system that is deeply and acutely racist and xenophobic (Bernal, 2006; Jureidini, 2010, 2011).

Similarly, while this study highlights the racism pervasive within this society, it is necessary to make clear that not all Lebanese people embody a xenophobic attitude toward migrant workers. Had it not been for the Lebanese anti-racism activists and volunteers who devote their lives and time in the service of others and to fighting racism and other human rights abuses, this study would not have been possible. I want to stress that racism is not particular to any one country, or any one group, or any one ethnicity. Prejudice of others based on skin color, class, gender, sexuality, or other difference is pervasive in every country, not just Lebanon. In short, racism is a global problem and need to continue to be examined and exposed in every country.

Abuses of Power: Experiences of Migrant Domestic Workers

As mentioned in Chapter 1, there are about 300,000 migrant domestic workers from African and Southeast Asian countries laboring in Lebanon (Kassamali, 2021). Many of these women are vulnerable to physical, emotional, and sexual abuse due to the lack of laws protecting this population (Jureidini, 2010, 2011, 2019). Too often, power brokers, such as job agents and employers, attempt to subjugate the oppressed, rather than empower them.

Migrant domestic workers report employers intentionally enforcing isolation of the worker by prohibiting access to social networks, prohibiting communication with family members in their home countries, monitoring their every movement, not allowing privacy, practicing wage garnishment for the slightest infraction, or holding back wages altogether.

In Ethiopia, Amara,[3] a student at the Migrant Center who has worked as a migrant domestic worker for six years, was told by a job agent that she would have a good work situation when she arrived in Syria. She would make decent money taking care of children, but the reality was quite different:

> كذب كله. المكتب [مكتب العمل] قال للبدو يشتغل. اذا لازم تنضف بتنضف البيت.
> اذا لازم تربي الاولاد, بتربي الاولاد. بدك تنامي اذا تعبت, بتنامي. بس ماكان في وقت للنوم.
> مالقيت منه شئ. بس ياخذ (عمولته) بيفركها. ولابيسال عنيك وين انتي.

> Everything was a lie. [The Agency] would say to the worker [being recruited] that if you're told you are going to clean the house, then you clean the house, if you're told to take care of the children, then you're going to take care of the children, you can sleep if it is tiring for you- [but] there was no time to sleep. I did not find anything that he [the recruiter] had told me [to be true] – nothing. The agency recruiter [did not care] he only wanted his money, once he received his money, he cut ties [with the employees]. The recruiter doesn't even ask about you or your whereabouts.

The same recruiting practices happen in other African countries as well. In Kenya, Faith submitted her resume to employment agencies, which reflected her college degree in the hotel industry and experience with community development. They told her she would be working in a hotel in Beirut for two years. It was only when she arrived in Lebanon that she learned she would be working in a private home as a domestic laborer for the duration of a three-year contract. She has no legal recourse because of the *kafala,* or sponsorship system, which makes employers of migrant domestic workers responsible for securing their visa and for their legal status once they enter the country. Employers who wish to have a domestic worker pay upwards of 3,000 USD to employment agencies for a three-year contract.

Even if it is stipulated in the written contract that the migrant domestic worker will be provided health insurance, food, private living quarters, and 40-hour work week, these conditions are not typically upheld (Amnesty International, 2019). Almost all of the migrant domestic workers I interviewed report some form of abuse during a previous or their present contract, and, for some migrants, the mistreatment starts as soon as they arrive at the airport. Laurencia, a migrant domestic worker from Madagascar, came to Beirut in 1996 and recounts the first moments of her arrival at the airport in Beirut:

> Et en plus à l'aéroport, c'était très sale, car c'était en 96. Ce n'est pas comme maintenant. J'ai été surprise que la police nous a enfermés dans une chambre et a pris tous nos passeports. On était 14. Et après, il y a eu trois heures d'attente debout pour que mon patron vienne me chercher. La salle était très sale partout, il y avait des Kleenex, ça sentait le pipi par terre. Après mon patron est venu me chercher de l'aéroport et je n'étais pas très contente quand j'ai vu le monsieur. Tu sais ce qu'il a fait, il m'a acheté de la glace, et le jour même sur la route, il m'apprend comment on mange la glace. Tu sais je lui ai répondu: "Monsieur je m'excuse, même à Madagascar il y a de la glace". Et dès que j'arrive à la maison, à la montagne la dame a pris mes affaires et fouille toutes mes affaires et écrit tout ce qu'il y avait dedans. Et elle m'a présenté ma chambre, il y avait un matelas par terre, sans drap, sans

> rien du tout, sans fenêtre, seulement une porte. Et je lui ai dit: "Mais c'est la première fois de ma vie que je vais dormir par terre". Parce que je lui ai dit depuis que je suis petite jusqu'à ce que je quitte le pays, on a toujours quelqu'un qui travaille à la maison, chez nous et qui nous aide et qu'on traite comme notre famille. Même les gens qui travaillent chez moi, ils ont des jolies chambres, plus que chez les autres. Et tu sais elle m'a dit? "Va prendre un bain, lave-toi". et elle m'a donné un shampoing anti-poux. A ce moment-là, j'ai commencé à pleurer.
>
> The airport was very dirty because it was in 1996. It wasn't like it is now. I was surprised that the police locked us in a room and took our passports. They were 14 of us. And then, I had to stand up for three hours, waiting for my boss to come and pick me up. The room was so filthy, there were Kleenex lying on the floor and it smelt like piss. Then, my boss came to pick me up from the airport and I wasn't very happy when I saw him. Do you know what he did? He bought me an ice cream and later on, on the road, he explains me how to eat the ice cream. "You know", I told him, "I am sorry but even in Madagascar there is ice cream". And as soon as I arrived at the house, in the mountains, the lady took my things and she went through all my things and wrote down a list of all my things. She showed me my room and there was a mattress on the floor, without sheets on, without anything, there was no window, only a door. And I told her, "It is the first time in my life that I am going to sleep on the floor, because since I was little until I left the country, we have always had someone working at home who is helping us and whom we treat like a family member. Even the people working for us had pretty rooms, which was not common". And do you know what she told me? "Go take a bath and scrub yourself off". And she gave me a de-lousing shampoo. At that moment, I started crying.

A lack of labor laws protecting migrant workers from forced labor, servitude, and slavery contributes to the exploitation of the domestic employment sector. Many migrant domestic workers who opt to leave their inhumane working conditions endure sexual assault or threats of assault at the employment agency. Laurencia continues,

> J'ai refusé de travailler, je suis restée deux mois dans un bureau. Pendant des mois je mangeais que du pain arabe et du bœuf. Il n'y avait pas d'eau potable, y'a que l'eau du robinet que je buvais. On était 14 filles qui refusaient de travailler. Et après tu sais ce qu'il arrive aussi au bureau? Il n'y a pas de lits pour dormir, seulement pour se reposer. Les filles malades elles dormaient sur les lits superposes, les filles qui n'étaient pas malades elles dormaient en bas comme ça. J'en ai eu marre d'attendre deux mois, parce qu'on ne mangeait même pas de fruits, de

> salade, pas d'eau potable. Après j'ai décidé de travailler même si c'est dur. J'ai oublié même dans les bureaux aussi lorsqu'on était 14, il reste deux filles, moi et une fille, parce qu'on était 14 filles au bureau et les autres ont décidé de travailler. Les gens du bureau nous ont aussi menacées de faire l'amour avec eux. Il y a un monsieur qui est venu et il voulait que je travaille avec lui et j'ai accepté car j'avais peur qu'il fasse l'amour avec moi. Quand j'arrive dans la deuxième famille (ça c'est la deuxième patronne), je suis seulement restée dix jours, parce que c'était une 23 pièces. La maison était trop grande. 23 pièces et 6 salles de bain. Et je suis trop fatiguée et toute seule, et ce qu'il y avait à manger aussi c'était très insuffisant. Et la dame m'a frappée aussi parce je refusais, j'étais fatiguée donc j'ai refusé de travailler.
>
> I refused to work and I stayed at the employment agency for two months. For months, I would only eat Arabic bread and beef. There was no drinkable water, only tap water, and we were 14 girls – all refusing to work. And also, do you know what happened at the office? There was no bed to sleep, only to rest for a while. The girls who were sick would sleep on the bunk beds and the girls who were not sick would sleep on the floor. I got fed up with waiting like that after two months because we wouldn't eat any fruits, any salad, or drink any drinkable water. So then, I decided to work, even if it would be hard. I also forgot to tell you that at the office, at some point, when the other girls decided to work, there were two girls left – I and another girl, and the people at the office threatened us to have sex with us. There was a gentleman who came and wanted me to work with him and I said yes because I was scared that he would have sex with me. When I arrived in the second family, with the second madam, I stayed only 10 days because there were 23 rooms. The house was way too big: 23 rooms and 6 bathrooms. I was too tired to take care of all of it on my own and I didn't get enough food. And the lady hit me because I didn't want to work because I was too tired.

Physical violence is a common theme in the migrant interviews. If they had not experienced it firsthand, they would have observed it; Giftee, an Ethiopian migrant, reports,

> جفتي: جارتي كثير بتعذب الناس. كثير بتضرب. مافي اكل. 23 ساعه مافي راحه.
> ش. ك: جارتك؟ وغير ناس؟
> جفتي: ايه, في جارتي تحت
> ش.ك: اي وقت يضربها؟
> جفتي: اكيد مو هيك بتشوفي في الكلب. الكلب هنده احتلاام اكثر.
> ش. ك: كام عمرها جارتك اللي بتشوفيها؟
> جفتي: مابعرف. بس هي اصغلر مني. مابحكي معها ليصير مشاكل.
> انا مابدي احكي لان المدام مو كويسه. انا شو بدي فيها.

GIFTEE: My neighbor tortured them [the workers] a lot, they always beat them, they would starve them and left them 24 hours without a rest or break.

S.K.: You saw this with your neighbor and anyone else?

GIFTEE: Yes, with my neighbors below me.

S.K.: At any time, they would beat her?

GIFTEE: Absolutely, it was something you wouldn't even see with a dog. A dog is given more respect.

S.K.: How old is this neighbor [the migrant worker] that you see?

GIFTEE: I do not know, but she is younger than me. I would not talk to her because it causes problems. I also did not speak to them [neighbors and migrant worker] because the madam was not good.

The abuse can be life-threatening, as it was for Faith, who describes the madam as threatening to kill her, forcing Faith to run away for fear her life was in danger. In Lebanon, every week two migrant domestic workers die of unnatural circumstances; in most cases, authorities rule the death a suicide (Azhari, 2020). These crimes are not fully investigated by the police nor are they treated with much seriousness. In 2012, Lila Aacharya, a Nepali migrant, allegedly committed suicide, but further investigation of her corpse revealed bodily mutilation, the absence of her internal organs, and her gold jewelry missing from her ears and nose (Pattisson, 2012). This tragic case brought international attention to the migrant worker plight in Lebanon and the Arab Gulf region, prompting human rights organizations to report the atrocious human rights violations. According to Dakshi, a Nepali community leader in Beirut (and Suba's husband) who follows up on the criminal investigations and works with migrant advocacy agencies,

> Daily at least fifty to sixty women enter Lebanon from Nepal to work as domestic workers. Most are between the ages of 18 [and] 25 years old and some come under false employment contracts. A lot of Nepali men traffic women from Nepal because they earn a commission from local Lebanese agencies once the woman is hired.

Lila Aacharya's mother was physically assaulted by the Nepali job agents at her own daughter's funeral:

> We have now food to eat, no one to turn to and two children to look after. In this [emotional] state, I went to see her body. When I was on my way back, crying and supporting myself with a stick, that woman [the agent's mother] beat me demanding £45. How could we pay them with our daughter dead? Our heart and soul is lost. Our hearts are broken and they react like that – they beat me! What could I do? I'm poor,

so I have to put up with these things. I found no one to support me. I could do nothing – just put up with it. I cry all the time. (Pattisson, 2012)

The second event that captured international attention happened in March 2012. Alem Dechasa-Desisa, an Ethiopian migrant domestic worker, was filmed being beaten in front of the Ethiopian consulate in Beirut ("Alem Dechasa Kidnapped", 2012). The man beating her was the job agent for the employment agency through which Ms. Dechasa-Desisa came to Beirut. She is moaning and crying throughout the video while passers-by watch and do nothing to intervene on her behalf. He slaps her and drags her into a waiting car ("Ethiopian Migrant Suicide", 2012). A week later, on March 14, 2012, she committed suicide by hanging in a psychiatric hospital. The beating video began circulating widely, drawing attention from the United Nations special rapporteur on slavery, which demanded Lebanon's labor and justice ministries conduct a thorough and transparent investigation into the matter ("UN Urges Lebanon", 2012).

Faith describes in detail how she was able to survive a work situation with a madam who was psychologically abusive and threatening her with bodily harm and murder:

FAITH: I was very close to the boy [the son of the madam]. He reminded me of my son. He was that age of my son so I was very close to the boy. The mother was jealous. So one day me and the boy we were talking. And I knew the character of this woman. So one day I told the boy, "Stop misbehaving. Because if you keep misbehaving, your momma will beat you. And if your mama beats you I will cry. And when you cry, I do not like it. It affects me. I don't like it". And it so happened, that I arrived at that house four days after the other domestic worker. Apparently, the madam had tried to strangle the other domestic worker, the other domestic help. So the boy told me, "My mama tried to strangle the other house worker who left right before you came". I asked him, "What did your mama do? Show me what your mama did". He showed me the action. "My mom did this to Evelyn". [Faith demonstrates to me by putting her hands around her neck, simulating choking].

ME: So he put his hands around his neck to show you the action of strangulation?

FAITH: Yes. I said to the boy "Are you sure?" He said yes and he said, "Evelyn cried Evelyn cried Evelyn cried". I said "Okay..." I kept this information for myself. So one day, I said to the madam to test her, to measure her... Every time I do something, something she doesn't like, the smallest little thing, she shakes with anger. One day I was feeding the small baby who was two months old. And I dropped a little bit of food on the floor. And the two-year-old girl was eating some chocolate and it fell on the floor. So I was taking care of these two little ones at the same time and I did not want her to eat the chocolate that had fallen on the floor so I blocked her with my leg. Can you imagine? A 5 ½ year-old boy, a 2 ½ year-old girl, and the two-month-old baby. And the madam, she is sleeping. This one is breaking things. The other one is fighting with this one...What are you supposed to do? And when the madam calls for me to help her, and if I make the mistake in delaying to help her...So on that day, when the chocolate fell down, she happened to wake up, and she saw the chocolate on the floor while I was in the middle of managing all these children. She said to me, "Hey! Don't you have eyes?! Don't you see that there's some chocolate on the floor here? Why didn't you pick it up?" I said to her, "Excuse me madam, you can see that I'm feeding these young babies. And this one here, was eating chocolate, and it just now fell. And it's not that I did not see it, I did see it. As you can see, my leg is blocking the girl, so she does not try to eat it or step on it". And you know what she said to me? "You don't know what will happen to you one day!" She threatened me. And I kept quiet. And I finished feeding the baby. And when I was finished, the madam was sitting on the couch. And I said to her, "Excuse me madam, did I hear what you said correctly? That I don't know what will happen to me one day?" So she immediately went to her room, and stayed in there for about 10 minutes, to gather her courage, to make up stories. So I went to do my washing in the kitchen. She found me there. She said to me, "What you think I meant?" I said, "You don't remember what you said? It was only 10 minutes ago. You don't remember?" She said to me, "You want to make up stories for yourself?" I said to her, "What stories? You said it with your mouth. I just wanted to confirm it. That's why I asked you, did I hear you correctly?" So she became angry. She started shouting. And I said "Excuse me madam, I have kept quiet. I have been observing you. And let me tell you, I know you... Did you do this to Evelyn who was here before me?" [Made motion of strangulation around her neck]. She was shocked. She said, "What are you saying? That I wanted to kill Evelyn?" I said, "I did not say anything about killing. Don't put words in my mouth. I just ask you if you did this to Evelyn". So it was a fight. I told her, "Your son told me what you did to Evelyn. Your son is not a baby. He is a five-year-old boy and he can talk. And he can tell me so-and-so said this or so-and-so told me this". And my madam said, "He told you I would kill you?" And I said, "Calm down immediately, and call my agency immediately". There was a lot of drama in that house that day. And the husband was not there, he was at work. And the boy, did not know what to do. He was my friend. He would tell me, "When you are not here when I wake up in the morning, I cry every day". In that house, smiling was forbidden. And if you stay in that house for three years like that, they mess with you. So my madam said to me, "Go into your room! I don't want to see you!" And she said, "You think I am going to kill you? Then I'm going to kill you". And I said to her, "excuse me madam, before you lay a hand on me, I will be off the balcony".

SK: Wow, wow. Thank you for sharing that. When she threatened you, did you tell anyone? What did you do with that information to show she threatened you?

FAITH: I took note of what she said. I wrote it down in my journal. And the date. Because in case anything happens, someone will know, she tried to threaten me. After all, she did try to strangle the other housemaid. I was expecting anything from her. I wrote it down. And I told my agent, "I want to change my house. I want to go to another house. If I stay here, I will be affected psychologically". Unfortunately, I just finished my papers and when they have your papers, you are their prisoner. She has paid maybe $2000 to bring me to Beirut. She thinks she can do whatever she wants with me.

When some migrant domestic workers attempt to seek assistance from their own embassies and consulates in Beirut, they report it is difficult to secure any kind of help at all, as Alem Dechasa-Desisa's story reveals. Faith experienced apathy and indifference when she attempted to receive counsel from the Kenyan consulate; her experience suggests they do not care about the plight of migrant domestic workers in Lebanon. When she ran away from her employer's home because the madam threatened to kill her, Faith went to her consulate in search of social services or legal assistance. She reports,

> It was unfortunate that this person received me, because she did not even allow me to enter into the office. She wanted to throw me outside the door. Inside the office, I see my president's [picture] and my flag is waving inside the office. And you don't want me to enter into the office? My taxes are paying you!

It is a chief complaint among many Ethiopian and Kenyan migrants working in Lebanon that their consulate does nothing to assist them. After the death of Ms. Dechasa-Desisa, Ethiopians gathered in front of the consulate to protest the callousness of the consular officials regarding the migrant domestic worker's suicide (Salhani, 2012).

Mental and sadistic cruelty inflicted by the madam upon migrant domestic workers is very troubling. Faith reports how the madam would run to the balcony when she heard a plane flying over Beirut, and point to the sky, and say, "Look at the stupid people coming to Beirut!" referring to the migration of women about to arrive to work in domestic servitude. Another migrant reports,

> Some madams even make the maid a sandwich and tell her, “This is what you are eating for the day”. …Madam say to the girl “I paid a lot of money for you, I did not pay it for you to sit”. They invent work for her even when everything is in order. (Shakr, 2012)

As these stories illustrate, some domestic workers encounter insurmountable obstacles in their lived realities in Lebanese society. They report employers who intentionally enforce isolation, prohibit access to social networks, prohibit privacy, forbid the migrant domestic worker from taking one day off a week, and refuse to pay these women their wages. Employers attempt to suffocate the confidence and agency within the migrant domestic worker to maintain control of her autonomous self, such as when Laurencia was forced to use de-lousing shampoo. Similarly, other migrant domestic workers reported employers forcing them to wear a maid’s uniform. Helena recounts this experience:

فرضوا علي الاوفرهول في المنزل. كان عندي مشكله فيه. كثير بتشاجر معها.
كنت اضبط شعريبشعري او بخصوص ملابسي. لانها تجذب انتباه الرجال. وانا
ماعندي رجل بحياتي. انا هنا للعمل فقط. في ناس بيشتغلوا ومابيحكوا ابدا. اذا ما
اذاماعجبك شغلي. ماعندي مشكله. اما ان ترجعوني على بلدي او الى مكتب التشغيل.
وادفعوا لي راتبي. لالبعد مرمر عام على عملي انا اريد ان ارحل واريد راتبي.
بعد مرور عام على المشاكل في عملي. ذهبت الي مكتب التشغيل وطالبت براتبي. ولم نتفق. واللي حصل انهم استبدلون.

> They [both the agency and the madam] would even make me wear the uniform when in the house and I had a problem with that. We argued a lot about that and she would tell me to fix my hair or argue with me about my clothes because they will catch the attention of men. I have never had a man in my life. I am here for work and that is it. There are people who work and who do not speak up. If you don’t like the way I work I do not have a problem with that. You can either return me to my home country or the agency. And give me my salary. After a year of problems, I needed to go and told them to give me my pay and the backpay they owed me. We [the agency and I] did not agree. The last thing to happen was them exchanging me.

Abaynesh reports a similar experience with her employer, though with more restrictions:

شي انه كانوا بيجبروني على اشياء مابدياها. الواحد مابيرتاح. مثلا الام كانت تقول لي قصي شعرك
ملابسي موعا جبينها. ماكنت احب اقص شعري. لازم انه اقص شعري. لانه ممنزع اطول شعري.
ممنوع اغير الموضه او اي شي.

> They forced me to do things I did not want. For example, one could not relax, the madam would say cut your hair, [she would complain about my] clothes. I could not relax because she had to force me to do things. [order me around]. For example, I did not like to cut my hair, I had to cut my hair, because it was against the rules to let it get long. It was against the rules to change the style or anything.

Other migrant domestic workers report how they are not permitted to wear the clothes of their homelands, nor were they allowed to cook the foods of their African countries, nor wear their hair in braids and styles that outwardly looked "African". As many migrant domestic workers noted above, the intentional alienation and isolation from social networks, be it friend networks, church networks, community involvement, or isolation from family communication, is akin to depriving these women of their language as well, as one's language is tied fundamentally to one's identity construction (Brice-Heath, 1983; González, 2006; Wyman, McCarty, & Nicholas, 2013) and empowerment (Ruiz, 1997). These markers of cultural identity were forcefully stripped from these women for the duration of their employment terms. These employer practices are motivated by feelings of superiority over "the other" and xenophobic sentiments toward the African peoples steeped in justified racism, which plays out in the master/slave dynamic; Jureidini (2011) notes,

> there is a sense that when some Lebanese "confess" to such racist attitudes, it is not out of a sense of shame, but almost pride, for it serves to confirm a sense of superiority. Related to this is the view that the domestic worker does not belong to the same moral circle or community. This may be because she is from a different religion, or is racially different or otherwise stereotyped as ignorant, sinful, dirty, uncivilized, uncontrollable, and so on. Constructions of the "other" allow employers to construct the idea that "she is not one of us" and therefore are not required to treat her as they would treat one of their own. (p. 10)

In a country that still refers to migrant domestic workers, whether they from Africa or Southeast Asia, with the Arabic term *el abed*, which means both "Black" and "slave" (Jureidini, 2011), suggests that Lebanese society is immersed in a pervasive, explicit, and overt racism that permeates and replicates from a young age. To be sure, several migrant domestic workers reported that the Lebanese children in their care replicated racist attitudes. Makeda, a migrant domestic worker from Ethiopia, said that a child told her that Lebanese people came from God and Black people came from Satan. Faith, the migrant worker from Kenya, relays the following story:

> I was with my madam's son, and he was watching the Olympics. A Black man from Germany was running in a race. I said, "Ah, you mean there are Black people who are citizens of Germany?" I just wanted to get his opinion. "I have never seen in Beirut, Lebanon, a Black person who is a citizen of Lebanon", I said to the boy. And he said, "That's right we don't have". And I said, "But why?" So, the boy said, "Well, we have Black Indians". "I'm not talking about Black Indians; I was talking about Africans". And this 11-year-old boy, he said to me, "Those are gangsters". So, I cracked a joke and said "Yes we are the gangsters". So, one day I said to the boy, "What am I missing to be a gangster?" And he said to me, "The only thing you're missing is a gun".

Here we see the young boy framing African people as gun-wielding "gangsters", a group associated with violence and bloodshed; such racist trope uttered by children exemplifies how deeply embedded the dehumanizing ideology is within Lebanese society. According to Fanon (2008), "...[N]egrophobes exist. It is not hatred of the Negro, however, that motivates them; they lack the courage for that, or they have lost it. Hate is not inborn; it has to be constantly cultivated, to be brought into being..." (p. 37). Racism and xenophobia, a disdain for "the other", is a taught and observed phenomenon, one that rears its head and repeats itself, as we see with the children here, who repeat what they observe in their households.

How to Oppress: An Analysis Using Foucault and Bourdieu

To understand power, it should be deconstructed to reveal its anatomy, its inner workings, and how it subjugates and mitigates on the one hand, and uplifts and renders one agentive/powerful on the other. The tools I call on to deconstruct power are the ideas of Bourdieu's (1986) habitus, the field, and capital, and Foucault's (1984) conceptualization of disciplining the body via the panopticon. By applying these theoretical groundings of power dynamics by way of the lived realities of migrant domestic workers, I provide a framework which will be helpful in understanding how marginalized groups attain a resistance to the disempowering discourses in the employment and social space and how empowerment is appropriated for further activism.

An individual's associations with their culture vis-à-vis language, food, and bodily adornment and their social networks, according to Bourdieu, is a social conditioning in which "the way society becomes deposited in persons in the form of lasting dispositions or trained capacities and structured propensities to think, feel, and act in determinate ways..." (Wacquant, 2005, p. 318). We as participants in the social world are "endowed with habitus, inscribed in [our] bodies by past experiences" (Bourdieu, 1997,

p. 138). Such bodily inscription generates, according to Bourdieu, "a permanent disposition, a durable way of standing, speaking, walking, and thereby feeling and thinking" (as cited by Lukes, 2005, p. 141). In essence, we are an embodiment of inscribed social and cultural meanings and experiences. Vygotsky's (1978) sociohistorical theory asserts that the social actor's cognition is embedded in their social and cultural worlds; and, as Moll (2014) notes, the concept of the "cultural mediation of thinking" captures "the plurality of social relations, cultural practices...and the importance of individual agency in the formation of particular subjectivities and in establishing the significance of meditational means and actions" (p. 2). By framing one's identity, persona, and social makeup within the ideas of habitus and sociohistorical theory,[4] that is, by acknowledging that we are the sum of our deeply embedded cultural and social parts which function in dialectical fashion, we can understand that the attempt to suppress this social conditioning has the potential to be analogous to leaving the social actor in an agentless state.

The Panoptic Effect of the Maid's Uniform

The attempts of employers (i.e., madams/misters) to oppress migrant domestic workers can be seen in the above narratives. Another such way is by requiring the domestic worker to live in the employer's home, locking her inside when the madam leaves, not allowing her any privacy, and forcing her to wear a maid's uniform, a common sight on the streets of Beirut, sold in shops and worn by migrant domestic workers.

The maid's uniform is symbolic of wealth and status for the madam, granting her a higher social standing in the eyes of her peers; however, the uniform for the migrant worker represents domestic servitude. Several of the women interviewed were forced to wear a maid's uniform. As Helena relayed above, her madam expected her to wear her uniform even outside of the house when running errands for the madam, such as picking up dry cleaning or walking the family dog. For every moment she wears the uniform, she is reminded of her subordinate position. According to Blackman's (1985) chapter that examines the service sector of the American economy,

> The uniform actually helps to extend management influence to actions of its service technicians; the uniform is an ever-present reminder of management. When a service technician puts on his uniform, he is subordinating part of himself (his freedom to choose his own dress) to company control. (p. 301)

The combination of the physical action of the wearing of the uniform, the constant tactile sensation of it which reminds the wearer of her subordinate status, and the enforcement of it by the employer/madam/oppressor lends to what Foucault (1995) refers to as "disciplines", or methods "which made possible the meticulous control of the operations of the body, which assured the constant subjection of its forces and imposed upon them a relation of docility-utility" (p. 137). The disciplining of the body "produces subjected and practiced bodies", or "docile bodies" (Foucault, 1995, p. 138), which is the ultimate attempt of the employer/madam/oppressor in order to create workers who are disciplined, orderly, submissive, and subordinate.

For the migrant domestic worker, living in the home of the madam and mister renders her at the mercy of the people occupying that space. Even in her own private moments, she is reminded of her servitude, because that uniform and that space and place surround her 24 hours a day, 7 days a week. These visual and tactile reminders of the ever-present space of the private home and the wearing of the uniform act as a panoptic presence of control and "discipline", though it is

> ...as discreetly as possible, as well articulated on the other functions of these multiplicities and also in the least expensive way possible: to this correspond anonymous instruments of power [the uniform], coextensive with the multiplicity that they regiment, such as hierarchical surveillance, continuous registration, perpetual assessment and classification...[it is] a power that insidiously objectifies those on whom it is applied.... (Foucault, 1984, p. 209)

While Foucault is referencing the public institutions of school or government bodies which are co-opted as a state-functioning panopticon, it can be asserted that living and working in the exploitative space of the home and the wearing of the maid uniform function in the same covert way, due to its ever-presence and its subtlety in reminding the wearer of the uniform that she is under control. The panoptic effect of her work situation is registered in the reactions of the migrant workers – they report that they feel "constantly monitored", "under control", and the uniform made them feel "inferior", "owned", and "like a nobody, like a slave". In the public space, they were visibly marked as working in the domestic sector, a service job "only good enough for migrants" (Wood & Boswall, 2021).

If habitus is the embodiment of one's cultural, social, political, and religious historicity, and she experiences a forced removal of these markers when she is required to wear the maid's uniform, which is meant to remind the African woman that she is under the subjection of the superior Lebanese woman, it can be asserted that the migrant domestic worker interprets the uniform as an attempt to control her, undermine her agency, and remind her of her inferiority. While the home space and the uniform are covert in their attempts to control, they simultaneously have the intentionality to objectify, to feel constantly under watch; and, coupled with the fact that the majority of migrant workers live in the homes of their employers, this objectification and sensation of constant scrutiny is magnified.

These attempts to control at the micro level, in the private workspace, are also intended by the madam to ensure the migrant domestic worker is keenly aware of her place in the social hierarchy. Some domestic workers report that the madams feel threatened by their presence in the home, stemming from feelings of jealousy, insecurity, and loathing toward the migrant domestic worker; such feelings lead the madam to employ control over the worker by way of physical abuse (Jureidini, 2011).

Gratitude in Servitude

As mentioned in Chapter 3, the migrant participants of this study were students at either the Migrant Center or their sister site in central Beirut attending EFL or computer classes, or they were participating in Rakeb's play practice after language classes. The migrant workers were not only given their Sundays off, but their madams also allowed them to attend language classes and play practice. In several of the interviews, the participants expressed thanks toward their madams for allowing them to participate in these educational endeavors; here, Antsa, a migrant domestic worker from the Ivory Coast, speaks with appreciation for her employer:

SK: Qu'est-ce que tu penses de la famille?

ANTSA: Waouh, elle est juste formidable, je sais pas comment le redire. Ils sont bien, ils sont bien. Par rapport aux autres, moi je suis bien.

SK: D'accord! Tu peux demander à ta patronne de ne pas travailler le dimanche, c'est le jour de repos?

ANTSA: Sur ce problème, là, normalement, quand je devais venir, ils m'ont dit… tous les dimanches, c'est ton jour… pas tous les dimanches, une seule fois dans le mois c'est ton jour de repos.

SK: Une seule journée dans tout le mois?

ANTSA: Oui, voilà, dans tout le mois. Et donc, c'est comme ça dans les contrats qu'on signe. Et donc, au fur et à mesure que je suis avec elle, elle m'a dit tu peux sortir le dimanche, et par exemple, aujourd'hui, j'ai toute la journée à moi. Mais les autres dimanches, je sors le matin, et quand j'ai fini les courses, je rentre. Quand il n'y a rien à la maison, je peux faire ce que je veux. Mais moi, pour la confiance qu'ils m'ont portée et qu'ils ont en moi, j'ai pas envie d'exagérer, je veux être toujours correcte. Donc les autres jours que je fais rien à l'école, et juste quand je fais rien, je rentre à la maison. Mais bon, y'a pas de problème, elle peut me laisser, mais bon avec les enfants, il faut que je sois quand même avec elle. Souvent elle a du travail. Je peux pas tout le temps être… voilà. Moi je la comprends. Ça me ferait plaisir, mais moi je la comprends.

SK: Tu peux me dire combien tu gagnes?

ANTSA: Ils me payent comme tout le monde je pense, 150 dollars.
SK: What do you think of your employer?
ANTSA: This family is ... just amazing. I don't know what else to say. They are great. They are great. Compared to the others, I am lucky...She helped me to find this place [Migrant Center]. She even called Maha to find out where it's located and the times of the classes.
SK: Ok! Can you take Sundays off?
ANTSA: Well, when I was planning on coming to work for them, they told me I would get all Sundays off – I mean not every Sundays, but one Sunday a month.
T: Only one day in the whole month?
ANTSA: Yes, only one day. That's how it is in the contracts we sign. And gradually, she told me I could leave on Sunday, and for example today, I have all day to myself. But on other Sundays, I go out in the morning and when I am done with the grocery shopping, I get back home. When there is nothing to do at the house, I can do whatever I want. But because they trust me, I don't want to take advantage of the situation and I always want to be decent. So when I am not doing anything at school, or when I am not doing anything at all, I go home. It's not a big deal, I can leave, but when she is with the kids, I have to be home with her. She has often work to do. I can't always be away, you know. But I understand her. I would like to have more time off, but I understand her.

I ask her later in the interview the amount of money she makes as a domestic worker:

SK: What is your salary?
ANTSA: The same as everyone else I think, I make $150 per month.

In the domestic industry in Lebanon, the male employer is called "mister" and the female employer is called "madam" by the migrant domestic worker. These labels are reminiscent of the enslaver/enslaved dynamic during the historic period of enslavement in the United States and in Europe. The required use of the "madam" and "mister" monikers produces a subtle coercion to remind the migrant domestic worker of her position of obedience and subservience. Also worthy of recognizing is that Antsa frames her madam as being generous for allowing her to go to the Migrant Center every Sunday. Antsa was even reluctant to pursue these educational opportunities for fear of appearing as if she were taking advantage of her "madam's generosity". This "gratitude in servitude" dynamic is reminiscent of Foucault's notion of the modern form of covert discipline, which is "...different from service or slavery...[It] involves a larger 'scale of control', a 'subtle coercion' of the various parts of the 'mechanism' itself including such minutiae as 'movements, gesture, attitudes, rapidity'" (Foucault, as cited by Constable, 2007, p. 15). That Antsa would assume a positionality of admiration for her madam's gesture, and feel a sense of indebtedness for being allowed to attend classes, especially when she is paid wages that do not meet Lebanon's minimum wage guidelines, suggests a "project of docility" (Foucault, 1995, p. 136), a disciplining of the body that manifests in an "attitude of gratitude", or, as Freire (1970) calls it, a "false generosity", that being "Any attempt to 'soften' the power of the oppressor in deference to the weakness of the oppressed almost always manifests itself in the form of false generosity...In order to have the continued opportunity to express their 'generosity,' the oppressors must perpetuate injustice as well" (p. 44). Indeed, the oppressor in the above situation, the "madam", bequeaths upon Antsa the opportunity to steal away to the Migrant Center for a few hours every Sunday. In this way, the oppressor/madam can feel like a generous humanitarian, especially because Antsa feels very grateful for her good work situation when she compares her situation to that of other migrant workers. However, the oppressor/madam even does not provide her any full days off, nor a wage that meets Lebanon's wage guidelines.

The Oppressor as Savior

The oppressor can also be framed as the "savior" (Cammarota, 2011), in that the oppressed and marginalized attempt to escape their situation "through the guidance and agency" of a White savior figure (p. 243). A frequent theme in the interviews, as mentioned, was viewing a good work situation and madam as someone who "saved" them from certain doom. However, it does not serve the oppressor/madam to "free" the oppressed/migrant domestic worker too much; Cammarota (2011) asserts, "The savior requires exploiting his or her status to procure leadership positions and thus denying people of color the process of developing the agency required for long-term systematic change" (p. 256). This exploitation of one's position of power at the micro level is evidenced again and again among the women whom I interviewed for this research project. Indeed, macro-level entities, such as empires, societies, governments, and communities, have also perpetuated abuses of power and position throughout history by way of enslavement, empire-building, human trafficking, and colonization in order to marginalize, colonize, and otherize vulnerable groups, such as migrants, refugees, and women and children (Anzaldúa, 1987; Du Bois, 1903; Fanon, 2008; Said, 1978; Spivak, 1988).

The Interplay between the Habitus, Capital, and the Field

According to Bourdieu, the habitus is not a remote entity unaffected by the interactions of other entities, those being capital and the field. Capital is defined as "the 'energy' that drives the development of a field through time.

Capital in action is the enactment of the principle of the field" (Moore, 2012, p. 102). The field is defined as the "social arena", the space in which "interactions, transactions, and events occurred" (Thomson, 2012, p. 65), where the habitus and capital inform, impact, align, and create; what is created is "theory of practice", or praxis[5] (Robbins, 2014). The following is an amalgamation describing the interrelationship between the habitus, capital, and the field, producing practice: "[(habitus)(capital)] + field = practice" (Maton, 2012, p. 50).

The necessity of laying out this structure is, again, for deconstructing the interplay between these entities. In this realm, the habitus is the social and cultural conditioning of migrant domestic workers. The cultural capital, in this case, would be the level of education, the number of languages spoken by the migrant domestic workers, and their literacy level; examples of social capital would be access to social networks, such as religious social networks and friend/family social networks. The field here is the space of Beirut, Lebanon, a contested social space where migrant domestic workers' social and cultural capital is appropriated more for physical, emotional, and mental survival and navigation of these social spaces, thereby leading to "practice", the end result of a dialectical relationship between the three entities of the habitus, capital, and field, according to Bourdieu.

In the following recounting of the women's life stories, we will see how migrant domestic workers call on their agency, social and cultural capital, and funds of knowledge (González, Moll, & Amanti, 2005) to inform their lived trajectories in order to not only survive in this contested social space, but also to create successful economic endeavors under the most dire of circumstances. We will also learn that the attempts to stifle, oppress, marginalize, and enslave do not limit the agency of some migrant domestic workers; rather, the women have constructed epistemologies of everyday resistance, empowerment, and activism.

Migrant Workers and Empowerment

Migratory patterns have increased in the past decade due to an influx of natural disasters, armed conflict, economic hardship, and social and religious persecution. The act of migration, especially when brought about by the above conditions, makes an already vulnerable population even more so in the receiving country, as they are viewed as a liability (Cox, 2011). Of concern for this population are issues of social justice and social welfare, access to healthcare, economic opportunities, and educational opportunities, for both migrant children and adults. Structural and societal racism and xenophobia are significant problems for migrant populations in the United States (De Genova, 2005; Gonzales, 2011), in North Africa (Bachelet, 2013; Daoud, 2016; Errazzouki, 2013; Maidhof, 2011), in China (Constable, 2007), and in the Middle East region (Adelkhah & Olszewska, 2007; Jadaliyya Reports, 2013; Jureidini, 2010).[6] In many countries, refugees and migrant workers cannot access educational opportunities by virtue of their migrant, refugee, undocumented, or asylum status (Hoodfar, 2007) and/or their children face bullying and harassment (Johnston, Baslan, & Kvittingen, 2019; Tinker Sachs et al., 2017). In the United States, undocumented children are legally able to attend K-12 public schools. However, children of undocumented adults may grow up unaware of their undocumented status, only becoming cognizant of it when they desire to find employment, get a driver's license, or attend college. Such a quandary is referred to as "learning to be illegal" (Gonzales, 2011).

As the literature asserts, formal and nonformal systems of education are rife with unjust, harsh, and racist treatment toward migrants and other vulnerable populations. While it is necessary to continue to study and document these uneven systems of power, we must also bring to the forefront stories of hope, resilience, and determination. In the following pages, I will present the counter-narratives that surround acts of empowerment, resistance, and activism by migrant domestic workers at the micro level. Even within an incredibly corrupt system under abject conditions, the women at the center of this study have not just persevered, but have created powerful lived experiences, which encourage and empower each other. By way of this analysis, we will learn their ways of knowing, deconstructed through the lens of a Third World feminist resistance framework (Abu-Lughod, 1990; Bernal, 2006; González, 2006; Mohanty, 2003; Sharma, 2008). First, we will explore the concepts of agency, power, and empowerment, which will help us better understand how migrant domestic workers are able to grapple with and navigate within the hegemonic power structures in Beirut, Lebanon.

Notes

1 In Abu-Lughod's (1990) ethnography of the Awlad 'Ali Bedouins and their "complex workings of social power", she reveals the everyday ways in which women who belong to the Bedouin community enact their resistance. She calls for "using resistance as a diagnostic of power" (p. 48) instead of conflating constructs of power and resistance as if one is synonymous for the other; in so doing, she dismantles the tendency to romanticize resistance. Instead of obfuscating discourses of resistance, one can locate the historical, cultural, and social mechanisms of power in the everyday ways migrant women navigate the interstitial third spaces they inhabit (Bhabha, 1994).

2 As noted in Chapter 3, my research questions examine the constructions of power and the empowerment of migrant domestic workers; as such, I privilege the input of the research participants within the scope of this research project. In honoring the migrant domestic workers' requests to highlight their daily struggles, this aligns with the core ideology of the community-based participatory approach of my research methodology.

3 The names of all the research participants have been changed to protect their anonymity.

4 Within educational theory literature, parallels between Vygotsky's sociocultural theory and Bourdieu's ideas of habitus have been noted as being complementary; see Panofsky (2003).

5 While the term "praxis" has been in use in association with Bourdieu's seminal work, *Outline of a Theory of Practice* (1972), it has been noted that Bourdieu did not explicitly use this term: "I really must point out that I have never used the concept of praxis which, at least in French, tends to create the impression of something pompously theoretical..." (as cited by Robbins, 2014, p.38).

6 Racism, colorism, tribalism, and anti-Blackness persist and have a long history in the Middle East region and have been documented in the scholarly literature (Asgharzadeh, 2007) and in policy reports (Johnston, Baslan, & Kvittingen, 2019; Tayah, 2012) yet such topics have historically been met with denial in much of the Arab and Persian world, as noted by Eltahawy (2008) and Whitaker (2006). However, racism is being discussed more openly in public discourse such as the online news sources Al Jazeera English (Abulhawa, 2013; Shebaya, 2017; Sheen, 2018; White, 2016), the ezine Jadaliyya (Bachelet, 2013; "Jadaliyya Reports", 2013; Errazzouki, 2013; Maidhof, 2011), and Middle East Eye (Fahim, 2020; "Yemen Ramadan", 2021). The death of George Floyd has had reverberations throughout the region (Malekian, 2020; Salloum, 2020). In the United Arab Emirates, for instance, it was noted, "Floyd's tragic death has also sparked a conversation about racism in the Middle East creating space for black Arabs to give voice to their own experiences" ("George Floyd", 2020).

References

Abulhawa, S. (2013, July 7). Confronting anti-black racism in the Arab world. *Al Jazeera English*. Retrieved from https://www.aljazeera.com/

Abu-Lughod, L. (1990). The romance of resistance: Tracing transformations of power through Bedouin women. *American Ethnologist*, *17*(1), 41–55.

Adelkhah, F., & Olszewska, Z. (2007). The Iranian Afghans. *Iranian Studies*, *40*(2), 137–165. DOI: 10.1080/00210860701269519

Amnesty International. (2019). "Their house is my prison": Exploitation of migrant domestic workers in Lebanon. Retrieved from https://www.justice.gov/file/1156951/download

Anzaldúa, G. (1987). *Borderlands - La Frontera: The new Mestiza*. San Francisco, CA: Aunt Lute Books.

Asgharzadeh, A. (2007). *Iran and the challenge of diversity: Islamic fundamentalism, Aryanist racism, and democratic struggles*. New York, NY: Palgrave Macmillan.

Azhari, T. (2020, April 7). The desperate final days of a domestic worker in Lebanon. *Al Jazeera English*. Retrieved from https://www.aljazeera.com/

BBC. (2012, April 13). UN urges Lebanon to investigate Ethiopian maid's death. Retrieved from https://www.bbc.com/news/world-middle-east-17598437

Bachelet, S. (2013, August 9). Migrants in Morocco: "Go home or face death". *Jadaliyya*. Retrieved from https://www.jadaliyya.com/

Bernal, D. D. (2006). Learning and living pedagogies of the home. In D. Delgado Bernal, C. A. Elenes, F. E. Godinez, & S. Villenas (Eds.), *Chicana/Latina education*

in everyday life (pp. 197–213). Albany, NY: State University of New York Press. DOI: 10.1080/10665684.2012.698149
Bhabha, H. (1994). *The location of culture.* New York, NY: Routledge.
Blackman, B. (1985). Making a service more tangible can make it more manageable. In J. A. Czepiel, M. R. Solomon, & C. F. Suprenant (Eds.), *The service encounter: Managing employee/customer interaction in service businesses* (p. 291). Lanham, ML: Lexington Books.
Bourdieu, P. (1972). *Outline of a theory of practice.* Cambridge: Cambridge University Press.
Bourdieu, P. (1986). The forms of capital. In J. Richardson (Ed.), *Handbook of theory and research for the sociology of education* (pp. 241–258). New York, NY: Greenwood.
Bourdieu, P. (1997). Bodily knowledge. In P. Bourdieu (Ed.), *Pascalian meditations* (pp. 128–163). Stanford, CA: Stanford University Press.
Brice-Heath, S. (1983). *Ways with words: Language, life and work in communities and classrooms.* Cambridge: Cambridge University Press.
Brochmann, G. (1993). *Middle East avenue: Female migration from Sri Lanka to the Gulf.* New York, NY: Routledge.
Cammarota, J. (2011). Blindsided by the avatar: White saviors and allies out of Hollywood and in education. *The Review of Education, Pedagogy, and Cultural Studies, 33*, 242–259. DOI: 10.1080/10714413.2011.585287
Constable, N. (2007). *Maid to order in Hong Kong: Stories of migrant workers.* Ithaca, NY: Cornell University Press.
Cox, P. (2011). Issues in safeguarding refugee and asylum-seeking children and young people: Research and practice. *Child Abuse Review, 20*, 341–360. DOI: 10.1002/car.1200
Daoud, K. (2016, May 2). Black in Algeria? Then you'd better be Muslim. *The New York Times.* Retrieved from https://www.nytimes.com/
De Genova, N. (2005). *Working the boundaries: Race, space, and "illegality" in Mexican Chicago.* Durham, NC: Duke University Press.
Du Bois, W. E. B. (1903). *The souls of Black folk.* Chicago, IL: A.C. McClurg and Co.
Eelens, F., Schampers, T., & Speckmann, J. D. (1992). *Labour migration to the Middle East: From Sri Lanka to the Gulf.* London: K. Paul International, Ltd.
Eltahawy, M. (2008, November 10). The Arab world's dirty secret. *The New York Times.* Retrieved from https://www.nytimes.com/
Errazzouki, S. (2013, August 1). Complicity and indifference: Racism in Morocco. *Jadaliyya.* Retrieved from https://www.jadaliyya.com/
Fahim, J. (2020, June 25). Racism in the Middle East: The Arab films and TV that promote hatred. *Middle East Eye.* Retrieved from https://www.middleeasteye.net/
Fanon, F. (2008). *Black skin, white masks* (New edition). London: Pluto Press.
Foucault, M. (1984). Panopticism. In P. Rabinow (Ed.), *The Foucault reader* (pp. 206–213). New York, NY: Pantheon Books.
Foucault, M. (1995). *Discipline and punish: The birth of the prison.* New York, NY: Random House.
Fits Fit. (2012, April 16). *Alem Dechasa kidnapped and dragged into a car* [Video file]. Retrieved from https://www.youtube.com/watch?v=4AqY1tjGIlk
Freire, P. (1970). *Pedagogy of the oppressed.* New York, NY: Herder and Herder.

Gamburd, M. R. (2011). Female labor migration from Sri Lanka to the Middle East. In J. Holt (Ed.), *The Sri Lanka reader: History, culture, politics*. (pp. 687–694). Durham, NC: Duke University Press.
George Floyd: Honouring his legacy one month on. (2020, June 25). *The National Editorial*. Retrieved from https://www.thenationalnews.com/
González, N. (2006). Testimonios of border identities: "Una mujer acomedida donde quiera cabe". In D. Delgado Bernal, C. A. Elenes, F. E. Godinez, & S. Villenas (Eds.), *Chicana/Latina education in everyday life* (pp. 197–213). Albany, NY: State University of New York Press.
Gonzales, R. G. (2011). Learning to be illegal: Undocumented youth and shifting legal contexts in the transition to adulthood. *American Sociological Review*, *76*(4), 602–619. DOI: 10.1177/0003122411411901
González, N., Moll, L. C., & Amanti, C. (Eds.). (2005). *Funds of knowledge: Theorizing practices in households, communities, and classrooms*. New York, NY: Routledge.
Hoodfar, H. (2007). Women, religion and the "Afghan education movement" in Iran. *The Journal of Development Studies*, *43*(2), 265–293. DOI: 10.1080/00220380601125115
Jadaliyya Reports. (2013, December 6). Ethiopian and Yemeni migrants under the Saudi Crackdown. *Jadaliyya*. Retrieved from https://www.jadaliyya.com/
Johnston, R., Baslan, D., & Kvittingen, A. (2019). Realizing the rights of asylum seekers and refugees in Jordan from countries other than Syria with a focus on Yemenis and Sudanese. Norwegian Refugee Council. Retrieved from https://reliefweb.int/sites/reliefweb.int/files/resources/71975.pdf
Jureidini, R. (2010). Trafficking and contract migrant workers in the Middle East. *International Migration Special Issue: Special Issue on Human Trafficking*, *48*(4), 142–163. DOI: 10.1111/j.1468-2435.2010.00614.x
Jureidini, R. (2011). *An exploratory study of psychoanalytic and social factors in the abuse of migrant domestic workers by female employers in Lebanon*. Beirut: Human Rights in Lebanon.
Jureidini, R. (2019). Vagaries in the management of migrant domestic workers from the Philippines: A case study from Lebanon. In S. Rajan & S. P. Irudaya (Eds.), *India's low-skilled migration to the Middle East* (pp. 77–97). Singapore: Springer Nature.
Jureidini, R., & Moukarbel, N. (2004). Female Sri Lankan domestic workers in Lebanon: A case of "contract slavery"? *Journal of Ethnic and Migration Studies*, *30*(4), 581–607. DOI: 10.1080/13691830410001699478
Kassamali, S. (2021). Understanding race and migrant domestic labor in Lebanon. *Middle East research and information project*. Retrieved from https://merip.org/2021/07/understanding-race-and-migrant-domestic-labor-in-lebanon/
Kelly, P., & Lusis, T. (2006). Migration and the transnational habitus: Evidence from Canada and the Philippines. *Environment and Planning A*, *38*(5), 831–847. DOI: 10.1068/a37214
Lukes, S. (2005). *Power: A radical view* (2nd ed.). London: Palgrave Macmillan.
Malekian, S. (2020, June 2). George Floyd vigil in Iran leads to online backlash. *ABC News*. Retrieved from https://abcnews.go.com/

Maidhof, C. (2011, March 1). The Arabs in Africa. *Jadaliyya*. Retrieved from https://www.jadaliyya.com/
Maton, K. (2014). Habitus. In M. Grenfell (Ed.), *Pierre Bourdieu: Key concepts* (pp. 48–64). Durham, UK: Acumen Publishing.
Mohanty, C. T. (2003). "Under Western eyes" revisited: Feminist solidarity through anticapitalist struggles. *Signs*, *28*(2), 499–535.
Moll, L. C. (2014). *L.S. Vygotsky and education*. New York, NY: Routledge.
MEE Correspondent. (2021, April 25). Yemen Ramadan show sparks outcry over use of Blackface. *Middle East Eye*. Retrieved from https://www.middleeasteye.net/
Moore, R. (2014). Capital. In M. Grenfell (Ed.), *Pierre Bourdieu: Key concepts* (pp. 98–113). Durham, UK: Acumen Publishing.
Oishi, N. (2005). *Women in motion: Globalization, state policies, and labor migration in Asia*. Stanford, CA: Stanford University Press.
Panofsky, C. P. (2003). The relations of learning and student social class: Toward re "socializing" sociocultural learning theory. In A. Kozulin, B. Gindis, V. S. Ageyev, & S. M. Miller (Eds.), *Vygotsky's educational theory in cultural context* (pp. 411–431). Cambridge: Cambridge University Press.
Pattisson, P. (2012, January 30). *Beirut death of Nepalese migrant worker Lila—video* [Video file]. Retrieved from https://www.theguardian.com/news/video/2012/jan/30/beirut-death-nepalese-migrant-video
Robbins, D. (2014). Theory of practice. In M. Grenfell (Ed.), *Pierre Bourdieu: Key concepts* (pp. 26–40). Durham, UK: Acumen Publishing.
Ruiz, R. (1997). The empowerment of language minority students. In A. Darder, R. Torres, & H. Gutiérrez (Eds.), *Latinos and education* (pp. 319–328). New York, NY: Routledge.
Said, E. (1978). *Orientalism*. New York, NY: Pantheon Books.
Salhani, J. (2012, April 2). Ethiopians in Lebanon protest their consulate's apathy, callousness. [web log comment]. Retrieved from http://satenawzehabesha.blogspot.com/2012/04/ethiopians-in-lebanon-protest-their.html
Salloum, S. (2020 June 9). The killing of George Floyd sparks controversy over African-Iraqi rights. *El-Monitor*. Retrieved from https://www.al-monitor.com/
Scott, J. (1985). *Weapons of the weak: Everyday forms of peasantry resistance*. New Haven, CT: Yale University Press.
Shakr, R. (2012, March 19). Migrant students demand "Justice for Alem". [web log comment]. Retrieved from https://mwtaskforce.wordpress.com/2012/03/19/migrant-students-demand-justice-for-alem/
Sharma, A. (2008). *Logics of empowerment: Development, gender, and governance in neoliberal India*. Minneapolis, MN: University of Minnesota Press.
Shebaya, H. (2017, October 21). Lebanon has a racism problem. *Al Jazeera English*. Retrieved from https://www.aljazeera.com/
Sheen, D. (2018, March 29). Black lives do not matter in Israel. *Al Jazeera English*. Retrieved from https://www.aljazeera.com/
Spivak, G. C. (1988). Can the subaltern speak?. In C. Nelson & L. Grossberg (Eds.), *Marxism and the interpretation of culture* (pp. 271–314). Urbana, IL: University of Illinois Press.
Tayah, M. L. (2012). *Working with migrant domestic workers: A mapping of NGO services (1980s-2012)*. Beirut: ILO-ROAS.

The Guardian. (2012, April 11). *Ethiopian migrant suicide: "I can't tell my daughter her mother is dead"* [Video file]. Retrieved from https://www.youtube.com/watch?v=ykTB9VgXNtc

Thomson, P. (2014). Field. In M. Grenfell (Ed.), *Pierre Bourdieu: Key concepts* (pp. 65–80). Durham, UK: Acumen Publishing.

Tinker Sachs, G., Clark, B., Durkaya, M., Jackson, A., Johnson, C., Lake, W., & Limb, P. (2017). Decolonizing pedagogies: Disrupting perceptions of "The other" in teacher education. In *Culturally* Responsive Pedagogy (pp. 73-97). Palgrave Macmillan, Cham.

Truong, T., Gasper, D., Handmaker, J., & Bergh, S. I. (2014). *Migration, gender and social justice: Perspectives on human insecurity*. New York, NY: Springer.

Vygotsky, L. S. (1978). *Mind in society*. Cambridge, MA: Harvard University Press.

Wacquant, L. (2005). Habitus. In J. Becket & Z. Milan (Eds.), *International encyclopedia of economic sociology* (pp. 317–321). London: Routledge.

Whitaker, B. (2006, September 8). The race taboo. *The Guardian*. Retrieved from https://www.theguardian.com/

White, B. (2016, February 25). In Israel, racism is the law. *Al Jazeera English*. Retrieved from https://www.aljazeera.com/

Wood, D., & Boswall, J. (2021 March 23). Why Lebanon can't kick its addiction to indentured labor. *Foreign Policy*. Retrieved from https://foreignpolicy.com

Wyman, L. T., McCarty, T. L., & Nicholas, S. E. (Eds.). (2013). *Indigenous youth and multilingualism: Language identity, ideology, and practice in dynamic cultural worlds*. Routledge.

Chapter 5

Subaltern Epistemologies, Part II: Articulating Agency, Power, and Empowerment

Agency, power, and empowerment are central themes in this work, and necessitate an understanding of how these terms are appropriated and utilized in the social sciences. Scholars frequently conflate these concepts or use them interchangeably, and do not differentiate nor dissect these terms for more nuanced meaning (Ahearn, 2010). Indeed, these concepts are complex (Roald, 2016) and are fraught with political, social, and cultural implications. Within the realm of social reproduction, Bourdieu asserts that agency and structure are invariably connected and should be framed within a "dialectical relationship" (Swartz, 1998, p. 8), which foregrounds the idea of the "reproductive tendencies of habitus" (Ahearn, 2001, p. 118) as a mechanism for reproducing social inequalities. Some scholars believe that Bourdieu is guilty of structural determinism, thereby limiting one's capacity for experiencing free will or agency and making it untenable for one to change their circumstances or to participate in social transformation (Ahearn, 2001; Sewell, 1992). If agency is the "socioculturally mediated capacity to act" (Ahearn, 2010, p. 28), then agency, coupled with the understanding of one's power, is the antithesis of structural determinism.

One of the main foci within the social sciences is the understanding of the concept of power in terms of its function, its nature, and the ways in which it is mis/appropriated. According to Kreisberg (1992), most theories of power were postulated from a relationship of domination (Foucault, 1995; Lukes, 2005; Scott, 1992) between the structure that held power and the structure that did not, or a "power over" position:

> Dominating relationships are characterized by inequality: situations in which one individual or group of individuals, in order to fulfill their own desires, have the ability to control the behavior, thoughts, and/or values of another individual or group of individuals. The relationship of domination is described through the *language of imposition*. Its vocabulary includes words such as *control, force, coercion, manipulation,*

DOI: 10.4324/9781003166566-5

> *sanctioning, obedience*, and *submission*...[Emphasis his]. (Kreisberg, 1992, p. 36)

Foucault reifies discourses of "power as domination" in that he asserts "...if we speak of the structures of the mechanisms of power, it is only in so far as we suppose that certain persons exercise power over others" (Foucault, as cited by Kreisberg, 1992, p. 53). However, the "power as domination" discourse, just as Bourdieu's structural determinism of habitus, is restrictive and narrow in its scope as it posits a static view based on episodes rather than the dialectic and heuristic attributes of one's life trajectory and also on the assumption that one's lived experiences will always be determined by social reproduction. For this reason, we look beyond the "power as domination" discourse to consider "power with" (Kreisberg, 1992), or discourses of empowerment. The term "empowerment" is not fully understood nor used in clear or precise ways in the scholarly literature (Ali, 2014; Page & Czuba, 1999) and is a complex, multidimensional concept (Chamberlin, 2013). What follows is an examination of the term "empowerment" used in philosophical, feminist, and educational discourses.

Empowerment

The central concern of empowerment is the notion of power, and, as such, it is helpful to dissect the etymology of both terms. Definitions of power, as Kreisberg (1992) notes, differentiate between two notions, the first one being that the person is imbued with a sense of their abilities: "the ability to do something or act in a particular way, especially as a faculty or quality". The second notion of power is the idea that one dominates another: "the ability or right to control people or things". The latter definition proposes a "power as domination" paradigm while the former definition of power informs the "power with" or "empowerment" paradigm. A definition of empower/empowerment reflects two ideas: "to give official authority or legal power to" and "to promote the self-actualization or influence of". Again, in these definitions the former is the granting of power from one entity to another, as if bestowing power to the powerless, while the latter suggests assistance, help, or improvement from the periphery.[1]

Several theories in the past decades explore meanings of the "power with" or empowerment discourse, and recognize that power is much more potent when it is attached to the experience of human interconnections, relationships, trust-building, and the desire to affect positive change within one's own group or network (Kreisberg, 1992). The use of the construct of empowerment in the literature can have different meanings from one context to the next. For instance, the reliance on the ideas of empowerment within international development literature is ubiquitous, given that the main and official objective of the development sector is to improve the lives of marginalized groups in underdeveloped nations, and that typically it is the "Global North" empowering the "Global South". The usage of empowerment is found prominently within the pedagogical discourses pertaining to critical education to challenge notions of the status quo, to develop a critical consciousness, and to "connect knowledge to power and the ability to take constructive action" (Giroux, 2010).

In the anthropological literature pertaining to women's migration, education, and development, one finds the following definitions of the construct of empowerment: "a pedagogic process that facilitates a transformation of both the self and society" (Sharma, 2008); Ali (2014) views it as "an intimate and personal journey which enables women to gain the capacity for strategic forms of agency" and it "involves the pain of being denied respect. Under such circumstances, empowerment should manifest feelings of self-respect and dignity" (p. 119). In Constable's (2007) study of Filipina domestic workers in Hong Kong, empowerment is not explicitly defined but is instead viewed through the lens of resistance. Within the development sector, approaches to empowerment can be categorized as political/educational;, socioeconomic;, technological;, and cultural/spiritual (Titi & Singh, 1995). For the purposes of this study, I focus on the political/educational and cultural/spiritual elements informing the empowerment of the women migrant workers.

What makes the counterstories of the migrant domestic workers all the more compelling is that they are able to transcend the very social conditions such as racism, classism, and economic disparity that were, according to Bourdieu's social deterministic views, supposed to predetermine their life trajectory. In the analysis of this transcendence of structural circumstances, these brave women are able to exceed these social and work conditions. In the following narratives, I explore these intimate portraits of their everyday experiences of empowerment and their counter-narratives of resistance in living and working in Beirut.

A discussion of this transcendence of structural circumstances is not meant to fetishize "the neoliberal doctrine of pulling oneself up by the bootstraps" (Sharma, 2008, p. 58) that is prevalent in the U.S. discourse regarding the overcoming of the structural inequalities that have been built into our legal, educational, political, and social systems. Rather, this analysis of empowerment is meant to unpack epistemologies of learning and resistance within an extremely oppressive social system. In doing so, we, as critical learners, scholars, authentic educators, and researchers, have a more nuanced understanding of how, within an oppressive system, social actors are able to harness agency and power of their own making to access social networks, governmental agencies, non-governmental organizations (NGOs), and other peripheral assistance to not only survive within that oppressive system, but also flourish.

The Counter-narratives: Recognizing Oppression and Enacting Agency

Because of the prominence of xenophobia, racism, and sexism in Lebanon aimed at migrant workers, and particularly domestic workers, I asked the women who participated in this study about their encounters with racist sentiment in the public space: their encounters with it, observations of it, and reactions to it; I was interested in learning how they were able to manage, cope, and/or escape the mistreatment and abuses they regularly are forced to confront; what skill sets are domestic workers using in dealing with being mistreated?. Twenty-four-year-old Helena from Ethiopia has spent four years in Beirut working as a domestic laborer. I asked her to name specific instances where she either observed or was the target of racism and abuse in the public space, and Helena responded in the following way:

مره بالمطار وانا راجعه للبنان. دخلوا اللبنانين اول واحنا لوحدنا. واحد لابس بدله اجانا. وسالنا.
شو صار؟ اقعدوا هون لا روحوا هناك. انتم مع بعض ؟ سالنا بدون ما يعرفنا. احنا حيوانات؟ بس كيف هيك يحكي؟
في الطريق هيك انا كنت احس. ليش هو يعمل هيك فينا؟ احنا ناس. اذا احنا سود. احنا لسا ناس. قال
لي [المفتش في المطار] : شو انتي بتحكي عربي؟ كيف بتحكي معي هيك؟ هو كان مستغرب كيف
انا باحكي معه عربي. ولماردیت عليه. قال لي: اسكتي. فرديت: ليه بدي اسكت؟انا باحكي اللي بدي اياه.
بعد ماحكيت معه هيك. زعل وقال لي روحي من هون. فقلت له: هذا شغل. ليش عم تعمل معنا هيك؟...
ليش هم بيفكروا انه نحنا مثل الحيوانات؟ما بسمعوا لشئ.

> One time in the airport, I was returning from a trip. They had let the Lebanese citizens go through [customs] first but stopped us [the migrant workers] and put us in an area by ourselves. [This immigration officer], wearing a suit, came up to me. He questioned all the girls, [telling us] "Go there and sit here! What happened while you were here? Are you together?" [assuming we were together and without knowing anything about us]. He [treated us like] animals. But why does he do that? From this instance on my way/travels, I felt [discrimination] very much. Why did he do this? We are human beings. If we are Black, aren't we human beings? [while in the airport] he asked me [in disbelief] do you speak Arabic? How [dare] you speak Arabic to me? [I guess he found it strange that a Black Ethiopian woman would speak Arabic]. I asked him: Why are you speaking to us like that? He then ordered me to "shut up". I told him why do you want me to be quiet? He became upset and left after I spoke with him like that. Why do they think we are like animals? They don't listen to anything [we say].

Faith, the domestic worker from Kenya, recounts the following experience she had with a taxi driver one day:

> When I take a taxi, when they see you, they think you are *sharmuta*, a whore. A prostitute. So one time in a taxi, a man said, "Ethiopians

> are *sharmuta*". I say to the man, "These Ethiopians, do they do *sharmuta* with themselves? Or do they do *sharmuta* with Lebanese men?" So I said to him, "You yourself, you are *sharmuta*! Don't say that Ethiopians are *sharmuta*! They are doing it with you! So you, yourself, you are the same thing!" So when you tell somebody like that, they zip up. I don't give them time. I am annoyed with these men. How can you tell me that? So you want to go behind the curtain secretly and say, "You Africans are *sharmuta*!" And you're also putting me in this thing [category]. But I won't give them a chance. And after we are finished talking, that person says to me "You are intelligent" or "You are wise".

Here we see women migrant workers publicly defending other women in the face of scorn and aversion, risking public humiliation or worse. In the above, the men in both excerpts construct the women's identities through the intersections of race, sex, and class, those being "African" and "poor migrant worker" and *sharmuta* or whore. However, we see that the women resist the deficit nature of this constructed identity; Helena asserts, "We are Black, but we are human", in a public effort to re-define and re-construct those markers of being. Within the popular mindset of many Lebanese people who employ migrant domestic workers, it is believed that they are "disposable"; "unfeeling"; like an animal; and can be worked like a robot without rest. Helena's public declaration that she is Black and human has the potential to re-calibrate in the mind of the observer, Lebanese or other nationality, a new framing of the women migrant workers while she asserts her agency. Her actions are rooted in human rights – the right to be treated with dignity and respect, driven by a deep sense of right and wrong. She enacts a verbal resistance to emotional violence within an unequal power differential. These acts of resistance by Helena and Faith in the public space have the potential to demarcate the sometimes visible, but oftentimes invisible, yet acutely felt, boundaries of power for both the Lebanese and African observer.

Faith, like Helena, was also classified by her race, class, and also by the imposition of a demeaning sexual category, that of a *sharmuta*, or whore. In Lebanon, most African women who work as prostitutes are Ethiopian. The taxi driver was attempting to re-cast Faith, who is Kenyan, as Ethiopian and "promiscuous". In Faith's rebuttal to the taxi driver, she uses his logic against him by casting him and other Lebanese men as "whores" for partaking in sexual activity. Not only does Faith defend her African sisters, she also resists the man's categorization of her sexuality and re-defines the boundaries of sexuality for men, casting *them* as unsavory "whores". Such a bold public dialogue is dangerous, given that Faith, as an undocumented migrant worker, is at the mercy of an unjust and cruel legal system.

These counter-narratives represent what Sandoval (2000) refers to as a form of oppositional consciousness. Morris and Braine (2001) define oppositional consciousness as "…an empowering mental state that prepares members of an oppressed group to act to undermine, reform, or overthrow a system of human domination" (p. 25). While the migrant domestic workers here do not indicate that they desire to overthrow the hegemonic power structure, we see how the women are willing to risk great harm for ideologies in which they strongly believe and uphold, those of human and gendered rights.

Such a firm endorsement of beliefs could be categorized as a desire for equal rights. In Sandoval's (2000) description of the five topographies of oppositional consciousness,[2] the "equal rights" category includes oppositional actors who

> …[A]rgue for civil rights based on the philosophy that all humans are created equally. Practitioners of this particular ideological tactic demand that their humanity be legitimated, recognized as the same under the law, and assimilated into the most favored forms of the human-in-power. (p. 56)

When the oppositional actor is faced with some kind of perceived human indecency or oppression and chooses, or, rather, is compelled to confront this inhumane act, it is her oppositional consciousness at work. She must first be in possession of an oppositional consciousness to react to the event; and, in this process of reacting, speaking out, protesting, and risking harm, she becomes, at times unknowingly, a change agent. For Helena, she does not consider herself an activist, yet desires to learn more about what activism is:

> لاماسمعت شي. احب ان ادافع عن الحق. بدي ادافع عن المظلومين. باحب بس ما بعرف.
> اذا شفت واحد مثلا في مسلسل [تلفزيوني] و كوب ماي وقع من يدها. ياالله, الست بتسب عليها. ليش؟
> حرام. ليش بتعمل هيك. وقعت ماي. تقول كلمه خفيفه.

> No I have not heard anything [about activism]. I would like to empower others of their rights. I would like to defend the oppressed. I want to be a participate in activism. I would like to but I don't know how. If I see someone, for example, on a TV show. If they [the migrant worker] spilled a cup of water, it just fell from their hand. Oh my god, the madam [employer] would curse at her. She would say why did you do this?! Poor [migrant worker] she just spilled some water; she should use soft language.

The experience of the social actor (publicly) contesting what she views as a violation of human decency, triggered by her oppositional consciousness, can be a catalyst for the formation of new bodies of knowledge. The migrant domestic worker develops "a critical analysis of inequalities that links their everyday experiences of injustice to a structural analysis of social inequality and to an awareness of collective forms of action" (Kwon, 2008, p. 60). Helena desires to become engaged in a larger struggle with like-minded people to defend the oppressed; according to Foley (1999), "For people to become actively involved in social movements something had to happen to their consciousness – they must see that action is necessary and possible" (p. 103). The critical consciousness of Helena and Faith has been triggered by not only experiencing injustices as a domestic worker at the hands of a madam/oppressor, or the interrogator at the airport, or the taxi driver, but by observing injustices against their fellow domestic workers.

What are migrant domestic workers' reflections on the blatant human injustices they experience in Beirut? How can change occur in this society? What can be done about it? I asked Thomas, a migrant worker from Nigeria, about racism in Beirut, his encounters with it, and how he considers it; Thomas is also a community leader, in that he is an assistant pastor at a local Nigerian church. Thomas told me about Lebanese people throwing eggs and other rotten food items at him with no provocation, and the discrimination he faces almost daily. His reflections regarding his own lived experiences, and how he conceptualizes and frames the hateful and xenophobic behavior, incorporate a spiritual component. Here, Thomas relays an experience he had with a Lebanese woman who refused to get on an elevator with him:

> I got on the elevator. I got on it first. And because I'm a Black man, she refused to enter into the elevator. So I choose to see it like this: She gave me priority to have the elevator all to myself! [laughter] So I didn't see it as anything [negative], though I know that she has a racist heart, but I don't have to be bothered by it. But I have to move on with my life. If not, I will be stuck. And when I got into the elevator I stepped in with boldness, with boldness...I did not care how anybody chose to see me. So I'm Black, I don't care. I don't choose to see myself in a negative way. I have to be positive in everything. I don't care how other people look at me, I care how God looks at me. But it's not everybody who has this kind of mindset. There are many Lebanese that don't want to sit on the same seat as Black people on the bus. Or stand in the elevator with them. And the Lebanese won't have anything to do with us because of the way they choose to see us [African people]. But you yourself do not have to feel inferior. Look at you...you must see yourself as God created you. If you look at the Book [the Bible] you will see that God says that we are special. So everybody is special. And everything God created was good. God said so. So I'm good. I'm okay. Regardless of my color. I am fine. We need to change our mentality.

SK: See, you embody power, where other people might embody inferiority, and feel like they have to acquiesce to a White person. Do you see that?

THOMAS: Yes.

SK: And what does that look like when you see that?

THOMAS: I feel very sad when I see that. I feel very sad the way some of them look at themselves. Because it is the way you position yourself that is how somebody respects you. If you feel inferior in front of somebody, the person will look at you as inferior. So here we need to overcome that inferiority complex. We need to change our mentality. We need to change our mindset. The way we think. The way we think about ourselves. Because it is you that is limiting yourself. One Sunday just go to a restaurant and say to yourself, I'm just going to sit here, that is the goal. Or, let's go to the movies. And if they look at you, look at them, look at them right back. And then do it again and then it becomes normal. They want to hear you speak English. But if you limit yourself, you will remain where you are. So we need to get out of this. I went to a shop again, a big shop. And I know they are thinking, "Does he have money to buy?" And, I went in, and picked up clothes, and they were shocked to see that I could pay for that. There was a guy and a lady, they were just looking at me. I went up to them and I said "How much is this?" They looked at me, they looked at each other. They said, "The cost is such and such". And I put my hand in my pocket. And they asked me, "Are you a tourist?" I said, "No, I am not a tourist". And they said, "Where are you working?" And I said, "I work here". And I said, "So do you have any problems?" And he said, "No no no". Because they thought that I could not afford that. So it's the impression you give to people. And every time I step into that shop, they give attention to me before they give attention to anybody else. So it depends on you. We limit ourselves. If we see ourselves as inferior… And so what if they look at you, let them look at you in that way. Just go to the mall and buy something. Even if it's a little something just buy it and leave. But we are the ones limiting ourselves. Yes we have this complex, but we can overpower it. I know that some of my people will say, "Oh, I don't like the way they look at me". I just say "Come on!"

SK: You tell them this? You tell your friends this? You tell your people this?

THOMAS: I said this in the church one time, I said to them, "You limit yourself. Move on. If you don't like the way somebody looks at you don't let it bother you. Just move on".

SK: So you provide messages of empowerment to your people?

THOMAS: Yes, sometimes, when I have the opportunity, if the messages goes that way. Like the other Sunday, I talked to them before the message about Africa, before I did my teaching. I told them, Africa today, God has arisen Africa. God has heard our cries. In the past, the White man came and took our people to America to work for them. They came, they took our resources. Everything we have. Africa is not a cursed country, we are blessed. Europe has nothing, they have snow. We have

> oil, and gold, when they came, they took it from us. But today, they are paying the price. Recession is everywhere. And the African economy is good. And why? Because of your cries to God. So don't see yourself as suffering. Look at Greece... They are paying the price for what they stole from you. Because God said whatever you sow, you will reap. Look at America today. What they stole from us, they are now paying the price. And why is the economy sinking? Africa is now having the fastest growing economy. Now you see China fighting to get to Africa. So God is hearing your cries. I tell them we are Black and we are proud. Africa is blessed. In my country, we have everything. But the British came and stole it. And now they are paying the price. And don't worry, God will fight for you. And God will speak for us. But stop seeing yourself as suffering. We are not suffering. We're not suffering. God is opening doors for us. And soon we will become number one in the world. Our economy will be number one in the world. God has to clean up all the political leaders that are putting all that we have to their pockets. God has to clean them. Those who are connected to the Western government, God will take care of them. And then I gave them the message from the Bible that day. The first message was political and the second message was Biblical. But it's the truth. And I have to tell them the truth.

In Thomas's narrative, he explains how it is possible to overcome within oneself the sense of inferiority triggered by the possession of a "double consciousness". Historian and civil rights activist W.E.B. Du Bois, explains this concept of being viewed and measured through the eyes of others:

> It is a peculiar sensation, this double-consciousness, this sense of always looking at one's self through the eyes of others, of measuring one's soul by the tape of a world that looks on in amused contempt and pity. One ever feels his two-ness, – an American, a Negro; two souls, two thoughts, two unreconciled strivings; two warring ideals in one dark body, whose dogged strength alone keeps it from being torn asunder. (1903, p. 3)

This idea of double consciousness also encompasses the sensation of "otherness"; this multifaceted conception of "self" influences how we view ourselves and defines our identity, particularly for those who have crossed borders as refugees or migrant workers; or, those who belong to two or more ethnic groups; and/or those who belong to a minoritized/marginalized group. Those who identify with the experience of in-betweenness understand the constant reconciling of belonging to groups with which they identify.

As mentioned in Chapter 4, human beings are "endowed with habitus, inscribed in [our] bodies by past experience" (Bourdieu, 1997, p. 138). According to social and cultural reproduction theory, our habitus is a subconscious programming that cannot easily, if at all, come undone. In the above narrative, Thomas challenges this fatalist idea that we are at the mercy of one's habitus. He does acknowledge the power that double consciousness can wield on how one views oneself by recognizing the feelings of inferiority experienced by migrant workers; however, he offers instruction on how to overcome this sensation. He encourages his fellow migrant workers to practice facing the discomfort of "looking at one's self through the eyes of others" by visiting shopping centers and other establishments, to come to terms with the feelings of inferiority that stem from being viewed through that double lens, a superimposed inferiority that can be cast off by way of one's oppositional consciousness. In his church sermons, he acknowledges how the Global North, specifically Europe and the United States, have stolen African resources and now they pay the price due to the recessions they experienced and continue to experience.

Like Thomas, Felicity, a 38-year-old domestic worker from Nigeria, also has a side business designing and sewing dresses, and has lived several years in Lebanon (her story will be told in more detail in the coming pages). She shares the following observations and reflections about dealing with racism in Lebanon. Like Thomas, Felicity believes education is necessary for changing the effects of racism; however, she suggests those who need to be educated are the Lebanese people:

SK: What do you think of racism in Lebanon? How can this change? What can be done?

FELICITY: It is part of living in Lebanon. The country and the people themselves must begin to educate this people on how to treat their maids, on how to be nice to people. That is the only way. But if they are not doing anything about it, we just have to keep trying. It's like trying a new lock, til you get to the right place.

Felicity's observation is that it is Lebanese people themselves who must be responsible for changing their own people's xenophobic mindset toward migrant domestic workers, as opposed to outside systems of assistance, e.g., Western NGOs. Felicity also iterates that "We just have to keep trying. It's like trying a new lock, til you get to the right place". Her spirit of persistence and resilience shines through in the face of much oppression and opposition. Her words are reminiscent of Martin Luther King, Jr.'s (1963) thoughts on resilience: "The ultimate measure of a man is not where he stands in moments of comfort and convenience, but where he stands at times of challenge and controversy" (p. 67).

Migration as Knowledge Production

The world is witnessing an unprecedented increase in migration in the Middle East/SWANA region, Africa, and Southeast Asia due to civil war and violent conflict, unstable economies, natural disasters, civil and political unrest, and hostile policies toward marginalized groups. For instance, the ongoing Syrian crisis over the past several years has prompted Syrians to flee into neighboring Jordan, Lebanon, and Turkey; the insurrection of the Taliban in Afghanistan has caused Afghans to migrate into Iran and Pakistan; gay and transgendered Iraqi men have sought asylum in Jordan and Lebanon; and the onslaught of natural disasters, such as drought and devastating cyclones, also forces populations to migrate, either internally or to another country. Such traversing of borders, sometimes several before getting to a final destination, and sometimes waiting in refugee camps for decades, creates within the migrating person a sensation of liminality, of in-betweenness (Bhabha, 1994) in the act of navigating within the third space (Soja, 1996). Most people who choose to migrate are prompted by some kind of trauma in their country of origin, and, to make matters more challenging, those who migrate are viewed as outsiders, unwelcome guests, interlopers, or even worse to the local populations, which only compounds the sensation of alterity in the migrating person.

Suarez-Orozco (1991) noted that coping strategies, or "dual frame of reference", were utilized by marginalized border-crossers to "psychologically remain in their homelands rather than in the host society" (p. 111); according to the author, this type of mental framing of their lived experiences was intentional in order to "help foster a psychosocial home and peer group atmosphere that immunizes immigrant children against the hardships they must endure" (p. 111) in dealing with issues of assimilation. This coping mechanism is indicative of the notion that migration, in and of itself, is a learning process (Rao & Hossain, 2012, p. 417). Transnational border-crossers hold powerful epistemologies (Kasun & Saavedra, 2013; Saavedra, 2020); further, education for those who traverse borders must be viewed within a broader definition of education "in order to shed light on the multiple and changing meanings ascribed to education as part of processes of physical mobility as seen from the perspective of individual migrants and in the life course of the individual" (Valentin, 2012). In the following narratives, migrant domestic workers illustrate their own learning and teaching and sharing of knowledge within liminal spaces.

Many of the migrant domestic workers I interviewed suffered much hardship in their childhood. Several women describe the death of a parent when they were young children and how this event impacted their lives. Usually, it meant an end to happy and carefree times and leaving school at a young age to work and contribute to the household financially. For others, it meant an end to the dream of pursuing a college education, like for

Amara, whose father died when she was 11 years old, leaving her mother to raise Amara and her siblings alone. She very much desired to go to college; here, she relays how she came to the decision to work abroad:

ش. ك: شو خلاكي تتركي اثيوبيا وتيجي لهون [على لبنان] ؟ اهلك دفعوا لك ام انت؟
اماره: مش اهلي. انا كنت بالجامعه بادرس two years. امي مافيها
تدفع لي الجامعه واخواتي. انا دفعت لحالي. اشتغلت كثير.دبرت اموري لوحدي.
ما حد جبرني.
ش.ك: شو القرار اللي خلاكي تيجي هون؟ لدفع [تكاليف] الجامعه؟
اماره: في البدايه نعم. بس الان لا. انا بادفع تكاليف دراسة اخوتي.
ش.ك: مين خبرك [عن برنامج العمل] لتيجي هون؟
اماره: ال agency في اثيوبيا. في يوم كانت صاحبتي [في اثيوبيا] رايحه
على ال [agency] فرحت معها. شفت الباسبورت وكل شي. من بعدها بدات اذهب لوحدي.
امي ما كانت تعرف شو بعمل بال agency. عملت كل شي بدون ما تعرف. ما حبيت ماما تعرف حتى
لاتحزن. لما جبت [تاشيرة] الفيزا هي عرفت وحزنت كثير. وسافرت مع صاحباتي.
ش.ك: هل قررت ان تاتي للبنان قبل ما تحكي مع امك؟
اماره: نعم. ما قلت لها شئ. بعد ما حصلت على الباسبورت والفيزا حكيت قلت لها.
حتى ماتزعل.

SK: What made you leave Ethiopia and come here? And did your family pay or did you?

AMARA: Not my family, I was at the university studying. I studied two years in the university. My mother was unable to pay the university [fees] for me or for my siblings. I went on my own, I had to work hard, and I got myself in line [built myself]. No one forced me to do it.

SK: Your decision to come was to pay [the expenses] of the university?

AMARA: Yes, for the university, but now no. My siblings go to school, and I pay their school expenses.

SK: Who informed you about the [job] program?

AMARA: There is an [employment] agency here. My friend wanted to go there. One time I went with her, I saw the passports and everything. After this I went on my own. My mother did not know but I would go to the agency, and everything was moving along but she didn't know. I travelled with my friends. I did not want her to be sad and such. She only knew when I got a visa. She was very sad. I left, travelled alone with my friends.

SK: Did you decide to go to Syria before you spoke to your mother?

AMARA: Yes, I did not tell her anything. Once I was got my visa did I tell her. I did not want her to be sad.

In the above excerpt, Amara stresses that she has to "get herself in line", or build herself by herself, which can be interpreted as indicative of Amara's autonomous sense of self, that she is responsible for her own interpersonal growth. Many of the women came to the decision to leave their home countries because of their family's financial situation, and, like Amara, many came to the decision to leave on their own volition, making a point to declare that they own that decision; Makeda, who is a 28-year-old Ethiopian domestic worker, says, "No one knew I was going [to Beirut]. Because of the bad way people talk about Lebanon, I did not tell anyone. Only after a year of being here, did I tell them". She pretended to her mother that she was working in a different part of Ethiopia for that year.

Helena's story is also indicative of self-reliance and strong sense of self. She is a 24-year-old Ethiopian woman who has labored as a domestic worker for four years. She recounts her story:

هالينه: ابي مكان يعرف بي [بوجودي]. امي ما كانت تخلي ابوي يعرف عني شي.
امي اخذتني عند بيت اهلها يربوني وابي ما كان يعرف شي عني. كان عندي 24 سنه.
وابي ما عرف بي. انا بدي اعطيه حقه كاي اب. انا بدي اوقف مع حقه. ما بدي اظلمه.
لهيك بحب الحق.في يوم قلت لامي بدي اشوف ابي. قالت لي: كيف بدك تشوفي وانت ما تعرفيه؟
كيف هلا بدك تشوفيه؟ قلتلها انا بدي شوف ابي. هذا حقي. فاخذتني عند ابوي.
لما شفت ابي كثير بكيت. ابي متزوج وعنده بنت. لي اخت صغيره.
بقولوا اني باشبه ابوي [خاصه] راسي (بوشي).
انا ممكن اشتغل كمان هون [في لبنان]. بس مابدي. هلا الكونترا لسا ماخلص.

ش.ك: هو [ابوك] مستعد يساعدك؟
هالينه: اكيد بساعدني. هو عرض علي. بس مافيني اروحله. سالني كم تريدين لمدرستك؟
بدك مصاري؟قلت له: انا ما بدي شي. كان لازم يساعدني لما كنت صغيره. ماساعدني. انا
وصلت لهون بدون مساعدته ولازم اكمل لوحدي. الوقت فات. لما كنت بدي اياه. ما لقيته.
كان بدي والد حنون يعطف علي. بس ما كان موجود وقتها. انا ما بكلره ابي الان. بالعكس
بحبه كثير. انا ما بغارعلى اصحابي لان عندهم اب وام حنون يربوهم بعطف وحنان.
انا كنت ادبرس وباشتغل وبساعد امي كمان. وهلا كبرت وعندي 25 سنه. ابي اجا
متاخر. انا باحاول اكمل دراستي لوحدي. اذا بدي ابي بساعدني. بس انا بدي احاول
اكمل لوحدي.

ش. ك: هل ممكن تعيشي اسهل مع مساعدة ابيك؟
هالينه: انا ما عندي مشكله انه اشتغل اي شئ. ممكن اشتغل اي شغله, انضف بيوت او
ابيع حلويات مثلا. ما بهمني. وما حد بصدقني. مره اخي الكبير سالني:
كيف بدك تروحي على لبنان تتنضفي الحمام؟ بدك تخزينا؟... انا رح كمل في
المشوار حتى اصل نهايته. ما راح وقف. انا رح فرجي الناس كلها موش بس اهلي.
انا رح فرجيهم انه راح اصل للي بدي اياه. لهيك انا ما قبلت المساعده من ابي...
احيانا كثيره باشعر بالحزن والوحده هنا. باطلع يوم الاحد فقط. ما بشوف اهلي.
باشعر بالوحده. بس بدي احقق هدفي.

HELENA: My father did not know about me. To keep my father from having the ability to take me, my mother took me to her father's, for me to be raised there. My mother's family raised me and I did not know my father. How could my father have his lawful rights, I was 24 and did not know my father. I wanted him to have his rights. I did not want injustice,

I wanted him here. For this I would like rights. My mother would not take me to meet him. I had not seen my father's family. I was told I look very much like them like in the head and face. I went to Lebanon, [but] I did not even finish my contract there. How was I only going to see my father? I would cry a lot. I went to my mother to tell her I wanted my father. She said how are you going to do that, you didn't know anything until just now, what do you want now? Go to your father. I told her this is my right. I want to see my father. There is work for me there too, but I do not want to work. I just want my father, my rights. So I went to my father's and he is married and has a daughter. I have a little sister.

SK: Is your father willing to help you financially?

HELENA: Of course. yes, he helps me. He offered to help me. I do not have it in me to go to him [ask him for help]. He asked me how much my school is and whatever I want, just tell him. I did not want his help. The time I needed his help, was when I was young. He did not help me. I got to where I am now on my own and I want to see myself continue to finish on my own. At the time that was necessary for him to be there, I couldn't find him. And I wanted a caring/affectionate father, that I did not find. I do not hate my father now. I love him very much. I would not bother with all my friends with their mothers and fathers that raised them with so much affection. I was going to school and helping my mother with work. Now I am old, I am 25 years old. He came too late, I want to continue to finish [on my own]. I am trying, if I need him to, he can give me help, but I am trying to continue to finish on my own.

SK: You could live an easier life with the help of your father...

HELENA: I do not have a problem with working as a house cleaner or selling sweets, no one is convinced when I tell them this. My older brother said to me [frantically] why do you want to go to Lebanon, do you want to clean bathrooms? Do you want to shame us?... I am on a path I started and will keep going until the end. I will not stop. I want to show not only my family, but all other people. I want to show them that I will reach my goal through this work. And that is why I rejected my father's help.... There are many times when I feel sad and lonely here. I only go out on Sundays, and I do not see my family, and it feels lonely without them, but I want to achieve my goal.

While family financial strain compelled Amara and Helena to consider leaving their home countries in Africa, they frame their decision to leave their home countries as a choice, not as an imposition of circumstances or a last resort or lack of options. There is a clear intentionality in leaving to go abroad, which indicates an ownership of the decision and the use of their own will. The women articulate an agentive process that informs their decision-making. In the above excerpt, Helena makes clear that she is in Beirut as the result of her own determination – no one forced her, nor did she feel at the mercy of her life's circumstances. A consciousness in the decision-making process is articulated when she makes the decision to see her father, when she chooses to continue to labor as a domestic worker in Beirut even in the face of scorn and criticism from her family, even turning down monetary assistance from her father, because of her sense of pride and independence, and desire to "build myself up".

This theme of building oneself, which was also present in Amara's narrative, speaks to the drive and resilience of the women at the center of this study. Worthy of noting is the relationship between Amara and Helena. They were close friends prior to attending the Migrant Center, and started attending the Center at the referral of a shared friend. The two women always sat together in class, and Amara was very helpful to Helena, and would assist her in group work, help her when it was Helena's turn to speak out loud, and act as a scaffold in a gentle way. They studied together and shared personal time outside of class on their days off. This shared notion of "building" oneself and relying on oneself suggests that they provided emotional support for each other, shared empathy, encouragement, strength, and the sharing of everyday life experiences – this is an example of how social relationships facilitate the transmission of shared knowledges among social networks (González, Moll, & Amanti, 2005).

Faith, as mentioned in Chapter 4, is an undocumented migrant domestic worker from Kenya who ran away from her madam's home because of abuse. As such, it was critical for Faith to learn how to navigate the space of the city in order to not get arrested. In Beirut, arrest means imprisonment at the underground Adlieh Detention Center, notorious for sexual and physical abuse of the detainees.[3] Undocumented workers are imprisoned for several months in inhumane conditions. Faith has a friend who was imprisoned at the time of our interview, and she spoke with sadness and great concern for her friend, and also fear, as she knows her good fortune of not being stopped on the streets thus far could run out. Faith learned, from her friends, the times to avoid certain areas of Beirut, namely, the area of Naba'a, where the Migrant Center is located, because at certain times, the area is flooded with police officers who frequently stop migrant domestic workers and ask them for their identification cards and paperwork. She relays the story of how she avoided the police:

> My friend called me on my cell phone, and said, "Don't you dare come here to the side of the bridge". [A bridge separates Borj Hammoud and Naba'a, and it is in Naba'a the police frequently roam looking for undocumented workers.] And we were just crossing over. So we had to run back to our house and shut the door and close all the windows. And hide from the police. So then I left the house around 9 p.m. The police get tired too, they have to go to their families too. If they don't go home on time, these Lebanese women, they will kill them!

For migrant workers, especially women, the public space of Lebanon is a contested social space, that being defined as "geographic locations where conflicts in the form of opposition, confrontation, subversion, and/or resistance engage actors whose social positions are defined by differential control of resources and access to power" (Low & Lawrence-Zúñiga, 2003, p. 18). Bourdieu refers to the social space as a "field", the space in which forms of capital are enacted, appropriated, and utilized (Thomson, 2012, p. 67). Within this space, Faith must call on her social capital, that being her friend network, to assist her in navigating the cityscape and avoiding arrest. Also noteworthy is how she calls on her implicit understanding of the dynamics and social relations between (Lebanese) men and women to inform her decision-making process. For Faith, success is measured in the days she remains free of bondage by a system that tricked her into human trafficking.

Another migrant domestic worker's story that exemplifies everyday resistance and empowerment is Felicity's. She is 38 years old and has labored as a domestic worker in Beirut for the past 15 years. Felicity is originally from Nigeria, and speaks four languages: Yoruba, the language of her father's province, and Delta, the language of her mother's province. She also speaks English, which is the official language of Nigeria. Additionally, she speaks Arabic, and is in the process of learning French. While she is fluent in these four languages and in the process of learning a fifth, she cannot read or write in these languages. I came to meet Felicity at the Migrant Center as she was there because she wanted to learn how to read and write English. I was paired up with her and we clicked beautifully: She was an eager student and I was eager to assist her in meeting her educational goals. She was shy at first, but warmed up quickly; she had a wonderful demeanor, emitting positive energy and a quiet confidence. For two hours, we sat with our heads crammed together, trying to hear each other over the ruckus of other classes and students and teachers, and going over her notebook of previous notes of the alphabet.

As I got to know her, I learned that Felicity is what is referred to as a "freelancer", or a migrant worker who is not bound to any contract, so they can make their own work schedules, essentially. However, most freelancers are undocumented, which creates a perilous situation for them, as some employers can use that information against the freelancers to get a cheaper price or refuse to pay the worker all together. In Felicity's case, I learned, her employer/madam is assisting her with her paperwork so she will be "documented". Felicity's formative years were marred by many obstacles: As a child in school, she struggled with learning to read and write, and her parents were too occupied with work to assist her. She began to hate school due to the frustration at learning how to read and write. She encountered one teacher who tried to go above and beyond to help her, but she still struggled. Eventually she quit school. Felicity was not diagnosed with a learning disorder as a child, but from her story and from my experiences working closely with her, I believe she was experiencing an information-processing problem. She explains her frustration with illiteracy here:

SK: How did it feel for you to see your colleagues be able to read and write?

FELICITY: It was the most frustrating thing in my life. So I was very frustrated and very... it was very discouraging. Though my parents were pushing me, they did not want me to quit school, they believed that there was hope, but I had already given up. I have begun to realize myself that I gave up. I was not patient to wait for the time. I was not patient. So I dropped. [Quits school]. And I don't want to say I have a block brain [laughter]. But my younger brothers and sisters they are making it, they can read, they can write, but for me I cannot read, I cannot write. It's difficult for me to memorize what you teach me today. When you asked me tomorrow, I forgot them all. I was a very frustrated person at that time.

Her parents were impoverished and had six other children to care for, and no resources existed at her school for diagnosing learning disabilities, so Felicity's learning needs were not addressed.

Even still, Felicity attended a "job school" (vocational training school) to learn sewing skills. She speaks of her mentor in Nigeria who taught her how to sew and who made a significant impact on her life trajectory:

FELICITY: She was a nice woman...she was a Believer [Christian]. She understood my case also. She was like a mother, and she cared for me and she understood my stubbornness, and not wanting to do... Not taking responsibility in something. When this dress, this style is very difficult for me, I just push it aside and I say "Oh this is too difficult, I cannot sew this". And she would say to me, "You must sew it". She made me to sew what was difficult... And then when she was doling out what we could sew that day, she would give me the difficult part even if I was swearing, sweating, I was not happy when she told me I had to had to sew it, she said, "I do not care, you just have to sew it because tomorrow I'm not going to be there for you". And I really... I really see now she did a very wonderful thing for me... A wonderful job for my life, because I am now facing the same things that are difficult and I cannot go run to her and tell her "Hey can you help me?" [Laughter]

SK: She forced you to rely on your own self.

FELICITY: Exactly. She has this language: "Use your brain, stop borrowing people's brains".

SK: That's interesting because remember when you... Remember when you were doing the spelling? [In class I was helping her with spelling out words] I said, "You want me to help you with that?" and you said "No, I can do that myself".

FELICITY: [Laughter]

SK: So this lesson this woman taught you...

FELICITY: It helps me in life also because...When I'm in Lebanon, I have no family, I have no brother, no sister. I try to do things myself. I have to go out... I cannot read the signs...You just have to go and do it. You cannot wait for somebody. You have to be bold and just do it. So I like it so much. I say "God, thank you so much for this woman, because she made me to be strong".

In addition to working as a domestic worker, Felicity also has her own business as a seamstress/fashion designer. Here she talks about her love for her work as a fashion designer and how she promotes her business:

> I love it so much, I'm so interested in this job. It's so much fun, I don't know how to describe it, but I have so much love for what I'm doing. I cannot imagine myself, who cannot read and write, making dresses for people who can read and write. And they like my work. And people tell me my work is good, and that I am wonderful in sewing, I'm so happy with it, I love the job so much.

Felicity was in the process of combining African and Western style to create a hybrid of fashion and describes how she creates original patterns:

FELICITY: I would like to combine them [African wear and Western wear] because there's no way I can keep away from my African...for me personally I'm so proud of African wear. And now the way the modern is going, we can use our African fabric...we can sell it like your dress. [She refers to the dress I am wearing] So, this is why I like it so much now. So I get to be creative.

SK: Do you use a pattern? Do you see it in your head? Do use a sewing machine?

FELICITY: Yes I use a sewing machine...And the way I... I don't use a pattern the way you people use the pattern. But I can sketch my own pattern... I look, I see the style...Then I have to figure out how to how to fix it together... So if the style's very difficult for me, that I do get a sheet of paper, and cut it out, and it's an original pattern, So, so I sketch it out on the paper then I see that I can make a pattern. Then I make this dress.

Felicity explains how she sells her products:

FELICITY: So they come, and they bring their material, I have material too, from Nigeria, so I sell what you want and you buy, you choose your style, I have my catalogs, from Nigeria you choose the style you want, and I'll make you a dress.

SK: And how do they learn about you? Word-of-mouth?

FELICITY: First time when I began to sew in this country, I had two friends, so I use them as my showgirls, from the church, so people would ask them "How did you get your dress where did you get your dresses? Who is your tailor?" I tell them that I'm the one who sewed these dresses.

Like many migrant workers, Felicity's educational, migratory, and economic trajectories have been impacted by structural forces beyond her control (González, 2006). And, as stated previously, Lebanon is a hostile country toward migrant workers, and more so for a person who cannot read or write. Yet, in Felicity's quest for creating a livelihood for herself under the most dire of social and economic conditions, she has been able to carve out gratifying employment opportunities that capitalize on her existing knowledge bases. These funds of knowledge are defined as the "historically accumulated and culturally developed bodies of knowledge and skills essential for household or individual functioning and well-being" (González, Moll, & Amanti, 2005, p. 72). In the above narratives, we see Felicity tap into several of her own accumulated funds of knowledge and create her own epistemological space by way of "reconfigured notions of teaching and learning" (González, 2006, p. 197). Felicity cites her mentor and sewing teacher who not only taught her the valuable skill of sewing, but also taught her perseverance in the face of adversity and discomfort, to move beyond her comfort zone and to "quit borrowing other's brains". This lesson on perseverance is one she cites today as serving her in the hostile space of Lebanon. Felicity expresses how grateful she is to have developed that ability to persist in the face of adversity.

Felicity also refers to her cultural capital as being a resource in developing her business model – she sews African styles and often combines them with modern, Western wear, to create her own fashion designs. Also remarkable is how Felicity is able to, without literacy skills, create complex patterns for her designs. She also demonstrates an appropriation of her social networks by utilizing her friends as show models for her dresses among her church community; such marketing savvy illustrates Felicity's business acumen without having any formal training in business or marketing.

Central to Felicity's and other migrant domestic workers' agentive experiences within this contested social space of Beirut is the idea that the migrant domestic workers interviewed here engage in the production of new epistemologies. By virtue of coming to a foreign country without access to language, social services, friends or other social networks, and being particularly vulnerable, even more so than their male migrant worker cohort, they set out on a learning journey of trial and error, and sometimes at great detriment to their lives. This process of learning is ever occurring and never faltering. These funds of knowledge (González, Moll, & Amanti, 2005) build like a savings account; the longer one can live, survive, and accumulate that knowledge over a continuum, and then share that knowledge for the group's survival and success, that account gains interest, to the point where such knowledge informs the empowerment and resistance of that shared group. Naomi explains this phenomenon of the accumulated knowledges:

احنا بنساعد بعضنا. احنا اكتسبنا خبره كثيره. صار لنا 9-10 سنوات. اكثر خبره من
اللي الهم 2-3 سنوات بيشتغلوا في لبنان. ما بيعرفوا شئ. بكفي انه احنا عزمنا ان
نعلمهن ونفسر لهن شو لازم يعملوا. ما لازم يعيشوا 10 سنين حتى يحصلوا ع نفس الخبره
اللس عنا. ممكن يخصلوا على الخبره بسنه او سنتيت. لازم ان نضل مع بعض. نساعد بعض.
لازم نكون يد واحده.

> We help each other. What we have acquired [knowledge] over 9 or 10 years is far more experienced than the new migrant workers that are here for only 2 or 3 years. They do not know anything. It is enough that I have the determination and intention to teach them or interpret for them what they need to do. [They do not need] to stay here for 10 years to get to where I am now. The can [obtain] the knowledge [experience] in one or two years… It is a must for us to be together, helping one other, we must be together hand in hand.

Here, Naomi articulates the sharing of knowledge within the migrant domestic worker social networks so as to make the transition for the newly arrived migrant worker easier than her own trial-by-fire experiences ten years ago. González (2006) explains how border-crossers (or any subaltern group who has traversed borders) have created these epistemologies of learning and how the transmission of accumulated knowledges acts as a catalyst for power:

> As discourses come to recognize the situated nature of knowledge and the partiality of all knowledge claims, the metaphor of borders and border-crossers has been foregrounded. However, the ultimate border – the border between knowledge and power – can be crossed only when…lived experiences become validated as a source of knowledge, and when the process of how knowledge is constructed and translated between groups located within nonsymmetrical relations of power is questioned. (p. 42)

In Naomi's understanding of shared accumulated knowledges, we see that, within a hegemonic space, nonsymmetrical relations of power are being contested by the transmission of accumulated knowledges. While the intent to challenge dominant power structures is not explicitly stated, it nonetheless becomes a by-product by virtue of this transmission of knowledges, because those shared knowledges teach the newcomer how to access social services and social networks; how to traverse the physical spaces of the city and mitigate the chance of arrest; and how to navigate the bureaucracy of employment agencies, embassies, and other government agencies. Thus, marginalized groups become more empowered to challenge the notions of dominance within a disproportionate power structure.

As the migrant domestic workers re-told and reflected on their stories of struggle and survival within the hostile terrain that is Beirut, it becomes evident that the women have shared experiences in which one finds many commonalities. They have lived outside of their home countries as migrant workers for anywhere from five to fifteen years, returning to their home countries perhaps every two years, or not at all, and they have cultivated a production of knowledge based on shared experiences that illustrate struggle and survival, resistance and hope, in that in-between, subaltern, contested social-physical space.

Knowledge Production in Interstitial, Subaltern Spaces

The term "subaltern" originates from the postcolonial and subaltern studies discourses, which sought to provide a historiography "of India from below" to counter the "colonial elitism" that dominated the field of the history of India (Buras & Apple, 2006, p. 18). For the purposes of my study, "subaltern" is used to denote a social group who has been rendered dispossessed, powerless or less powerful than, having often crossed political or natural borders and inhabiting and dwelling (sometimes forcefully) within the social, cultural, economic, racial, and spiritual margins and in-between spaces of the hegemonic power structure. The subaltern are refugees, asylum seekers, and migrant workers; they are internally displaced persons or internally colonized (Arteaga, 1996, p. 24); they flee the violent conflict of their homelands, or natural disasters, or economic despair; they often experience in their daily lives the threat of violence; poverty; illness; hunger; prejudice, racism, and xenophobia. This subaltern group's shared "culture" is not defined by a shared language, nor shared social mores, but rather, a shared space of struggle, of survival, of marginalization, of cultural differences, and of "in-betweenness" to achieve a shared resistance of hope and success in an oppressive and racist society. Here, Bhabha (1994) conceptualizes interstitiality:

> The move away from the singularities of "class" or "gender" as primary conceptual and organizational categories, has resulted in an awareness of the subject positions – of race, gender, generation, institutional location, geopolitical locale, sexual orientation – that inhabit

> any claim to identity in the modern world. What is theoretically innovative, and politically crucial, is the need to think beyond narratives of originary and initial subjectivities and to focus on those moments or processes that are produced in the articulation of cultural differences. These "in-between" spaces provide the terrain for elaborating strategies of selfhood – singular or communal – that initiate new signs of identity, and innovative sites of collaboration, and contestation, in the act of defining the idea of society itself. It is in the emergence of the interstices-the overlap and displacement of domains of difference – that the intersubjective and collective experiences of nationness, community interest, or cultural value are negotiated. (p. 2)

Within the gaps created by the juxtaposition of the local and "the other" are those liminal spaces where "the overlap and displacement of domains of difference" (Bhabha, 1994, p. 2) are located. Herein lie systems of knowledge of which the subaltern groups formulate, assess, accumulate, share, and apply. It is this epistemological process from which a pedagogy of the other (Burney, 2012) emerges.

The cultural markers shared by migrant workers as subaltern actors are not anchored to fixed geographical places but rather, by virtue of migrant workers' shared alterity and cultural, social, and racial differences from the oppressor within the liminal space, and are defined by an either collective or individual experience – a camaraderie is formed in the face of opposition. Recall how Faith has learned to navigate a racially charged social system by relying on and trusting her friends to help her navigate the city and avoid arrest; these are the shared cultural traits of interstitiality: The commonality of struggle and survival in the third, "in-between" space, and the calling upon one's funds of knowledge formulated by survival, endurance, and, sometimes, tragedy.

As evidenced in these narratives, migrant workers often contend with the alterity particular to the immigrant experience. "The Other" (Said, 1978) or "otherness" (Bhabha, 1994) is "the process of creating and maintaining a dichotomy between ones-self, as marked by a particular (Western) identity, and the Other(s)" (Bresner, 2010, p. 11). In the case of Beirut, it is the Lebanese people who frame themselves as "Western/modern" and impose upon migrant workers an otherness so as to make the other strange, foreign, otherized. The created dichotomy that is perpetuated by the madam/oppressor objectifies the migrant worker so as to reduce her into a "thing" that is not human, therefore, absolving the employer from any guilt when the madam and mister mistreat/abuse migrant domestic workers. In turn, the migrant domestic worker is constantly reminded of her subaltern state, her sense of liminality, which is reinforced by macro-level institutional laws, like the *kafala* system, and the everyday xenophobia of her workplace, at the micro level. Such disciplinary power acts as a tool of perpetual marginalization to remind the migrant domestic worker of her secondary status, her subjugated situation, and her subaltern position.

To understand how migrant domestic workers as subaltern actors inhabit and appropriate "culture as a strategy for survival" within the interstitial, socially contested spaces and how these practices segue into the formation of empowerment and resistance frameworks via social networks, educational opportunities, and activist participation, we turn in the next chapter to a critical pedagogical analysis of the educational opportunities accessed by migrant domestic workers at the Migrant Center in Beirut's neighborhood of Naba'a.

Notes

1 This type of power dynamic is reminiscent of the ideas of the Zone of Proximal Development and instructional scaffolding which are constructivist notions that will be discussed in greater detail in Chapter 7.

2 Sandoval's topography of oppositional consciousness as described in *Methodology of the Oppressed* (2000) is in reference to and description of the historiography of feminism in a Western/U.S. context, which is utilized in the Chicana feminist literature (Moya, 2002 [Moya asserts Sandoval's postmodernist project of oppositional consciousness "partially undermine[s]...theorizing the experiences of women of color" and suggests Sandoval is in alignment with "postpositivist realist theory of identity" p. 62]; Pérez, 1999) and referenced in other postcolonial and transnational feminist literature (Mohanty, 2003). I justify a borrowing of aspects of her topography as a framework because Chicana/Borderlands literature and feminisms speak to the interstitiality and alterity the migrant domestic worker in this study experiences as she inhabits a foreign and cruel third space in the face of much adversity, much like the migrant/borderlands women who traverse borders in González's (2006) "Testimonios of Border Identities: 'Una Mujer Acomedida Donde Quiera Cabe'".

3 For more information, see *The Daily Star*'s news report, " Inside Adlieh's Infamous Detention Center" at http://www.dailystar.com.lb/ and the web blog post, "The Adlieh Detention Center: A Living Hell" at https://hummusforthought.com/.

References

Ahearn, L. M. (2001). Language and agency. *Annual Review of Anthropology*, *30*, 109–137. DOI: 10.1146/annurev.anthro.30.1.109

Ahearn, L. M. (2010). Agency and language. In J. Jaspers, J. Östman, & J. Verschuere (Eds.), *Society and language use* (pp. 28–48). Amsterdam: John Benjamins Publishing.

Ali, R. (2014). Empowerment beyond resistance: Cultural ways of negotiating power relations. *Women's Studies International Forum*, *45*, 119–126. DOI: 10.1016/j.wsif.2013.05.019

Arteaga, A. (1996). Bonding in difference: Interview with Alfred Arteaga (1993-1994). In G. Spivak & D. Landry (Eds.), *The Spivak reader: Selected works of Gayatri Chakravorty Spivak* (pp. 1–14). New York, NY: Routledge.

Bhabha, H. (1994). *The location of culture*. New York, NY: Routledge.
Bourdieu, P. (1997). Bodily knowledge. In P. Bourdieu (Ed.), *Pascalian meditations* (pp. 128–163). Stanford, CA: Stanford University Press.
Bresner, K. (2010). Othering, power relations, and indigenous tourism: Experiences in Australia's Northern territory. *Platform, 11*, 10–26.
Buras, K. L., & Apple, M. W. (2006). Introduction. In M. W. Apple & K. L. Buras (Eds.), *The subaltern speak: Curriculum, power, and educational struggles* (pp. 1–42). New York, NY: Routledge.
Burney, S. (2012). *Pedagogy of the other: Edward Said, postcolonial theory, and strategies for critique*. New York, NY: Peter Lang Publishing.
Chamberlin, J. (2013). A Working Definition of Empowerment. Retrieved February 12, 2014, from http://www.power2u.org/articles/empower/working_def.html
Constable, N. (2007). *Maid to order in Hong Kong: Stories of migrant workers*. Ithaca, NY: Cornell University Press.
Du Bois, W. E. B. (1903). *The souls of Black folk*. Chicago, IL: A.C. McClurg and Co.
Foley, G. (1999). *Learning in social action: A contribution to understanding education and training*. London: Zed Books.
Foucault, M. (1995). *Discipline and punish: The birth of the prison*. New York, NY: Random House.
Giroux, H. (2010). Lessons from Paulo Freire. *Chronicle of Higher Education, 57*(9), B15–B16.
González, N. (2005). Beyond culture: The hybridity of funds of knowledge. In N. González, L. C. Moll, & C. Amanti (Eds.), *Funds of knowledge: Theorizing practices in households, communities, and classrooms* (pp. 29–46). Mahwah, NJ: Erlbaum Associates.
González, N. (2006). Testimonios of border identities: "Una mujer acomedida donde quiera cabe". In D. Delgado Bernal, C. A. Elenes, F. E. Godinez, & S. Villenas (Eds.), *Chicana/Latina education in everyday life* (pp. 197–213). Albany, NY: State University of New York Press.
González, N., Moll, L. C., & Amanti, C. (Eds.). (2005). *Funds of knowledge: Theorizing practices in households, communities, and classrooms*. New York, NY: Routledge.
Kasun, G. S., & Saavedra, C. M. (2013). Crossing borders toward young transnational lives. In J. Keengwe & G. Onchwari (Eds.), *Cross-cultural considerations in the education of young immigrant learners*. Hershey, PA: IGI Global. DOI: 10.4018/978-1-4666-4928-6.ch012
King, M. L., Jr. (1963). *Strength to love*. Boston, MA: Beacon Press.
Kreisberg, S. (1992). *Transforming power: Domination, empowerment, and education*. Albany, NY: State University of New York Press.
Kwon, S. A. (2008). Moving from complaints to action: Oppositional consciousness and collective action in a political community. *Anthropology & Education Quarterly, 39*(1), 59–76. DOI: 10.1111/j.1548-1492.2008.00005.x
Low, S. M., & Lawrence-Zúñiga, D. (2003). *The anthropology of space and place: Locating culture*. Malden, MA: Blackwell Publishers.
Lukes, S. (2005). *Power: A radical view* (2nd ed.). London: Palgrave Macmillan.
Mohanty, C. T. (2003). "Under Western eyes" revisited: Feminist solidarity through anticapitalist struggles. *Signs, 28*(2), 499–535.

Morris, A., & Braine, N. (2001). Social movements and oppositional consciousness. In J. J. Mansbridge & A. Morris (Eds.), *Oppositional consciousness: The subjective roots of social protest* (pp. 20–37)). Chicago, IL: The University of Chicago Press.

Moya, M. L. (2002). Chicana feminism and postmodernist theory. In *Learning from experience: Minority identities, multicultural struggles* (pp. 58–99). Los Angeles, CA: University of California Press.

Page, N., & Czuba, C. E. (1999). Empowerment: What is it? *The Journal of Extension*, *37*(5). Retrieved from https://archives.joe.org/joe/1999october/comm1.php

Pérez, E. (1999). *The decolonial imaginary: Writing Chicanas into history*. Bloomington, IN: Indiana University Press.

Rao, N., & Hossain, M. I. (2012). "I want to be respected": Migration, mobility, and the construction of alternate educational discourses in rural Bangladesh. *Anthropology & Education Quarterly*, *43*(4), 415–428. DOI: 10.1111/j.1548-1492.2012.01194.x

Roald, A. S. (2016). The nuances of Islam: Empowerment and agency for Palestinian women in the West bank. *Frontiers: A Journal of Women Studies*, *37*(3), 1–20. DOI: 10.5250/fronjwomestud.37.3.0001

Saavedra, C. M. (2020). Literacy as geographies of transnationalism and mobility: Diasporic experiences, identities, and knowledge production. *Research in the Teaching of English*, *54*(3), 285–287.

Said, E. (1978). *Orientalism*. New York, NY: Pantheon Books.

Sandoval, C. (2000). *Methodology of the oppressed*. Minneapolis, MN: The University of Minnesota Press.

Scott, C. E. (1992). Foucault, ethics, and the fragmented subject. *Research in Phenomenology*, 22, 104–137.

Sewell, W. H., Jr. (1992). A theory of structure: Duality, agency, and transformation. *American Journal of Sociology*, *98*(1), 1–29.

Sharma, A. (2008). *Logics of empowerment: Development, gender, and governance in neoliberal India*. Minneapolis, MN: University of Minnesota Press.

Soja, E. W. (1996). *Thirdspace: Journeys to Los Angeles and other real-and-imagined places*. Malden, MA: Blackwell Publishers.

Suarez-Orozco, M. M. (1991). Migration, minority status, and education: European dilemmas and responses in the 1990s. *Anthropology & Education Quarterly*, 22(2), 99–120.

Swartz, D. (1998). *Culture and power: The sociology of Pierre Bourdieu*. Chicago, IL: University of Chicago Press.

Titi, V., & Singh, N. (1995). *Empowerment for sustainable development: Toward operational strategies*. Halifax: Fernwood Pub.

Thomson, P. (2014). Field. In M. Grenfell (Ed.), *Pierre Bourdieu: Key concepts* (pp. 65–80). Durham, UK: Acumen Publishing.

Valentin, K. (2012). The role of education in Mobile livelihoods: Social and geographical routes of young Nepalese migrants in India. *Anthropology & Education Quarterly*, *43*(4), 429–442.

Chapter 6

Education, Empowerment, and Activism in Beirut's NGO Spaces

Most non-governmental organizations (NGOs) within international development focus on immediate needs of vulnerable groups such shelter, housing, and meeting medical needs of migrant workers, refugees, and asylum seekers. Most nonformal educational opportunities for these groups provided by NGOs in the Middle East/SWANA region have become a fairly recent development. For example, Jesuit Refugee Services began establishing tertiary educational programs for refugees beginning in 2010 in six different developing countries (McPherson, 2016). In Iran, Hami, an NGO that protects refugees, began providing education for Afghan children starting 2008 (Pournik, 2013) and in Jordan, several relief organizations such as Save the Children funds educational opportunities in Za'atari Camp, the largest refugee camp for Syrian for Syrian refugees ("Save the Children Delegation", 2017). Sawiyan for Community Development is a grassroots NGO established in 2018 and they provide community-led educational initiatives for Sudanese, Somali, and Yemeni refugee adults and children in Jordan (Johnston, Baslan, & Kvittingen, 2019).

Certainly, the education of refugees and asylum seekers is a very valuable and necessary endeavor. However, often left out of these opportunities are migrant domestic workers; and, given that they account for 1.6 million women from Southeast Asian and African countries in the labor force in Arab states ("Domestic Workers", n.d.), a pedagogical and epistemological examination of the teaching and learning of migrant workers is worthy of analysis. This chapter introduces a grassroots NGO system whose sole purpose is serving this demographic and examines its educational opportunities and how nonformal education acts as a conduit for empowerment and activism.

Language classes in developing countries, specifically the teaching of English, is predicated upon the notion within the development sector that mastering English will assuredly provide opportunities to participate in the labor market and is thereby directly related to one's social and economic mobility.[1] Such a notion contributes to an ideological and pedagogical

DOI: 10.4324/9781003166566-6

disconnect occurring within the world of development. Western-backed organizations funded by U.S. or European entities privilege Western organizational and managerial knowledge over local knowledges. This chapter disrupts this notion by demonstrating how Lebanese activists, volunteers, and migrant workers appropriate educational opportunities to serve purposes of their own making and not the goals superimposed upon them by outside forces such as NGOs of Western backing. I utilize the perspectives of migrant workers, program coordinators, and teachers as they reflect on their teaching and learning experiences and how these educational opportunities often contribute to a sense of empowerment and can segue into activism for some migrant domestic workers involved in this grassroots movement.

Context: The NGO System

Rarely do NGOs work in a vacuum, and the NGOs in which I conducted fieldwork were no exception: the Migrant Center (MC), the Migrant Workers Educational Group (MWEG), and Tamkin.[2] The MC itself was not responsible for the provision of educational opportunities, they only offered the space. As such, they welcomed the idea of the Center being used for teaching and learning. This resulted in a loose partnership between members of all three groups. Because of their shared members and overlapping ideologies, the relationship between these three groups was quite supportive and reciprocal. Tamkin is a well-respected and internationally known grassroots feminist organization located in Beirut. This organization worked in tandem with the MC and the MWEG to see that its objectives are met as a center that values the local knowledges of migrant workers and community leaders.

Tamkin: An NGO Feminist Collective

Tamkin describes itself as an organization that "…is a collective of feminist activists" who

> apply feminist analysis to their social justice work, meaning that they always have an eye on gender dynamics and oppression within social and political struggle, address the systematic structural problems rather than the symptoms, and place women's experiences and voices as central to any solutions and activist work. Feminism is a learning process for all of us and we are continuously figuring things out by listening to each other, challenging our opinions, and reflecting critically on our work and our theories of social change. ("About Nasawiya", n.d.)

In January 2010, Tamkin was borne out of a frustration of the existing NGO platforms that dominate Beirut's development infrastructure. Several factors set this organization apart from the traditional NGOs in Beirut.

Tamkin's organizational structure as a "collective" in which all members have an equal voice and have free choice to how they will contribute makes this group different from others. Tamkin provides the educational and activist space for members to convene, discuss, and put into action an initiative of their own creation. For instance, one such initiative supported by Tamkin is Sawt al Niswa, a feminist webspace with the intent of fostering a network for "a community of feminist writers, activists and artists working towards changing their realities by building a space that critically reflects on the social, political and intellectual experiences of women living in the Arab region or West Asia and North Africa..." (Sawt Al Niswa, n.d.). Another such initiative is the Anti-Racism Movement (ARM), which is a grassroots movement created by Tamkin activists in collaboration with migrant community leaders. According to their website, ARM's mission is to

> decrease racist discrimination and abuse in Lebanon on the social and institutional levels by advocating for changes in the systems that perpetuate racist exploitative practices, through sensitization, awareness raising, advocacy, and community building for more just social and institutional frameworks in Lebanon ("About Us", n.d., https://armlebanon.org/about-us).

According to Tamkin's Facebook page, they outline their interpretation of what it means to be a feminist:

> By feminists, we mean individuals who are committed to gender justice and equality. There is no one-size-fits-all feminism, but our collective has come up with a set of basic values that we all agree upon. Some people identify with the term "feminist" very strongly politically or personally. Others refuse to call themselves feminist and still have a lot of passion and commitment for women's issues and struggles. ("About Nasawiya", n.d., https://www.facebook.com/nasawiya/about_details)

The Migrant Workers Educational Group

While Tamkin, the MC, and the MWEG do not function under the same organizational umbrella per se (at the time of this research project), they work cooperatively in order to provide educational opportunities for migrant workers. The MWEG is a grassroots organization whose purpose is to provide educational opportunities to migrant workers by recruiting volunteer teachers to teach language classes and computer classes. The languages offered during my time with MWEG were English and French (there was talk about Arabic language classes becoming available when I left Beirut). MWEG does not have its own educational space so it relies on the generosity of local groups to provide a space; hence, the MC provides the space for MWEG to hold classes. MWEG is not an established NGO.

It is funded by private donations to cover overhead costs such as Xerox copies, teaching materials, and office supplies. Because MWEG relies on volunteers for teaching and the generosity of NGOs or other groups to offer the physical space to hold classes, they do not have the expense of a monthly rent payment, which keeps their overhead costs fairly low.

According to their website, MWEG defines itself as "a grassroots volunteer organization that leads initiatives for better treatment and social advancement of the migrant worker community in Lebanon" with the aim "to improve the situation of migrant workers in Lebanon through grassroots initiatives" by way of offering educational opportunities such as English and French classes as well as computer classes ("About Us", n.d., https://mwtaskforce.wordpress.com/about-2/). MWEG offers classes at different centers in Beirut. For the purposes of this study, I volunteered as an English teacher at the Naba'a location so I could provide continuity as an educator by having the same group of students every week and to be connected to my research site, the MC.[3]

The Migrant Center

The Migrant Center is located in the ethnically diverse and low-income eastern Beirut suburb of Naba'a. Naba'a is a diverse political, ethnic, and religious place, home to Sunni and Shi'i Muslims, Armenian Christians, and African and Southeast Asian migrant workers. The suburb is densely populated, with an estimated population of 12,000 in an area of three-square kilometers (Afifi et al., 2010). The MC was established in the summer of 2011 as a space

> where migrant workers meet, organize, build alliances, and access information, resources, and direct assistance. MCC's mission is to improve the quality of life of migrant workers, build their capacity to self-advocate and fight for their rights, and to contribute to a strong and powerful migrant community with women as leaders of change ("Migrant Community Center", n.d., https://armlebanon.org/migrant-community-center-beirut).

As previously stated, the on-site coordinator of the MC is Suba, a 25-year-old Nepali woman. She was hired as the on-site coordinator because, as a former migrant domestic worker, she is intimately knowledgeable about the migrant worker experience. This uniquely positioned her as an activist, a coordinator of the Center, and a comrade and friend to the women and men who seek services and refuge at the Center. Her husband, Dakshi, who is also Nepali and a former migrant worker, assists her with day-to-day operations. He is a Nepali community leader and participates in the migrant activist movement in Beirut.

The Center is open daily from 3:00 p.m. to 8:00 p.m., but often Suba is at the Center as early as 10:00 a.m. and stays as late as 10:00 p.m. to welcome migrant workers and make sure they have access to the computers. The

MC is often used as a space for get-togethers and parties. When the Center had its one-year anniversary, a huge celebration was held there, where volunteers, activists, and migrant workers from different nationalities came together to commemorate the establishment of the Center with food from their homelands, cultural dances, and socializing.

In Their Own Words: Narratives of Program Coordinators, Migrant Worker-Students, and Their Teachers

Several key themes emerged from participants' interviews, which include a Lebanese feminist-activist's reflections on Western humanitarianism and voluntourism in the Middle East/SWANA region; a migrant worker hired as the MC coordinator discussing the reasons migrant students learn English; Lebanese volunteer teachers' justifications for providing educational opportunities to migrant workers; and, volunteer teachers' reasons for teaching English and computer literacy skills. The following narratives are categorized by emergent themes.

Voluntourism in Beirut

In the following narrative, Fakira, the general director, talks about Tamkin, its ideology, and the NGO system in Beirut. She reveals how an organic, grassroots movement should involve local voices and input while also criticizing the orientalist views of Westerners who seek "voluntourism" opportunities in Beirut generally and Tamkin specifically.

FAKIRA: The Center is a space that is open to community leaders and migrant workers. The most urgent issue was that they needed a space...before all the other issues, such as shelter, they wanted a space to be able to use as a community space to do events, meetings, follow up on [legal] cases, have computers that have Internet, have phone access.

SK: Is this space [the Migrant Center] specifically for migrant workers?

FAKIRA: Specifically for migrant workers, yes. It's not an office space for us [Lebanese] to go use. It's supposed to be totally independent in its functioning. We coordinate every single day, me and Suba. We have common meetings, Suba, as part of Tamkin's other initiatives, of course many common things. But the MC space, it is supposed to have a totally different dynamic...it's not supposed to be a shared space for us, it's the migrant workers' space.

Fakira relays that if one wants to initiate a proposal for a project under the umbrella of Tamkin, it is important that the projects' values and motives run parallel to Tamkin's organizational values.

I asked Fakira how this organization came to into existence:

> We are registered as an NGO...But we do not refer to ourselves as an NGO because we don't have an NGO system and we have a problem with the NGO system, though we are on good terms with many NGOs around here. The reason that [our organization] was started was because there are many women's organizations around us in Lebanon. But none of them were able to fill the gap that we, as young women, wanted. We want to work on things, and feel ownership of things, and do changes in a certain way...None of those NGOs and organizations had this opportunity for us... This is why this space is safe and open for feminists and others and accepting of all people regardless of anything...

In the above excerpt, Fakira mentions an absence of a core feminist framework in other NGOs in Beirut. Most other NGO social service organizations in Beirut are usually aligned with a particular religious or political entity, be it Catholicism, Islam, or a Christian-Protestant group. For instance, Hezbollah, which is a powerful religio-political organization in Lebanon, provides millions of dollars in subsidies and assistance to Shi'i families throughout Lebanon, such as housing, food, medicine, health, and social services (Karakoç, Özcan, & Özcan, 2021). While Hezbollah considers itself a resistance movement and is not categorized specifically as an NGO, it does provide the social, educational, and health services to underprivileged and marginalized Shi'i (and some non-Shi'i) people.

Funding for NGOs in Beirut comes from internal partisan groups or international development organizations. Such funding can be fraught with problems such as bureaucratic red tape, political power grabbing, nepotism, and other problems. Additionally, funding is usually accompanied by stipulations as to how the funding should be spent; or, the funding source omits local partners from the decision-making process, leaving them with no sense of ownership. Fakira asserts that Tamkin's refusal to take money from U.S.-affiliated groups or over government groups allows their organization to be free of the political agenda of external organizations:

> The US Embassy has tried to contact us many times...they would love to fund us...they would love to build relationships with us...but we were never positive about it....they don't really get it when someone is not dying to get money from them, so this is why they insist!

Tamkin's funding during the time of this interview came from two international grants that fund women's initiatives and whose politics align with those of Tamkin's and do not impose conditions for receiving funding. The ultimate goal of Tamkin is to be 100% independent of all external funding.

To meet that goal, they opened a café located in the same space as Tamkin. Fakira explains the purpose of their café:

> We generate money [from the café] to support our collective. And we also have community events here. Of course, we are not self-sufficient after only being open [yet] but hopefully...everyone is volunteering their time to help the café. All the food is everybody chipping in just like everything around us is donation. Hopefully with time we will be able to reach a point where we will be self-sufficient.

Tamkin receives emails from all over the world asking how to visit, volunteer, or work for their organization. Its feminist stance, activist position, and collective nature make it a desirable organization in which to be involved. This can be problematic, however, especially if the ideological positionality of the interested parties not only contradicts but also undermines the core tenets of Tamkin's feminist stance. Here, Fakira explains her frustration with outsiders attempting to "help":

> This is an issue that we face at Tamkin every single day. Let's say five to ten emails a week. Of different people from around the globe, especially Europe and America, and the U.S., asking how they can come, and how they can join the collective....from Chicago, from Paris. The first twenty times, it was funny. But then when it reached you know, thousands. It wasn't funny anymore. It's a pattern you know. I shouldn't be surprised. It's shocking how rude people can be. And how, you know, not in touch with reality. One time I was corresponding with someone who lives in Toronto who has no roots whatsoever, nothing with the Middle East or Lebanon, who wants to join our collective from Toronto. If you're that much of a fervent feminist, why can't you join a collective there in Toronto and do local change wherever you are? What position are you to even email us with this? We have examples of a U.S. soldier who just finished serving in Iraq and asking if she could do an internship year at Tamkin. We have many examples of that. She saw how U.S. service people were treating women in Iraq. And she wants to come in help. We have lots examples of this. It's crazy...There's [also] a trend [in the NGO systems] of people working on behalf of people without consulting the people... Or talking on the behalf of people whether its refugees are migrant workers. There are many examples of this. That's a problem.

Fakira, as a Lebanese citizen, feminist, and activist, views the foreign policy of other countries (namely, the United States) as problematic for the political, religious, and social functionality for the Middle East/SWANA region.

English as Material Resource: Motivations for EFL Learning

In my interviews with migrant workers, I shared with them that some Lebanese activists question the utility of providing educational opportunities to migrant workers, because they think that resources can be better allocated for specific needs such as food, shelter, and medicine. I posed this assertion to frame my own inquiry to migrant workers about their own thoughts about education, English language classes, and computer classes for migrant workers: Why is it important? I interviewed Suba, a former migrant worker from Nepal who was hired to be the coordinator of the MC:

SK: What would you like to say to activists who think that educational opportunities like computer classes and English classes for migrants are not the best use of resources, and that food and shelter are more important?

SUBA: I think language classes are very useful. It's very important to have English. The first thing I advise my own Nepali people to do is learn English. I knew the [African] students before they started taking English classes, and we had a very hard time communicating with each other. It was hard to communicate. But now, when I speak to them, we can communicate. See, there is a lack of communication between different migrant communities. We need a common language. With the help of English classes, it is helping us [migrants] to communicate with each other. For example, I want to give advice to you. And you want to say many things to me. But how will we communicate? If we are from the same native country, we can communicate. But if we are from different countries, it is hard. So now, through language classes, you will learn from each other...how you feel, how I feel. And this will make something new. It's multicultural. We learn each other's culture, you can learn many things. It's very important, I think. That is what I'd let them [the activists who do not support language learning] to know.

SK: So in your experiences, in your work and professional experiences, you see learning English as serving a practical purpose, in the Center. And you have seen a migrant worker kind of change as they learn English?

SUBA: Definitely.

SK: Can you give me an example?

SUBA: Do you know Laurencia? From Madagascar? She takes English classes here. When I met her first, she did not know English at all. It was very hard to communicate. She has a child, she's four years old. Last year, I was going to give birth to my baby. Laurencia wanted to tell me many things about the delivery, about breastfeeding, about many things. She wanted to tell me what to expect. But we could not communicate. She knows French, I do not. She did not know English [yet].

> Now, since she has been taking English classes, we can communicate. She tells me many things, everything how she feels. She is even teaching her daughter English. Now, when she comes here, she only speaks with her daughter in English. I feel very successful about all that we are doing here at the MC.

In the above excerpt, Suba describes the practicality of migrant workers learning a common language in a place where many languages are spoken. On any given day at the MC, one will see people from Ethiopia, Nigeria, Sudan, Madagascar, the Ivory Coast, and other African countries. Migrant workers from Nepal, Bangladesh, Sri Lanka, and the Philippines also frequent the MC. These demographics represent numerous languages – in Ethiopia alone, there are between 45 and 86 different languages besides the official language of Amharic ("Language data for Ethiopia", n.d.) and in Nepal, there are 123 languages spoken as first languages in addition to the official language of Nepali (Khanal, 2019).

Also remarkable is how English became appropriated as a tool for the exchange of knowledge and information, for example, for giving birth and childcare. In Beirut, domestic workers often encounter discriminatory practices in hospitals when giving birth because some Lebanese people have xenophobic views about domestic workers, refugees, and their pregnancies. Suba and Laurencia were able to share their experiences giving birth in Beirut and act as a support system to each other while creating a network of knowledge to be shared with migrant women.

I also interviewed Thomas about the topic of education for migrant workers. As mentioned in the previous chapter, Thomas came to Beirut for migrant labor purposes and he became a born-again Christian and subsequently a pastor at a Nigerian church in Beirut. I asked Thomas his thoughts about the allocation of resources for education:

SK: There are some people who think that allocation of resources for migrant workers should be spent on immediate needs like food, shelter, or medicine, instead of educational opportunities. What are your thoughts on that?

THOMAS: We need something to go back home with. For someone, somewhere back home, it will help. Yes, we need clothing, we need medical help. Yes, we need that. But what if you give someone medicine, give someone a drug, but they don't know how to take it? I might overdose. What if I cannot read the letters on the side [of the bottle]? Education is not a waste of resources, we need this. So, if we have this kind of thing, it can help our lives and help us plan what to do next. Yes, food is important, but you pass it out [of the body]. Education will remain. And you can transfer that education to someone else. You cannot transfer that food to someone else. So, knowledge is power. And I prefer that they can use that knowledge. It will help them run their life, plan their life.

Thomas goes on to say that the knowledge migrant workers learn in the classroom in Beirut, whether it is English as a foreign language, Microsoft applications, or Photoshop, they then can return to their home countries and gain employment by teaching these new skills. Like Suba, Thomas has flipped the script to appropriate English language learning and computer skills not only for attaining employment in the migrant worker's home country, but also for the purpose of empowerment: His mention of food as nourishment passes from the body, but "education will remain". This powerful statement indicates an insight and wisdom about the nature of education for marginalized groups that also counters the West's intention of English language domination to serve their own economic, political, and cultural self-interests.

Perspectives from Volunteer Teachers

When I was volunteering as a teacher for MWEG, there were ten volunteer teachers: Six were of Lebanese heritage; one teacher was from Syria; and, the remaining three were from either the European Union or the United States. All of the teachers were undergraduate students, with the exception of Sofia, who was Italian and a graduate student in Islamic Studies. While none of the teachers were education majors or had any formal teacher preparation in pedagogy, practice, or teaching methods, most had prior formal and/or nonformal teaching experience. For instance, 21-year-old Omid, a Lebanese student who is in medical school, has held sexual health and education workshops for migrant workers and HIV+ seminars for Beirut's LGBTQIA+ community. Roby is 26 years old and he is originally from Syria. He has a bachelor's degree in pharmacy and has been living in Beirut due to the civil war in his country. He volunteers for the Red Crescent in Beirut and is looking for work with international NGOs. All MWEG classes are offered on Friday nights and Sundays only because these are the days off typically given to domestic workers. At the time of this writing, MWEG had established the computer and language classes and were providing educational opportunities to 130 migrant workers at their three locations ("What we Do", n.d., https://mwtaskforce.wordpress.com/our-initiatives/). The volunteer coordinator for MWEG at the MC location in Naba'a was Maha, who helped recruit volunteer teachers from American University Beirut (AUB) and Lebanese American University (LAU). Maha's duties were facilitating teacher meetings and teacher training, and also help with curriculum development. Maha has a master's degree in Social Justice and Intercultural Relations from an American university. She played an integral part in getting the classes established for the MWEG at the MC.

Maha often met one-on-one with teachers to provide guidance and to serve as a listening ear.

In the following pages, I present my observations in the teaching space and the narratives of the teachers. I then organize this data to reflect the common themes that arose in the data analysis that speak to issues of empowerment.

Volunteer Teachers' Understanding of Migrant Issues

Usually on Sundays prior to teaching, we would hold a teacher meeting to touch base about housekeeping details, such as making sure everyone had copies, could answer questions for the students, and for us teachers to discuss our own teaching experiences. During one meeting, we discussed the structural challenges of teaching migrant-students; one volunteer teacher, a medical doctor who teaches French, asked her students why they were inconsistent in their attendance. The students replied with a shrug of their shoulders, which left her perplexed. Other teachers also commented on this challenge. Another volunteer teacher said that they did not answer her out of respect. Another teacher commented it is difficult to push the students forward curriculum-wise when they do not attend classes. Someone else replied that these migrant domestic workers are often taken up to their employers' summer homes in the mountains for weekend-getaways, and they have no choice in the matter, they must go. Another teacher said that maybe they don't come regularly because they feel ashamed that they have not done the homework, or feel unprepared. A teacher went on to say that he believed the students came to the Center not only to learn, but also because they felt safe here. I also commented that one of the students I interviewed said they liked coming here (the MC) because she felt safe, and this is one of the students who has been sexually harassed on the streets regularly. Here, Maha said, "This is the point of social justice. While it's important they learn, it's not always the whole point for them. It's about providing a safe space and empowering them".

Twenty-one-year-old Alim is a business major and a Lebanese volunteer teacher; he discusses he discusses the migrant domestic worker contract and how it is not viewed as a legal-binding contract by the employers:

> The employee contract says that the employer should allow a day off for the employees and that day is usually a Sunday, and most [employees] do not give them that day off. And even when the domestic worker reports to the agency that the employer is hitting her, most of the time the agency might even beat her up, or not take her side and believe the employer. The employer might even lie when the domestic workers runs away and says she stole something, and that, of course, isn't true.

Here, Alim discusses the gendered differences in classroom attendance:

SK: Would you say that you have more females than males in your class? Or vice-versa?

ALIM: Usually like the females are the ones that are skipping[class]. It's because the males are Sudanese, and men do not work in the madam's house, they don't do domestic work. So, men migrant workers have more choice to come to class or not, unless their boss wants them to work on Sunday. But I think that it's that the females that may not be allowed, by their madam. They don't have choices like men migrant workers. But when women do [attend], my class is usually equal in males and females.

Personal Experiences, Empathy, and Allyship among Teacher Volunteers for Migrant Students

In my interviews with other volunteer teachers, many articulated their understanding of the myriad struggles migrant domestic workers face in Lebanon. Most of the Lebanese volunteers belong to upper-middle-class families, and, as such, their families employed (and continue to employ) migrant domestic workers. Omid, a Lebanese, 21-year-old medical student recalls specific incidents from his childhood regarding classism that prompted his present involvement with migrant activism:

OMID: When I was growing up, I was best friends with the domestic worker who used to work in my home. My parents were very much against that. They were like, there is classism that we cannot get over. We are from a different class than they are, they said. We should accept them but we cannot be friends. This person cannot be your best friend, you need to find friends elsewhere.

SK: Were you similar in age?

OMID: No, she was ten years older than me.

SK: So, when you were growing up, you saw these injustices... You are quite cognizant of these injustices... Did you see...

OMID: I saw them, but in the end, I got...shunned by all of my surroundings: my family, my friends, my principal at school... Even my therapist... Even my therapist told me know this cannot happen. You cannot be friends with your domestic worker. In my mind that never clicked, that made no sense.

Omid went on to tell this story of what prompted him to get involved:

OMID: The first domestic worker who worked with us, became my best friend, confessed to me later on, to tell me that, there was a rape in

> the family… My father committed rape against the domestic worker. Yes. And… She says she does not want to say anything about it now, because when I approached her, and asked her what she wanted to do, she said after she leaves the country or when she comes back, [she] shall talk to me. And she ended up not saying anything. A few years later, another domestic worker, came to stay at our house, and even though I did not become friends with her, but I came home one and I saw an open condom on the table. And I was like, "what is this?" So, I went and asked the migrant worker, I asked her, she was sort of avoiding the question running away from it, I asked her straight up, "did my father do anything to you? You can tell me, you don't have to worry". And she said the same thing as the other migrant worker, "Yes, he did, please don't tell anyone, please don't do anything, I don't want to make your mom angry, and I do not want to ruin my marriage". So, I respected what she said. I did not want to go against her will. But at the same time, I felt guilty, because perhaps if I had said something the first time, the second time never would've happened. But this time, I could not help myself. I got into a fight with my dad. I approached him with this issue. He got very upset, he got very nervous, of course he said that both of the migrant workers were lying. But from my perspective two different migrant workers, who never met each other, and they are both saying the same thing. So that was also a big push for me. To work with the [MWEG], to change migrant workers lives, to protect…Well I know protecting is not what we do, but to do something.

This life-changing experience affected Omid so much that he decided to participate in different groups and NGOs in Beirut that assist migrant workers. He talks about how his involvement made him come to terms with his own discrimination:

> When I came to [local NGO group], I learned more about discrimination. I also discovered that maybe myself had some discrimination in my mind. I used to discriminate without knowing. And that's how I got to realize that. Later on, I…From [local NGO group], that was a starting point. I got to know other human rights issues. I discovered other injustices in Lebanon.

Other volunteer teachers were prompted to volunteer due to experiences with migrants or refugees in their home countries. Twenty-six-year-old Sofia from Italy, who has lived in Syria prior to the war, speaks Arabic and is getting a master's degree in Islamic Studies from AUB. She had volunteered at an orphanage in Burundi, Africa, as a daycare worker and, in her native Italy, she volunteered as a tutor in a local high school to assist migrant students from Morocco with their schoolwork. She became very close to her students and visited them in their homes, which led to building relationships with the parents and other family members living in the home:

> One time I was invited to their home for Ramadan and they forced me to eat a lot [laughter] and I was like, "But I cannot keep eating!" And they said, "We are so happy for you to be here and eat with us". I think they were happy to have an Italian for a friend.

She relayed to me that other Italian students regularly called the Moroccan students she was tutoring racist names because they wore *hijab*, and teachers did nothing to intervene and at times encouraged bad behavior:

SOFIA: The 16-year-old, named Fatima, told me one day, "My head hurts so much". I was like, "Why?" She said, "Another student punched me in the head". I said, "Why was she punching you on the head?" And Fatima said, "Because she thinks I'm strange because I have the veil". I said, "When did this happen?" She told me, "During the class". I said, "What did the professor do?" She said, "He saw it happen, but did nothing". So, I went to the professor, and I said, "Do you know what happened today to Fatima?" And he said, "Well, you know, if she wants to integrate, she has to bear these kinds of things. They are kids. They will be like this". I said, "No, your job is about avoiding conflict between students. Your job is help other students understand that the differences between Fatima and other students are not bad". He said, "Ok, I apologize". But, no changes. Another professor actually told the girls to go outside the classroom for the beginning of the lessons so he could open the window because the professor said their smell [body odor] was so bad.

SK: The teacher said that to their faces?

SOFIA: Yes. Can you imagine? And imagine the other students. They follow the teacher. And they think they are justified when they see their teacher behave like this to the Moroccan students. I was so angry. I was so angry. You cannot imagine. Another interesting thing...the girls, when they lived in Morocco, they did not wear *hijab*. They only started wearing *hijab* after moving to Italy. The other students, they made them to feel so different, the Moroccan students wanted to look different, to embrace their own culture.[4]

SK: Do you think it was their parents who encouraged them to veil?

SOFIA: No, no. I asked them. It was their own choice.

SK: Ok. So what progress were you able to make with them in the year you worked with them?

SOFIA: In one year I was able to teach Fatima how to communicate, how to write and read a little bit, but mostly how to communicate. Because

I thought that was the most important thing. She was able to go to a vocational school.

SK: What is it about teaching you like?

SOFIA: I have always wanted to be a teacher, since I was nine years old. I knew I would love to teach. And I remember, when other students were behaving badly in the classroom, I would always feel sorry for my teachers. I am friends with many of my past teachers. Actually, about three years ago, I met my teacher from preschool when I was three years old, she still remembers me [laughter]. She said, "[Sofia], how are you?" And I was like, "How do you remember me?" [laughter].

SK: You make an impression on people!

SOFIA: I have many teachers who are now my friends.

SK: It sounds like you have a teacher's heart.

SOFIA: I guess so, I have always loved educational activities. I love them. It's a nice way to give something to other people. Something, that, you know, lasts. That's why I love teaching.

By virtue of experiencing some kind of marginalization (not necessarily with migrant workers), either personally or by observation, has motivated volunteer teachers to participate in a cause that aligns with the migrant worker allyship and activism. Alim cites childhood bullying, especially from classmates at a young age, as a reason for wanting to get involved in the MWEG:

> I don't think anyone should be treated that way. And I've had the situations, over the years, I was mistreated...by people I went to school with, or like classmates, so I know what every person might feel if he or she was mistreated. Of course, it [his experience from the migrant worker experience] differs, but I like generally got an idea.

Ashraf, a French-Lebanese volunteer teacher, is also a post-doctoral researcher and who also happens to be conducting fieldwork with migrant workers. I asked him his reasons for volunteering as a French teacher:

ASHRAF: I really like that this teaching opportunity was suggested by Suba. So, not from a Lebanese organization, to help migrants, it was more equal. And, because of this, my relations with the students is also horizontal, because it comes from Suba who used to be a migrant worker.

SK: Yes, I agree, probably the other migrant-students knowing that Suba supports your teaching, helped make you look trustworthy in their eyes.

Ashraf commented that there are some Lebanese people whom are encouraged to volunteer in some capacity by the university career services office, which can be listed on their resume:

> When you are sent from your university to do something good to benefit your CV, of course you don't have the same experience as someone else who is there for more altruistic reasons. Of course, the person who does it just to put it on their resume will also benefit, in some way.

I was also interested in Ashraf's motivations as a researcher, to work on migration and with migrant workers:

> My parents had a migrant worker from Ethiopia, and she stayed with us ten years, and she was really like part of our family, and I was close with her, sharing with her my life, she would share Ethiopian food with me, so it started as a curiosity for me, I wanted to know about her life? What is the Ethiopian situation in Beirut? What are the Ethiopian networks? And I have always been interested in migration, the idea of otherness, because of my own history...being in two places in one brain [laughter]...I always travel. It could also be that I have never really felt comfortable with many Lebanese [people]. I have lived outside of Lebanon, and my parents educated me in different ways, to respect everyone, and when you are in Lebanon, and everyone feels that they are the king.... at the end, I'd rather be alone than face people and their arguments. And usually with the migrant workers, life is just more simple.

Educational Opportunities for Domestic Workers and Migrant Activism: Access to the Struggle

I asked Abe, the Lebanese volunteer teacher who is studying to be an engineer, his ideas about education, empowerment, and activism: In his mind, why was he teaching English? What was meant to be gained for the migrant workers, seeing that they cannot earn college credit? To him, is teaching an act of activism, and why?

> Yes. This is a big, big big question for me. I have contemplated this a lot. I have asked myself, "Am I just helping? Or am I doing something to change? Why am I doing this?" And then I discovered something... other than the whole point of empowerment, the whole point that you're helping someone, and you're giving someone skills, that they can really use later on. With my students, I set the bar high, maybe too high. Why? Because I never wanted them to become students. I wanted them to become learners. Now, I know that, if I leave them now, and I never show up again to class, they can pick up the language by themselves. They have the tools. I was always teaching them tools. I have helped

> them to be independent learners. So, now, if they go back to their native countries, they can teach at least. It's not like I am only empowering them [through teaching], but they will go empower their children one day.

Abe went on to give one more reason for why he thinks teaching English to migrant workers is so significant:

> There is one more critical point that I discovered for teaching English. Are you familiar with the case of Alem Dechasa? She was the Ethiopian woman who was beaten in front of the Ethiopian embassy. She was dragged into a car, by the guy from the employment agency. One camera caught it and it was all over the news. She was taken to a mental hospital in Beirut, and a week later, she committed suicide. Now there is a group called "Justice for Alem". Then there was another case where the Daily Star [a Beirut newspaper] covered the story of Lila Aacharya, the Nepali migrant domestic worker, who was murdered by the family she worked for, this story was in the paper. There is a documentary showing her coffin being received by her family at the airport [in Nepal]. And then I realized that, it's not only empowering them with the language but also about the news about migrant workers...everything is reported in English. They need to know about their news. They are being pushed out of their own struggle just because they don't have the language. But if they know English, they can participate in their own struggle. They can read these reports in the Daily Star [an English-language Lebanese newspaper]. There are thousands of Lebanese groups and NGOs that supposedly help migrant workers...but do they get it? Can they participate? Can migrant workers understand their news? Their [NGO] posts [on Facebook or weblogs] that cover these issues? The key thing is, when migrant workers can capture the language, then they can participate in their own struggle. Also, when they learn the language, they can start networking internationally with other activists and advocates. That is power.

A case in point is Rakeb, an Ethiopian domestic worker-activist who is a student of Abe's and who has been laboring in Lebanon for more than two decades. As a child in Ethiopia, Rakeb attended acting and drama classes through an NGO that supported empowerment through education. When she was 20 years old, she came to Lebanon as a domestic worker. Her own experiences with xenophobia, human rights abuses, and sexual and physical harassment led her to write about her experiences to create theater productions in Lebanon. At the time of this fieldwork, Rakeb wrote, produced, and directed a play about the domestic worker experience titled, *Shouting Without a Listener.*

In this play, we learn of domestic worker exploitation and abuse. We also learn of the lives of domestic workers beyond the abuse; we learn of their thoughts, hopes for the future, and their moral courage and challenges. In my conversation with her, Rakeb detailed how she wanted to provide a message for Ethiopians coming to work in Beirut, beyond just surviving in their employment circumstances; she also wanted to deliver a message of encouragement for all domestic workers. Abe says that Rakeb has been contacted by other Ethiopians and migrant activists from all over the world. Rakeb's activism continues today – she has established an NGO with fellow Ethiopians in Beirut while also producing plays and movies that detail the lived experiences of migrant domestic workers.

I asked Abe if he himself, as an English teacher, ever brought up these issues of migrant abuse, racism, and sexism into his curriculum or classroom space? Do you ever explicitly say, "This is why you need to learn English, so you can have access to the struggle?" Do you ever verbalize this?

> I do incorporate it into the curriculum. On one test, for the writing assessment, I had a picture of Elizabeth Eckford, the first African-American student to be integrated into an all-White school in the United States. I asked them to write how they felt about this picture. The reading assessment was a paragraph about Elizabeth Eckford, and what she did in her life, and all the questions were on her life. Also, they had presentations. So, I gave them a piece of difficult writing, and they had to work in pairs. I gave them dictionaries, and they had to try to understand the overall idea, decipher it. Then they had to present it to the whole class. This was an in-class graded assignment. One of the topics was on racism. "What is racism? How do you recognize racism?" Vocabulary they came across in that piece of writing was "intentional segregation". If they didn't get it, I would sit down and explain these concepts to them. Another piece of writing they had to read and decipher was on Egypt and [Hosni] Mubarak, and another topic was the issue of the Nile and Sudan. Another topic was on floods in the Philippines, so I have tackled a lot in that level. Then, in the next level, I tackled even more social issues. So, I taught them how to write an argument, and then they would have an in-class writing assignment and they would have to answer the question, "Why do you think that migrant workers should get a day off? Please write a letter to an employer explaining why migrant workers should get a day off". And, "Write a letter to your friend back home about Lebanon and if they should come here as a migrant worker". And, "Your friend has run away from her employer. Write her a letter telling her what she should do; would you convince them to go back or not?" And, then I had them do creative writing. I told them to write about anything they wanted. One wrote a fictional piece; one wrote about her childhood. One wrote about why they are learning English.

SK: How do they answer that question, about why they want to learn English?

ABE: They have different answers. One says they want to go to university one day...he happens to be a refugee, and he is now in the United States. His English is at a high enough level that he could take the TOEFL [Test of English as a Foreign Language].

Computer Literacy and Access to the Struggle

Omid, the medical student I mentioned earlier, teaches computer classes as an MWEG volunteer. I asked him why he considers it important to teach computer literacy to migrant workers:

> Computers are the link between worlds...it is technology. Discovering this technology is a big plus. Communication between migrant workers and other migrant workers and migrants and their home countries and hometowns, this is the basic way of communicating with your families and parents. So, for example Skype, or Gmail, or Facebook, you can add people from your hometown, talk to them, you can have connections with them, you can talk to them, and in case there's something happening to you, it's easier to use the computer... And I have a lot of students, a lot of students who come to me and say, "Is there a way for me to get the Internet password? My madam does not give me the Internet password". Or, "I use the computer secretly when she is not at home, so I cannot use it in front of her".

I asked Omid what he taught in his classes:

> I teach them several things...many come into class not even knowing how to use a computer mouse, like how to get the arrow to where you want it on the screen. Then I had students who knew the basics, and just wanted to know how to type, how to use Google for research, or how to use Microsoft products like Word and Excel and PowerPoint. I teach them how to utilize social media, like Facebook, how to chat, how to upload videos to YouTube, or how to open an email account, and definitely how to use Skype, so they can Skype their family back in their home countries.

SK: Did any students ask to use Photoshop?

OMID: Yes, but I don't know how to use Photoshop. But now they know how to use Google and YouTube, so they can get tutorials online to teach themselves Photoshop. But first they need to learn the computer.

SK: What is it you'd like for them to gain by teaching them to use YouTube, besides accessing tutorials?

OMID: A couple months ago, an Ethiopian migrant worker, Alem Dechasa, was beaten in front of the Ethiopian embassy by her job agent. She was put in a mental hospital, and she killed herself. Someone took a video of her getting beaten by the agent and uploaded it to YouTube. So what we decided to do with that video, the [MWEG] grouped our students together, some of our students knew Alem, and we asked them what they thought of this. And they had a lot to say. And we used it to put together a YouTube video and it was put on the internet, it was very widely spread.

SK: Wow, that's powerful!

Omid talked about his beliefs about teaching:

SK: How would you define your teaching philosophy?

OMID: I think that if I know this information, why not share it with others? I hear from other people, I have a good way of sharing information... If that helps, then sure. I'm dedicated to other people. I'm dedicated to spreading this information. That's also sort of the...The medical...You know there's the certain ...oath....

SK: The Hippocratic oath?

OMID: Yes, the Hippocratic oath that says that the information that I learned, my job is to spread it around and give it to others. This information is not something I own, it's something that everybody should own. If I just happened to find it first, let me teach it to others....the [MWEG], that is what we are about, empowerment.

SK: So, did you create your own curriculum for your computer classes? How did you do this?

OMID: I looked back at my own computer curriculum when I was a student learning computers, which was in French, to try to help me develop my own. It was awful. It had a bunch of useless information for the purpose of my class...they did not need to know that html stood for hypertext markup language. To me, they needed to know how to access social media to communicate with family back home and friends here, and to use it to continue their education, and to use it for activist purposes as well.

SK: Tell me how you taught them Facebook.

OMID: Yes. I was asking myself should I teach on Facebook or not? Is Facebook useful for them or not? I know that it's very important to use Facebook for the social media thing, for the activism thing and it's also important for communication, but how do you teach Facebook, something that you use every day, that you take for granted? That was a really hard step. And that I was at that point that I started to realize, "Wait a second, what am I teaching? Is what I'm teaching really interesting? Is it really relevant?" Like, I started teaching them about

Facebook notifications, that they would get notifications about this and that everything else. And then I was like okay no. This is useless. But on the other hand… I wanted to get into, what is a profile? What do you put on your profile? What are privacy settings? And that came out of a lot of students approaching me and saying, "I have this photo, I don't want anybody to see it, I'm very scared, please help me". So okay let's work on the privacy settings. It's very important. And I told them, be careful because whatever goes on Facebook, it can be seen by everyone. So, be careful with what you put.

SK: It sounds like you did a lot of reflection on your teaching and curriculum.

OMID: I was afraid I would fall into the circle of teaching them useless information. Wasting their time, mine, and [other] students waiting for teachers in classrooms.

SK: How else do your students use Facebook?

OMID: Somebody approached me in class, and said, "Can you teach us how to create a Facebook group?" They wanted to learn that. Also, I heard that in the English classes, they're working on eliciting stories from them, and many of them have stories. Of friends of theirs, who died in Lebanon. Suicide… Killing themselves… Jumping off the roof… Being pushed off the roof… Rape… Many stories. So maybe we can combine the two.

SK: It sounds like Facebook is being used in a lot of different ways.

Pedagogy and Practice in the Classrooms at the Migrant Center

At the MC on a Friday night at 7:00 p.m., several migrant workers sit in a haphazard row of long desks and chairs to attend a two-hour French language class. The teacher, Ashraf, stands in front of the class. He and the students have a fun and lively chit-chat as they talk about their past week's happenings and gossip. It's clear a good rapport exists between students and teacher. Ashraf has an easy-going and kind demeanor, making him immediately likable and approachable. In tonight's class are a mix of African students and Nepali students. The majority of African students are Nigerian women with two Nigerian men are also present. One of the Nepali students is Suba, the MC coordinator. She is eager to learn French because she and her husband are planning to migrate to Canada soon. We sit together waiting for class to start. Class begins by Ashraf asking the class to recall the lesson of the previous Friday night; and with that, the two-hour session begins. Ashraf's manner of teaching is similar to his demeanor: laid back and calm. "How do you conjugate 'to go'?" he asks. Ashraf gives the students plenty of time to answer the questions, taking long pauses between questions. The students are at ease, taking advantage of the time given, pondering verb and sentence construction. They consult with one another to check answers; after some recollection and thinking, students start calling out answers. A student tries out loud to conjugate the verb but she is incorrect. Ashraf kindly prompts her to try again, and waits as she mulls over her conjugation. Ashraf writes on the white board, "je.... tu....il/elle....nous....vous...ils...."

With this visual prompt, she boldly rattles off the conjugation and we clap for her success.

This Friday night French class is independent of the MWEG Sunday classes and came about as a request from Suba to Ashraf:

SK: So, what made you decide to teach here?

ASHRAF: Suba asked me to teach here. She told me that they are looking for a French teacher. The problem was that all the French teachers who come through MWEG, they are here on Sundays only. And the Center needs teachers for the...freelancers. During the week it was easier for many of [the undocumented migrants and freelancers], and for many of the Nigerian migrant workers, they are only off during the week. Also, it's the only time that they go out specifically when they are illegal... So coming to the Center at night is really easy because they live around the place [the Center] so they come here and have their classes and hang out with friends. It's good for them.

Pedagogy and Teaching Methods

In Ashraf's class, he brings up issues of gender. During one class, he showed a video about speed dating; here, he explains his reasoning behind showing this video to his students:

SK: How did they respond to that video?

ASHRAF: It was only a three-minute clip about speed dating. It showed the women's responses, ideas about men, their image of the male while doing speed dating, and it was interesting.

SK: Wow, so what did the women say in the video about men?

ASHRAF: That women don't understand or think as men. I asked my students, "Do you agree with this?" And my students said, "No, we do not agree". Another French woman in the video said she needs a man to be dominant in a relationship with men. The woman said this in the video clip. She was a French woman who was well educated. And the female students agreed with her. But it was difficult in French to give an opinion.

SK: Why would you choose this video to show them? What motivated you, what was your process in choosing that clip?

ASHRAF: Well, the first reason is I wanted to show a video clip that was easy to understand. And usually the American movies and French movies, even translated, they speak too fast. It is quite difficult for migrants in the first level of learning [French] to understand. The second reason is, because the Migrant Center is created by the NGO [Tamkin] and it is a feminist movement, so, why not try to go with that idea and suggest these kinds of reflections in class? I knew that the students don't necessarily have the vocabulary to debate issues about gender, but....

SK: Was that the first time that you brought something into the class that had a feminist ideology behind it?

ASHRAF: Yes, first time. But I try to bring in subversive subjects into the class, about identities...even, in the end, we just talk in English, and not French, but it's good to debate these things.

SK: Can you give me an example of something that was subversive, as you say?

ASHRAF: Usually it's very spontaneous. Sometimes we talk about racism, issues of color, issues of gender, relationships...

SK: Did you get a sense that your students appreciated the discussions that would occur around issues of racism or other issues, even if it did occur in English?

ASHRAF: I think so because, except in their own communities, or with their friends, maybe this is the only time they can debate or discuss, when someone asks their opinion about something, and they express fears. Some of the students have been here 15 years, and some just arrived 5 months ago. So they speak from different backgrounds as migrant workers.

Classroom Interactions and Rapport

I also asked Ashraf about his pedagogy and teaching practice; as mentioned, the rapport with this class is positive, so I was interested in hearing his ideas on student-centered teaching and if he views relationship-building as an important component in the classroom space:

SK: In observing your class, it's clear that you have a good rapport with your students. Can you comment on this?

ASHRAF: Yes, I think...many people give me this feedback, about our relationships in class, and how the atmosphere of the course is positive, and I try to...I feel that they are here to learn French, but also to kind of exit their daily life...so after French class, sometimes we get together and eat, everyone brings something different, and I bring something, and the Nigerian students bring their food.

SK: Who's idea was that? To bring food and eat together?

ASHRAF: I think it was mine. It's nice because now they talk together and are friends together. Ya...it's more than just teaching class, I want it to be more than just teaching class.

SK: Yes, it seems like they have formed a strong network among themselves.

ASHRAF: Of course, like the Migrant Center, this class is an extension of that…a place where you connect and if you need help, you talk with others.

SK: How exactly are you able to form the strong relationships you have with your students? Because there are some teachers who aren't able to do that. In my observation, you really want to be on an even playing field with your students. Do you actively try to do away with a teacher-centered way of teaching? Do you use tangible ways that you are conscious of?

ASHRAF: I make some jokes. I try to….I don't know, it's a good question. I don't know how I do it. I try to do it, but I don't have a kind of strategy.

SK: It seems to come naturally to you.

ASHRAF: Not natural, because I do think about it, but…I do it naturally, but I don't know how I do it, it's not really clear.

Building Trust and Relationships

Other volunteer teachers commented on the importance of trust and building relationships with students:

SK: How do you feel the building of relationships is important in the classroom?

SOFIA: I think it is really important. First of all, when you want to teach someone, you need the other person to trust you. The other person has to trust you…to feel comfortable with you. So, I allow joking in class, not bad jokes, but we laugh, we have to be focused, but sometimes we have a five-minute break, and we just talk about our lives, what we do…since I have spent time in Ethiopia, I told my Ethiopian student where I was in Ethiopia, I told her the two or three words I know in Amharic, and she was impressed, and they told me about their lives, what they do, how they feel in Lebanon, and these kinds of things. The thing I like the best is that they are really happy when they see me. When I arrive, you can actually feel they are happy to see me, it's a nice feeling. Like, last time there was a new Lebanese guy, Salim, who came to the Center to observe and help us with teaching, and he did a really bad thing…he asked Mahmoud to pronounce, "p", and Mahmoud, he did the best he could, and to me, he did pronounce it "p". But Salim, he said, "No, you are pronouncing it as if it is 'b'. Say 'p'! 'p'!" See, in Arabic, there is no "p", and Mahmoud did the best he could. And then Salim said, "The reason why you do that is because you are Egyptian, you cannot pronounce the 'p' correctly". And Mahmoud was looking at me, like, "Is it true? Do I pronounce wrong?" And I told him, "It's not true, you are pronouncing it well, you are gonna improve, and

> you are doing a very good job, it's fine, it's ok". I was upset, because you should not say these kinds of things, "Your pronunciation is bad because you are Egyptian". I stopped Salim when he was saying this. Then he left to go have a cigarette, then came back, and was on his computer using the free internet. So, you come here to smoke cigarettes and use free internet? Good for you!" [sarcasm] [laughter]

Sofia described another disparaging comment Salim, the Lebanese guest teacher said toward Mahmoud:

SOFIA: Salim was trying to explain the "x" sound, he said, "Let's use a common word that Mahmoud knows for sure, 'sex'". I think they were all embarrassed...and I said, "Let's change it to 'box'".

SK: Why would he assume that Mahmoud would be familiar with that word?

SOFIA: That's what I'm saying, you don't say these kinds of things! That's what I am saying, people have to be comfortable with you, and then maybe you can talk about such topics, but if they don't know you, you don't talk about things like these. I really hated that. I really hated that.

SK: Good for you for stopping him from going further.

SOFIA: I could not bear it. He was so rude with them. When Salim was asking Mahmoud a vocabulary question, Makdes chimed in to answer. And Salim yelled at her, "No! I am asking Mahmoud! I am not asking you!" He was so rude! Hey, that's OK! It's not the end of the world!

What Sofia describes above about trust in the classroom parallels Omid's reflections as well:

SK: So, what about relationship building between the students in a teacher? What you think of that? And, how important is that you?

OMID: It's very important for the students to be very comfortable with you as a teacher. And here, it's a different setting, I'm a younger person who is teaching people who are older. So, this comes as a small challenge that you get over fast. They are saying you have this information...They are trusting you...So they're coming to you to get more information.

Another classroom practice that I observed and heard in interviews was the idea of reciprocal teaching, which is the idea that students teach the teacher as much as the teacher was teaching the students:

ASHRAF: I teach them in English, and my English is not perfect...and some of my students are Nigerian, and their English is much better than mine. Sometimes they know more English more than me. So I have to ask them, how to spell this word, or that word....so, to them, ok, if the teacher doesn't know something, we have a kind of new equality.

Sofia is also a student of Arabic (she has studied Arabic for four years), mentioned reciprocity in language teaching as well:

SOFIA: I was teaching Mahmoud [a migrant worker from Egypt] and we started from the alphabet. I was assessing what he knew and didn't know. We were communicating in Arabic. I think that for students who can speak Arabic they are comfortable with me because my Arabic is not as good as theirs, so they feel like they are teaching me, because I always ask them questions about Arabic. For Mahmoud, I can tell, he likes that he helps me and teaches me Arabic, at the same time I'm teaching him English.

Sofia mentions how the students help and learn from each other, creating dialogue:

SOFIA: We discovered that in Amharic [Ethiopian language], there is no difference between "planet" and "star". So, I was trying to teach Makdes, my Ethiopian student, what a star is, and she was telling me, "Sun?" and I was telling her, "Yes, 'sun' is a 'star'" and she couldn't really get it. And in Arabic, they use the same word for "planet" and "star" as well. So, it was interesting. So, Mahmoud helped me to explain the stars are the things you see in the night sky, next to the moon. He was rephrasing what I was saying in a way that she could grasp.

SK: And she got it after Mahmoud explained it to her?

SOFIA: Yes, yes.

Place-Based Curriculum

Also significant was the idea of using place-based curriculum that contextualized the lived experiences of the migrant workers. In my interview with Abe, who was an engineering student at the time, he talks about the importance of place-based learning:

> I remember looking at the EFL [English as a foreign language] textbook we were using, and it said, "John did this, Mary did that". And one of the students was like, "Why is it always 'John did this' or 'Mary did that'. Why is it never, Rahel, or Makda, or Gete [Ethiopian/Amharic names]?" I was like, "You know what? You're right. Let's change the names". So, we started changing the names and working with that. And I decided that, "You know what, let's just change the whole thing". So, I decided to write my own book for it.

Abe discussed the instructional issue of homework assignments, that is, being limited as an instructor and as a student by not assigning homework. Abe feels it is counter-productive to assign homework to his students because most students are not able to complete it given their time constraints and long work hours. He feels by assigning homework, the teacher sets up the student to fail. In order to accommodate this issue, Abe structures his class to test them at the end of the class session:

ABE: So, my idea is, to give them the class, and then give them an exam right after. My attitude, is "Show me what you know". So, then I would correct their test, and the next session I would give them their test back.

Discussion: Freirean Ideology in the NGO System and Its Spaces

The above descriptions and narratives of teacher practices, curriculum content, and classroom pedagogy of volunteer teachers in migrant worker classrooms contextualized within discourses of racial aggression, gender inequality, and class oppression is reminiscent of the work of Paulo Freire, the critical pedagogue and educator whose seminal work, *Pedagogy of the Oppressed* (1970) is significant to the education of oppressed peoples. Freire's early work is based on his teaching experiences in his native Brazil where he founded a national literacy campaign and taught literacy skills to peasant-laborers and slum dwellers. What differentiated Freire from other educators of his day was the incorporation of a radical socialist perspective he brings into the science of teaching and learning. *Pedagogy of the Oppressed* is not just an analysis of traditional, authoritarian system of education, but a political critique that links the passivity of the masses to a system of education that is representative of neoliberal policies. As a means of resistance, Freire advocated for a revolutionary pedagogy, one which endorsed a critical view of the world.

Pedagogy of the Oppressed: A Freirean Analysis

In Freire's work with illiterate peasants, he stressed the necessity of "reading the world" (Freire, 1985) instead of reading words. In his Portuguese classes, he would write a word, such as "slum" on the board, and then he and his students would discuss its meaning and what this word represented in their lives. Essentially, he and his students were deconstructing the social meaning of words. In so doing, he encouraged the building of a critical consciousness by way of dialogism, which is just one aspect of a liberatory and transformative pedagogy that seeks to counter the passivity expected of and, in essence, taught to students within the banking system of education. Here, I will outline benchmarks of a liberatory pedagogy that were evident in my participant observations, volunteer teacher interviews and social media artifacts in the nonformal educational spaces at the MC specifically and within the NGO system more broadly.

Reciprocity

In several of the interviews with volunteer teachers, it was pointed out by teachers that they often called on the language expertise of their students for instructional help. For instance, Ashraf's language of choice for classroom instruction was English because it was the common language among him and his students. While Ashraf has native-level Arabic and French language skills, he admits that his English language skills are not as good as his Nigerian students' knowledge of English; he often tapped into their language expertise for assistance in explaining vocabulary words or grammar. In my observations of his class, Ashraf asked for language help and the students readily and kindly provided it. Also, Sofia points out that her students help her in learning Arabic. She says, "I think that for students who can speak Arabic they are comfortable with me because my Arabic is not as good as theirs, so they feel like they are teaching me, because I always ask them questions about Arabic. For Mahmoud, I can tell, he likes that he helps me and teaches me Arabic, at the same time I'm teaching him English". Sofia, Ashraf and other volunteer teachers exemplify educators who feel she or he has as much to learn from his or her students as the students learn from their teacher.

An example of reciprocity is the privileging of local funds of knowledge, which was evident when Abe responded to his students who commented on the American-type names of "John" and "Mary" used in the EFL text. Instead of brushing off their concerns, he honored their insights by replacing the names in the textbook with Ethiopian names. He then went on to create a curriculum that responded to his students' wants and needs. According to Amanti (2005), "This process – of developing curricula based on local knowledge – is the reverse of the typical Anglocentric curriculum developed by education specialists usually located at a great distance, spatially and conceptually, from the classroom" (p. 132). In doing so, teachers demonstrate to their students that their input, their funds of knowledge, and their epistemologies are valuable to the teaching and learning endeavor. They show, as educators, that their students' voices matter in every step of the education process. When educators frame themselves not as "experts", "disciplinarians", nor "authority figures", but instead as simultaneous learners and teachers, believing that both positions are equally as important in the learning process, and privilege the local funds of knowledge (González, Moll, & Amanti, 2005) that students bring into the classroom space for all others, including themselves, to learn from, reciprocity in the teaching and learning process occurs (Freire, 1970).

Relationship Building and "Confianza"

As mentioned by the some of the teachers, the building of relationships in the context of *confianza*, or mutual trust/trust development, is an important aspect to this NGO systems as a whole and the teaching and learning experience. Ladson-Billings (1995) contends that, when a student feels that their teachers value them as individuals, despite their low-income status, these students excel as learners. She gives the example of a student who pointed out another student's academic shortcomings to the teacher, who rebuffed the student and gave the student in question a leadership position (p. 480). Sofia also demonstrated her nature as an authentic educator by defending and protecting her students from Salim's deficit model of teaching. When students observe their teacher exhibit a caring and concerned position in regard to her/his students, *confianza* becomes established. Sofia's interaction with Salim reveals two key points: that she is vested in her students for the sake of educational growth, and also as human beings for the sake of dignity and human decency. Moll, Amanti, Neff, and González (2005) state, "...[R]eciprocal practices establish serious obligations based on the assumption of *confianza* (mutual trust), which is reestablished or confirmed with each exchange and leads to the development of long-term relationships" (p. 74). The relationships being developed within Sofia's classroom between students and teacher are fomented by the mutual trust.[5]

In terms of relationship building and *confianza* as a functionality within this NGO system, several examples emerge. For instance, that Lebanese activists like Fakira and her colleagues recognized the deficit model of the existing NGO models in Beirut and sought out to center the ideas, insights, and input from the migrant community as integral to the missions and objectives of Tamkin and the MC is indicative of her allyship to the migrant cause. She sought to establish a system that creates equality between migrants and Lebanese. Recall Ashraf's reason for teaching – he stated that, because Suba was on board with the idea of French classes, and because she herself was a former migrant worker, it created a "horizonal" type relationship between him and migrant-students. Ashraf also commented that the classroom space was more than just a place to learn, it was also a space for building relationships, for "connecting if you need help". He observed that the classroom space is an extension of the MC, which illustrates how Freirean ideology resonates throughout the whole of this NGO system, and therefore acts as a conduit for empowerment.

Reflexive Thought

Several teachers commented on how they often reflect on their classroom experiences, their motivations for teaching, and pondering the purpose of offering educational opportunities to migrant workers; Abe often asked himself, "Am I just helping? Or am I doing something to change? Why am I doing this?" Omid also asked himself similar questions regarding his curriculum: "Wait a second, what am I teaching? Is what I'm teaching really interesting? Is it really relevant?" Other volunteer teachers often reflected on their own past prejudices; Omid commented, "I also discovered that maybe myself had some discrimination in my mind. I used to discriminate without knowing. And that's how I got to realize that....From [local NGO group], that was a starting point. I got to know other human rights issues. I discovered other injustices in Lebanon". By participating NGO work, it prompted him to confront his own discrimination.

For these teachers who lead classrooms whose students are from culturally, economically, racially, religiously, and socially different backgrounds, it is important that teachers engage in a rigorous reflexive process, as described by the volunteer teachers, especially in terms of interrogating one's own suppositions and prejudices regarding racial difference. Howard (2003) asserts that teachers must possess "...[T]he necessary skills to critically reflect on their own racial and cultural identities and to recognize how these identities coexist with the cultural compositions of their student" (p. 196). Ashraf, as someone who grew up in France and is also Lebanese, commented that he's always been interested in "the idea of otherness, because of my own history...being in two places in one brain. It could also be that I have never really felt comfortable with many Lebanese [people]. I have lived outside of Lebanon, and my parents educated me in different ways, to respect everyone, and when you are in Lebanon, and everyone feels that they are the king". Ashraf recognizes his own in-betweenness – having grown up outside of Lebanon, his lived experiences allowed for an etic, or outsider perspective. He was able to recognized the classism that exists in his country, which provides him with a point of reference for being able to understand some of the lived experiences of his students.

Dialogic Learning as Resistance Building

In the narratives above, several of the teachers and other participants commented on how dialogue played an important role in their teaching; for instance, Sofia mentions that, during her five-minute classroom breaks, she and her student will talk about their lives outside of the classroom. Sofia shared with her Ethiopian student that she has been to Ethiopia and knows some Amharic. She asked her student what it's like to be a migrant worker in Beirut. Ashraf also mentioned how he and his students would talk about their daily lives, and share meals outside of class. By way of students' sharing their lived experiences, which often includes racism, sexism, and other forms of oppression, a camaraderie is formed, a sense of community, a solidarity in oppression. As mentioned in Chapter 2, the act of dialoguing in a shared learning space about a common social struggle that is the essence of dialogic learning (Freire, 1985); In this way, dialogic learning is the framing of "dialogue" as a transformative work, one that seeks to bring to the forefront the oppressed/oppressor dichotomy. To dialogue is to engage in the "...[P]rocess that...is dedicated to the empowerment of students through disconfirming the dominant ideology of the traditional educational discourse and illuminat[e] the freedom of students to act on their world" (Darder, 1991, p. 94). Recall Abe and Omid's mention of Alem Dechasa's tragic end and the ways the MWEG addressed that death. Instead of ignoring the event or merely offering a consolatory word of sympathy, MWEG used class time to gather students in a dialogue about Alem Deshasa's suicide. The migrant-students were able to voice their concerns against oppressive systems, those of the Ethiopian consulate, the *kafala* [sponsorship] system, and employment agencies that seek to profit from the human trafficking of migrant workers. This is evidence of dialogic learning: naming the world, as Freire describes, naming the oppressors, and seeking just means for the end of oppression.

A dialogic space in which students, teachers, and other community members participated contributes to an intentionality, a purpose, a deliberateness of thought and dialogue. This critical dialogic space creates the conditions for the fomentation of *conscientização* [conscientization], or critical consciousness, which contributes to foundations for new knowledge. Freire and Macedo (1998) assert, "Dialogic experience is fundamental for building epistemological curiosity. Dialogue also implies a critical posture; it implies a preoccupation with the raison d'etre of the objects that mediates the subjects of the dialogue" (p. 100). In the example of students coming together to discuss Alem Dechasa's death, all conditions aligned to bring to fruition an activist stance and new bodies of knowledge.

Dialogic learning was evident not only in the classroom space but also as part of Tamkin's mission statement. Recall that Tamkin is based on feminist ideology, which encapsulates a learning process for members, activists, and migrants and they are "continuously figuring things out by listening to each other, challenging our opinions, and reflecting critically on our work and our theories of social change ("About Nasawiya", n.d., https://www.facebook.com/nasawiya/about_details). This illustrates the importance of Tamkin participants to engage in a metacognitive process, to challenge their assumptions about their own knowledge production, and challenge each other in engaging and critical ways.

This chapter illustrates how educational opportunities, supported through grassroots efforts, inform powerful migrant epistemologies while resisting Western-backed NGO agendas. These interviews encapsulate stories of resilience and perseverance and speak to the construction of epistemological spaces that reconfigure learning and teaching (González, 2006) while also developing tools to help navigate a social system that is deeply and acutely racist and xenophobic (Bernal, 2006; Jureidini, 2010, 2011).

As these migrant workers re-told and reflected on their stories of struggle and survival within the hostile terrain of Beirut, it became evident that these women and men have shared experiences in which one finds many commonalities. They have lived outside of their home countries anywhere from one to fifteen years returning home perhaps every two years, or not at all, and they have cultivated a production of knowledge based on shared experiences that illustrate struggle and survival, resistance, and hope in that contested social space.

By providing a study that examines the local voices and knowledges of the migrant workers, coordinators, and members of a grassroots educational initiative under the auspices of a grassroots organizational system, we gain insight into their views of the development sector, both foreign and local, how material resources should be allocated, and migrant workers' own motivations for learning English. Consequently, we as practitioners and scholars learn of the localized epistemologies for better practices in the delivery of educational opportunities in order to create a dialogic space to mediate a transformative and revolutionary experience for resistance against social, gendered, and class oppression.

A migrant worker's epistemological curiosity, in conjunction with a critical posture and spurred on by an oppositional consciousness, and of course fostered by educational opportunities, precipitates a need for a critical subaltern pedagogy, which will be the topic of the next chapter.

Notes

1 See Álvarez, Amanti, Keyl, and Mackinney (2016), especially Chapters 10, 11, and 12, for insights and critiques on English language teaching within the development sector.
2 Names of organizations and research participants have been changed to protect their identity.
3 As of 2015, the ARM and the MWEG joined forces and now work together under the ARM banner.
4 The appropriation of *hijab* as a political tool and a symbol of resistance (Duderija & Rane, 2019, p. 183), an advertising tool for *sigheh*, or temporary marriage (Haeri, 1989) and a utility for covert activities (Varzi, 2006) establishes the *hijab* as not just a marker of piety, but an instrument of both social reproduction and social and political resistance. In this example, the Moroccan sisters opt to wear the veil, even though it will further mark them as different and foreign, to the point of provoking xenophobic reactions from both students and teachers alike. The resistance and resilience of these young students is remarkable, especially when they could easily choose not to wear the veil.
5 One Sunday in my classroom at the MC, a well-known international correspondent and her camera crew came to the Center to report on the MWEG's classes. They interrupted my class session to announce that they wanted to film us and interview the students and me. I respectfully declined. She informed the students that she was going to interview them (did not ask), and they were nervous, as some of the students were undocumented. I asked

the students slowly if they wanted to be interviewed; most of the students declined by shaking their heads no. When I told the crew that we were not interested in being filmed, they were quite adamant that they have access to our classroom and the students. I was firm. They then left, but I caught the camera crew attempt to film us covertly. I then told them that they were violating our boundaries and that the Center is a safe space and they were making it unsafe for my students. I include this story because, as Moll et al. (2005) state above, the establishment of *confianza* (mutual trust) is an important aspect in the teaching and learning cycle. I established to my students in that exchange with the reporter that student safety is of utmost importance, and the learning space is their sacred space.

References

About Nasawiya. (n.d.). Retrieved May 5, 2021, from https://www.facebook.com/nasawiya/about/?ref=page_internal

About Us. (n.d.). Retrieved May 5, 2021, from https://mwtaskforce.wordpress.com/about-2/

About Us. (n.d.). Retrieved May 5, 2021, from https://armlebanon.org/about-us

Afifi, R. A., Yeretzian, J. S., Rouhana, A., Nehlawi, M. T., & Mack, A. (2010). Neighbourhood influences on narghile smoking among youth in Beirut. *European Journal of Public Health*, *20*(4), 456–462. DOI: 10.1093/eurpub/ckp173

Álvarez, J. A., Amanti, C., Keyl, S., & Mackinney, E. (Eds.). (2016). *Critical views on teaching and learning English around the globe: Qualitative research approaches*. Charlotte. NC: Information Age Publishing.

Amanti, C. (2005). Beyond a beads and feathers approach. In N. González, L. C. Moll, & C. Amanti (Eds.), *Funds of knowledge: Theorizing practices in households, communities, and classrooms* (pp. 131–142). Mahwah, NJ: Lawrence Earlbaum and Associates. DOI: 10.4324/9781410613462-13

Bernal, D. D. (2006). Learning and living pedagogies of the home: The mestiza consciousness of Chicana students. In D. Delgado Bernal, C. A. Elenes, F. E. Godinez, & S. Villenas (Eds.), *Chicana/Latina education in everyday life* (pp. 113–132). Albany NY: State University of New York Press.

Darder, A. (1991). *Culture and power in the classroom*. Westport, CT: Bergin and Garvey.

Domestic Workers. (n.d.). Retrieved from https://www.ilo.org/beirut/areasofwork/domestic-workers/lang–en/index.htm

Duderija, A., & Rane, H. (2019). *Islam and Muslims in the West: Major issues and debates*. Cham: Palgrave Macmillan. DOI: 10.1007/978-3-319-92510-3

Freire, P. (1970). *Pedagogy of the oppressed*. New York, NY: Herder and Herder.

Freire, P. (1985). Reading t.he world and reading the word: An interview with Paulo Freire. *Language Arts*, *62*(1), 15–21.

Freire, A. M. A., & Macedo, D. (1998). *The Paulo Freire reader*. New York, NY: The Continuum International Publishing Group.

González, N. (2006). Testimonios of border identities: "Una mujer acomedida donde quiera cabe". In D. Delgado Bernal, C. A. Elenes, F. E. Godinez, & S. Villenas (Eds.), *Chicana/Latina education in everyday life* (pp. 197–213). Albany, NY: State University of New York Press.

González, N., Moll, L. C., & Amanti, C. (Eds.). (2005). *Funds of knowledge: Theorizing practices in households, communities, and classrooms*. Mahwah, NJ: Lawrence Earlbaum and Associates. DOI: 10.4324/9781410613462

Haeri, S. (1989). *Law of desire: Temporary marriage in Shi'i Iran*. Syracuse, NY: Syracuse University Press.

Howard, T. C. (2003). Culturally relevant pedagogy: Ingredients for critical teacher reflection. *Theory into Practice*, *42*(3), 195–202. DOI: 10.1207/s15430421tip4203_5

Johnston, R., Baslan, D., & Kvittingen, A. (2019). Realizing the rights of asylum seekers and refugees in Jordan from countries other than Syria with a focus on Yemenis and Sudanese. *Norwegian Refugee Council*. Retrieved from https://reliefweb.int/sites/reliefweb.int/files/resources/71975.pdf

Jureidini, R. (2010). Trafficking and contract migrant workers in the Middle East. *International Migration Special Issue: Special Issue on Human Trafficking*, *48*(4), 142–163. DOI: 10.1111/j.1468-2435.2010.00614.x

Jureidini, R. (2011). *An exploratory study of psychoanalytic and social factors in the abuse of migrant domestic workers by female employers in Lebanon*. Beirut: Kafa (enough) Violence & Exploitation Organization.

Karakoç, E., Özcan, M., & Özcan, S. A. (2021). Beyond identity: What explains Hezbollah's popularity among non-Shi'a Lebanese? *Politics and Religion*, 1–29. DOI: 10.1017/s1755048321000018

Khanal, R. (2019). Linguistic geography of Nepalese languages. *The Third Pole: Journal of Geography Education*, *18*(19), 45–54. DOI: 10.3126/ttp.v18i0.27994

Ladson-Billings, G. (1995). Toward a theory of culturally relevant pedagogy. *American Educational Research Journal*, *32*(3), 465–491.

Language data for Ethiopia. (n.d.). Retrieved from https://translatorswithoutborders.org/language-data-for-ethiopia

McPherson, G. (2016). *Providing hope, investing in the future: Education in emergencies & protracted crises*. Washington, DC: Jesuit Refugee Service.

Pournik, M. (2013). *Civil society organizations and empowerment of women and girls in Iran*. Washington, D: Institute for Global and International Studies.

Save the Children delegation checks on projects in Zaatari camp. (2017, October 20). *Jordan Times*. Retrieved from https://www.jordantimes.com/

Sawt Al Niswa صوت النسوة (n.d.). About [website]. Web blog. Retrieved May 5, 2021, from https://sawtalniswa.org/about

Varzi, R. (2006). *Warring souls: Youth, media, and martyrdom in post-revolution Iran*. Durham, NC: Duke University Press. DOI: 10.1215/9780822388036

Welcome to the Migrant Community Center. (n.d.). Retrieved from https://mccbeirut.wordpress.com/

Chapter 7

Critical Subaltern Pedagogy and Practice: The Ideology and Functionality of Beirut's Migrant and Activist Communities

Given the ever-increasing migration in the neoliberal era, I argue for a paradigm shift in the theory and practice that informs how the international development sector "does" development work. In this chapter, I will discuss a critical subaltern praxis which draws from three main critical theoretical frameworks: Third World feminisms (Abu-Lughod, 1990; Bernal, 2006; González, 2006; Saavedra & Nymark, 2008; Saavedra, & Pérez, 2017; Sharma, 2008; Yegenoglu, 1998), critical pedagogy (Freire, 1970; Giroux, 2010), and a critical spatial analysis (Butler, 2012; Soja, 1996, 2010). This latter idea in particular situates marginalized, subaltern groups in their liminal context. Critical spatial analysis takes into account how the space one inhabits impacts their social, cultural, and economic worlds, thereby affecting their life and learning trajectory. The Migrant Center (MC) is a gendered, critical, and activist space and migrant patrons of this space often cite how it operates as a type of sanctuary in terms of its empowering presence. Critical subaltern praxis utilizes the funds of knowledge of migrant workers, refugees, asylum seekers, and other marginalized groups to create progressive and culturally relevant development agendas and plans-of-action. For instance, migrant community leaders and Lebanese non-governmental organization (NGO) focal participants have worked together to establish the MC that is run by migrant workers. Also noteworthy is the united activist front between Lebanese and migrant workers fighting the *kafala* (sponsorship) system and myriad other forms of abuse at the hands of employers and job agents.

Aronowitz and Giroux (1993) maintain, "There has been an overemphasis on how structural determinants promote economic and cultural inequality, and an under-emphasis on how human agency accommodates, mediates, and resists the logic of capital and its dominating social practices" (p. 91); also salient to a class analysis and its interrelatedness to human agency is an understanding of the subaltern experience of women whereby the categories of race and gender intersect, especially as it pertains to the constructing of a pedagogy and practice. By way of grounded theory

DOI: 10.4324/9781003166566-7

(Charmaz, 2006), I posit a critical subaltern praxis, a pedagogical project that theorizes classroom pedagogy and NGO community practices. I attempt to answer one of the driving inquiries of this study which explores how power and knowledge production produce a liberatory pedagogical model that speaks to the human agency of subaltern groups and informs resistance to systems of injustice.

This study has examined how both the Lebanese activist community and the migrant worker community from African and Southeast Asian countries were able to work together to harness knowledge, agency, and power to inform a critical consciousness and appropriate this collective empowerment into a transformative and liberatory educational movement by employing a critical subaltern praxis, that is, a subaltern pedagogy and practice that operates as such because of the spatial analytical, postcolonial/Third World feminist, and critical pedagogical ideologies of these communities and its constructivist functionality working in a dialectical and synergistic fashion.

As discussed in Chapter 2, I utilize a grounded theory approach to examine the dynamics of knowledge production and power so as to posit a theoretical contribution that fills the existing gaps in pedagogy and development studies as they pertain to the education and assistance to subaltern groups. Because this work was grounded in the social, the historical, and the local, it strengthens its theoretical position and allows for generalizability. According to Charmaz (2006), "The generality arises here from scrutinizing numerous particulars and after developing a substantive theory may include analyzing and conceptualizing the results of multiple studies to construct formal theory" (p. 180). I stress the comparison is not intended to create binaries, a "better than/worse than" position, but rather to conceptualize how a critical subaltern praxis could be applied in other social, historical, and local situations.

I seek to theorize an understanding of how the social phenomena of knowledge production, subaltern student empowerment, and appropriation and utilization of space engage in a dialectical manner. This theoretical construct, that is, a critical subaltern pedagogy, attempts to explain how the reification of an empowered and activist space organized by local, grassroots entities (the Migrant Workers Educational Group (MWEG), the MC, and Tamkin), knowledge production (in nonformal educational experiences and learning in social action), and power (agentive processes and building of critical consciousness) work in a dialectical fashion to produce subaltern epistemological spaces for critical teaching and learning.

The theorizing process of producing a critical subaltern pedagogy adopts a processual approach. According to Nayak (2008), "Processual theory construction directs our attention towards the process of going about the task of theory construction. This moves the emphasis from evaluating the theory to the different stages in the process of being-on-the-way to theorizing" (p. 184). This "on-the-way to theorizing" encapsulates the processual, the grappling with the conceptual to answer for the social phenomena emerging through events; Moore (1987) asserts, "...[P]rocess conveys an analytic emphasis on continuous production and construction without differentiating in that respect between repetition and innovation. A processual approach does not proceed from the idea of a received order that is then changed" (p. 729, as cited by González, Moll, & Amanti, 2006, p. 41).

In the following pages, I provide a justification for and discussion on a critical subaltern pedagogy and practice.

Describing Critical Subaltern Pedagogy: Spatiality, Third World Feminisms, and Critical Pedagogy

Resistance in the Margins: A Justification for a Subaltern Pedagogy

A justification for a critical subaltern pedagogical theory and practice lies in an urgency for how we "do" education for subaltern groups in nonformal and formal educational spaces. We live in a day and age where migration and transnational movement is unprecedented since post-World War II – according to the United Nations High Commissioner for Refugees, today there are 82.4 million people worldwide who were forcibly displaced ("Figures at a Glance", 2020) resulting from geopolitical conflict, natural disasters, civil war and conflict, sexual violence, economic hardship, poverty, and famine. Just in the past decade, the world has witnessed unprecedented movement: The Islamic State of Iraq and Syria (ISIS) insurgency in Iraq in 2014 caused more than 6 million Iraqis to flee the civil conflict to neighboring countries such as Turkey and Syria, or trek to the Kurdistan region (Reid, 2019); along the Mexico-U.S. border, over 172,000 migrants from Latin American countries fleeing extreme violence have been placed in holding centers along the border regions and throughout the United States (Canipe & Rosenberg, 2021); the Russia invasion of Ukraine has caused over 4 million Ukrainians to flee to neighboring countries over the span of six weeks ("Ukraine Refugee Situation", 2022); and, events caused by climate change such as drought, coastal flooding, and hurricanes are estimated to cause 1.4 billion forced migrations by the year 2060 (Geisler & Currens, 2017). Such internal and transnational movement is a global trend that experts predict will not abate any time soon.

These groups, be they asylum seekers, internally displaced, transnational refugees, border dwellers, and/or migrant workers, are what Spivak (1988) calls the "subaltern". These groups generally are poverty-stricken, driven to migrate for the above reasons. Within the new space subaltern groups inhabit lies the premise for an ontological beginning in how we interact

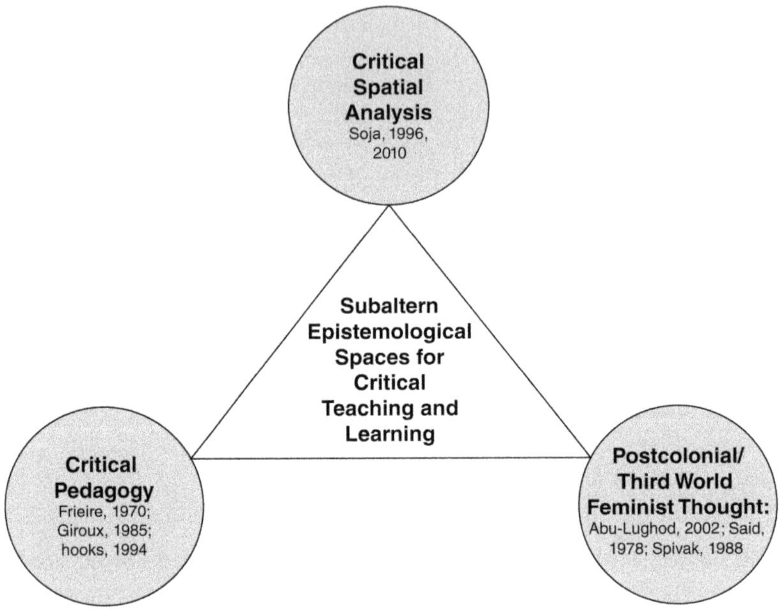

Figure 7.1 Critical subaltern pedagogy model

with new surroundings and new spaces. The subaltern are "...[I]nescapably embedded in the geographies around us...as we are integral actors in social contexts and always involved in...our individual biographies and collective histories" (Soja, 2010, p. 71). What factors differentiate the subaltern experience from those of privileged groups such as expatriates and "third culture kids" (Pollock & Van Reken., 2009) are the limited social, cultural, and economic capital of subaltern groups, their inability to access social networks if no family members are already established in the host country (or, no knowledge that they even exist), and the social and economic oppression in the host country and marginalization coupled with a sense of alterity.

In the following, I describe a critical subaltern praxis, based on my work with this NGO community. Figure 7.1 is a reification of a subaltern pedagogical theoretical model, comprised of a triad of three critical spheres: critical spatial analysis, postcolonial/Third World feminist thought, and critical pedagogy.

The Spatial Dimension

The "double consciousness" (Du Bois, 1903) subaltern groups encounter resulting from living in these liminal spaces is often an experience of the duality of self: how one sees oneself and how others view the self, as "other". This duality potentially impacts myriad functions: the cognitive, the epistemological, the social, the ontological, within the everydayness of life, which shapes and re-shapes how one inhabits the marginal space. As often happens for subaltern groups, host countries view marginalized border-crossers through a xenophobic lens, casting them as interlopers, parasitic, less than, and so on. As this study has shown, for some members of a subaltern group, resistance becomes a reality of their making in reaction to the oppressor's prolonged racism, sexism, abuse, and human rights violations. hooks asserts marginality is the central location for the "production of a counter-hegemonic discourse" as it is a site of production of "habits of being and the way one lives...[marginality is] a site one stays in, clings to even, because it nourishes one's capacity to resist";

> Understanding marginality as position and place of resistance is crucial for oppressed, exploited, colonized people. If we view the margin as a sign, marking the condition of our pain and deprivation, then certain hopelessness and despair, a deep nihilism penetrates in a destructive way.... I want to say that these margins have been both sites of repression and sites of resistance.... (hooks, 1990 as cited by Soja, 1996, p. 98)

The migrant workers at the center of this study demonstrate how the thirdspace of Beirut, Lebanon is simultaneously a site of repression and resistance – the more they participate in acts of resistance, be they micro acts of defending a fellow African migrant worker to a Lebanese man in a taxi, asserting oneself to the madam, attending language classes or cultural events at the MC, posting messages of empowerment on social media platforms, or participating in migrant worker protests, the thirdspace becomes transformed from being a space of subsistence and survival to a space of empowerment, activism, and resistance.

Central to a justification for a critical subaltern pedagogical theory and practice is the inclusion of a critical spatial perspective. Soja (2010) contends almost all knowledge that exists today is based upon a "twofold ontology linking dynamically and dialectically to the social and historical dimensions of individual and societal development" to the neglect of the spatiality of our sociohistorical being (p. 70). As such, he stresses the importance in including the spatial/geographical dimension in any critical theoretical analysis, as the "spatial turn" can potentially affect every form of knowledge production "from the abstract realms of ontological and epistemological debate to theory formation, empirical analysis, and practical application" (p. 15). And, an increase in transnational movement for subaltern groups precipitates an understanding of the spatial: "thirdspace" (Soja, 1996, 2008); "liminality" and "alterity" (Villaverde, 2008); and, "interstitiality" (Bhabha, 1994) as they relate to the ontological and epistemological processes of subaltern groups in the new spaces they inhabit.

Subaltern groups who are subjugated by those in positions of power are often faced with resigning themselves to the dominant power structure, or they can resist,[1] "drawing upon their putative positioning, their assigned 'otherness' to struggle against the power-filled imposition"; either choice they make are spatial responses, "individual and collective reactions to the ordered workings of power in perceived, conceived, and lived spaces" (Soja, 1996, p. 87). The sensation of "otherness" expedites new meanings and new learning by way of lived experience, while also expediting resistance. Recall the Moroccan girls living in Italy who chose to veil because of the Islamophobia they experienced from their fellow students; as a result, they chose to capitalize on their "otherness" by choosing to wear the veil as a form of resistance. The historicized and cultural knowledges the Moroccan students in Italy and the migrant workers in Beirut bring into the thirdspace merge with newfound knowledges produced in new spaces and places. As this study describes, knowledge production among subaltern groups is facilitated by and is most likely accelerated by a critical subaltern space and place, that being the MC. Its establishment and use as a space for knowledge production is a form of spatial resistance.

Third World Feminism

Tamkin calls itself a feminist collective because its ideology aligns with the subaltern, postcolonial, and Third World feminism which seeks to analyze issues of inequity and inequality not just along the gender binary, but also within the categories of race, class, and sexuality, as per their strong commitment to migrant worker issues. In Chapter 6 in my interview with Fakira, the director of Tamkin, she describes how the NGO system she helped to establish is different from traditional NGO structures in Beirut, in that the typical organizational structure relies on a hierarchical system, with power concentrated at the top, and that they are overly competitive over funding, usually from Western sources. She criticizes how typical NGOs are out of touch with the needs of people they attempt to serve. Fakira stresses the lack of territoriality or competition Tamkin has with other NGOs and that its collective nature creates a community of practice with the very people who need assistance.

The resistance to outside funding is evident in Fakira's interview. Recall her comments about Westerners desiring to come to Beirut to volunteer with Tamkin (p. 129), and her strong reaction to it. She relays to me that some of the inquiries she receives are worded in such a way as to suggest that they are "doing Beirut a favor" by offering their volunteer services for a month and carry a sense of Western hubris and entitlement. What Fakira is referring to is called "voluntourism", or the combining of volunteerism with a vacation/tourism experience for the purpose of an internship or merely for volunteering.[2] Most people who desire such an experience possess the expendable material resources for such an endeavor, and most voluntourists come from a developed/First World country. Her words are reminiscent of Mohanty's (2003) analysis of First World feminism's academic foray into the Third; she exposes "...[T]he power-knowledge nexus of feminist cross-cultural scholarship expressed through Eurocentric, falsely universalizing methodologies that serve the narrow self-interest of Western feminism" and highlights the "connection between feminist scholarship and feminist political organizing while drawing attention to the need to examine the political implications of our analytic strategies and principles" (p. 501). Fakira's positionality of resistance to Westerners' attempts of voluntourism/volunteerism is informed by a privileging of the local, or Third World, feminist subaltern voice over the First World feminist foreign voice, which typically lacks an understanding of the complexities of the local's "micropolitics of context, subjectivity, and struggle" (Mohanty, 2003, p. 501). This privileging of the feminist subaltern voice is evident in Tamkin's and Anti-Racism Movement's establishment of the MC at the request of the migrant population, the selection of Suba, a former migrant domestic worker as the major leadership of the MC, and support of migrant-proposed initiatives, such as language and computer classes.

While Fakira does not suggest that it was a policy of Tamkin to avoid Western interest in their organization, she does stress that Tamkin is a local collective; she, as a representative of Tamkin, does voice a strong resistance to accepting any kind of funding originating from any intergovernmental organization like the United Nations or from any source originating from a United States governmental entity, such as the U.S. State Department. Given the history of Western colonization and empire building, it is the preference of Tamkin and its members to take into account a critical understanding of global politics and foreign policies of Western countries and enact their own agency in convening as a feminist NGO that will not tolerate Western interference nor hubris.

The "Otherizing" Lens

The ideological framework that informs Tamkin's functionality as an advocacy and action group and as a non-governmental entity partly stems from the ideas of Edward Said (1978) and his seminal text titled *Orientalism*, a postcolonial discourse that asserts Western constructs of the "other" are viewed through an exoticized, romanticized, uncivilized and largely xenophobic lens in the study and understanding of the Middle East/SWANA region. Said asserts, "...[E]very European, in what he could say about the

Orient, was consequently a racist, an imperialist, and almost totally ethnocentric" (p. 204) and,

> Along with all other peoples variously designated as backward, degenerate, uncivilized, and retarded, the Orientals were viewed in a framework constructed out of biological determinism and moral-political admonishment...Orientals were rarely seen or looked at; they were seen through, analyzed not as citizens, or even people, but as problems to be solved or confined or – as colonial powers openly coveted their territory – taken over. (p. 207)

Fakira and some of her colleagues find it problematic that those from the West, be they lay people, volunteers, researchers, development practitioners, or students desire to volunteer in Beirut when they have no vested interest in the region. She is wary of the Orientalist gaze as it is this fetishization and exoticizing of the "other" that perpetuates a knowledge production that "mimics Western imperialism" (Kapoor, 2004, p. 633). That the leadership of Tamkin refuses to accept any funding from a Western/U.S. source is an act of political and organizational resistance, which is exactly what they exemplify in their mission as a Third World feminist NGO.

The Intersection of Race and Class

Socioeconomic class of migrant workers is a determinant to the absence of socialization between migrant domestic workers and Lebanese people, according to some of the research participants. Omid mentions that his parents were against his friendship with their Ethiopian domestic worker when he was growing up. According to Omid, his parents said to him: "There is classism that we cannot get over. We are from a different class than they are" (p. 134). The literature reiterates the existence of class segregation, pointing out that female employers, or, "madams" feel threatened by the domestic worker's presence in the home, stemming from feelings of jealousy, insecurity, and loathing toward the migrant domestic worker; such feelings lead the madam to employ control over the worker by way of physical abuse (Jureidini, 2011). Ashraf, the Lebanese volunteer teacher, mentions that in Lebanon, "everyone feels like they are king". Jureidini (2011) notes how some Lebanese people take pride in their racist attitudes toward migrant workers, as such sentiments somehow pardon their elitist behavior and distances the Lebanese from those they deem to be "ignorant, sinful, dirty" (p. 10).

As in any system, micro-level incidents of classism are indicative of broader, institutional levels of classism and racism, and Lebanon exemplifies this case. When it is caught on video that an Ethiopian woman is not allowed inside a beach resort and she is falsely told it is a "members only" resort, the incident was brought to the attention of Fadi Abboud, from the Ministry of Tourism in Lebanon, to which he commented, "If people think that we are a racial [racist] country, I think we can kiss tourism goodbye, so for me this is very serious, and [discrimination] can only happen once", he said. "We let them know if it happens (another) time, we close them for one week – if it happens again, we close them for good" (Damon, 2013). His comment emphasizes the capitalist concerns and economic implications of Lebanon being deemed a racist country by the international community, while disregarding the classism and racism migrant workers experience daily. That he was more concerned over the appearance of racism and lost tourism revenue and not the everyday atrocities migrant workers face is indicative of the blatant disregard of the welfare of migrant workers.

Politics of Representation

Fakira's concerns about politics of representation are reminiscent of post-colonial literary theorist and philosopher Gayatri Spivak's work. She writes extensively about the representation of the "other", the Third World, and the subaltern in Western intellectual discourses. The topic of Spivak's (1988) most recognizable work, *Can the Subaltern Speak?*, examines how British colonizers and other power brokers viewed self-immolation in India to the detriment of neglecting the very voices of those who partake in the act, those being the subaltern class. Knowledge production from the Western sphere of influence produces on a continuum epistemic violence. Kapoor (2004), through an analysis of Spivak's work, problematizes the West's interpretation and representation of subaltern groups by asking critical questions such as,

> What are the ethico-political implications of our representations for the Third World, and especially for the subaltern groups that preoccupy a good part of our work? To what extent do our depictions and actions marginalise or silence these groups and mask our own complicities? What social and institutional power relationships do these representations, even those aimed at "empowerment", set up or neglect? And to what extent can we attenuate these pitfalls? (Kapoor, 2004, p. 628)

While Fakira does not iterate the above questions verbatim, her sentiments regarding Western involvement in the Middle East/SWANA region echo Kapoor's interrogation of one's positionality in working or conducting fieldwork in the Third World broadly and the Middle East/SWANA region specifically; as such, Tamkin and its leadership act as advocates for marginalized groups such as migrant workers and refugees while endorsing civic engagement and collective action at the grassroots and *local* level, as opposed to a top-down, foreign, hierarchical NGO system. In essence, Tamkin and its leadership are advocates for oppressed groups and advocates against the intrusion of a "help" or "assistance" that resembles a Euro- and Western-centric "White savior complex". Abu-Lughod (2002) discusses the orientalist and imperialist sentiment in the post-9/11 era that circulates throughout Western media and perpetuates the idea that Muslim women are in need of Western intervention for their own good; she asserts,

> Projects of saving other women depend on and reinforce a sense of superiority by Westerners, a form of arrogance that deserves to be challenged. All one needs to do to appreciate the patronizing quality of the rhetoric of saving women is to imagine using it today in the United States about disadvantaged groups such as African-American women or working-class women. We now understand them as suffering from structural violence. We have become politicized about race and class, but not culture. (p. 789)

It is precisely the notion of "white men saving brown women from brown men" (Spivak, 1988, p. 296) that postcolonial scholars and activists like Fakira resist.

In the following, I will describe how Paulo Freire's critical pedagogy informs the third ideology within the critical subaltern pedagogical framework (see Figure 7.1), using as an example Abe's choice of curriculum as a way to help his students "read the world" (Freire, 1985).

Critical Pedagogy: A Freirean Perspective

In most situations where a migrant or refugee inhabits new spaces, available educational opportunities for adults are typically offered through NGOs.[3] An important aspect to a critical subaltern pedagogical theoretical framework is approaching the question of how to teach adults who have transcended borders.[4] While the focus of the Western educational model consists of the intent of changing the student into a "rational" or educated person, constructed by the acquisition of knowledge that is not within their social context (e.g., physical sciences, geography, social studies, etc.), the work of the NGOs and grassroots collectives at the center of this study is inherently transformative and liberatory, as evidenced by the classroom practices, curriculum, pedagogy, and teaching philosophies of the volunteer teachers. The inclusion of the social contexts of the migrant workers' lived experiences is apparent in the reference to the deaths of migrant workers; in two separate interviews, volunteer teachers mention the suicide of Alem Dechasa, the Ethiopian migrant domestic worker and how this tragedy was utilized by MWEG as a way to "read the world" and transform the world through political and social action by holding a discussion in lieu of language classes (Freire, 1985). Many migrant workers chose to participate in the dialogue by voicing their concerns, writing their messages of dissent on placards, and participate in the YouTube video.

Many of volunteer teachers incorporated their students' lived experiences with racism, classism, and sexism in Lebanese society into their curriculum; as such, the classroom space became a site of contestation. In his in-class exam that he created, Abe refers to a monumental event in United States Black civil rights history of racial desegregation: the attempt of 15-year-old Elizabeth Eckford to enter Little Rock Central High School in 1957. That Abe chose to situate the Black resistance to racism and the civil rights movement in his EFL curriculum validates migrant-students' experiences with racism in Beirut. As Giroux (1985) notes, "Freire's view of power...stresses that there are always cracks, tensions, and contradictions in various social spheres such as schools where power is often exercised as a positive force in the name of resistance" (p. xix). The classroom space becomes both liberatory and resistant to the hegemonic power structures that perpetuate a classist and racist "us-them" binary.

Critical Subaltern Practice: Functionality of the NGO Community

In order to explain the functionality of this NGO system which consists of migrant and Lebanese activist communities, it is important to contextualize the NGO systems within the broader development sector of Lebanon. Beirut is currently home to 1,000 registered NGOs. The proliferation of NGOs was impacted by Lebanon's 1975–1990 war, in which the NGOs provided the necessity of healthcare, social services, and educational opportunities usually fulfilled by the government (Jamali & Keshishian, 2009). As mentioned in Chapter 6, most funding for these NGOs is tied to the international development sector, intergovernmental agencies, and its Western counterparts, such as USAID, United Nations Children's Fund, the World Bank, and the International Monetary Fund. This saturation of NGOs has led to competition among organizations for funding, resulting in a lack of cooperation, bureaucratic rivalry, and general territorialism between NGOs. NGO services provided by participants within this system of competitiveness and monetary motives can be subpar. Additionally, NGOs in Beirut are affiliated with and supported by certain political or religious parties, which makes these organizations partisan in terms of who is eligible to receive their services.

Another key feature of the NGO system in Beirut is the traditional managerial hierarchy. Universally, the organizational structure of most NGOs is such that power is concentrated at the top of the hierarchy, and is distributed in a top-down manner, so those who are at the very bottom are not valued as members of the larger organization as much as the manager or director at the highest level. What differentiates Tamkin and its partner initiatives, the Anti-Racism Movement and the MC, is that it functions in a horizontal, reciprocal style, driven by local community politics, organized in a bottom-up, grassroots style. No one has power over anyone else, and this idea is reiterated in the interview I had with Fakira. She stresses that the grassroots functionality of Tamkin is what makes it successful. Its organization is intentionally styled to be the antithesis of traditional power structures of other NGOs, which are hierarchical and authoritative.

In the following section, I outline the functionalities in what I assert to be a critical subaltern praxis as observed within the NGO system examined in this study.

First I will describe how the entirety of the NGO system creates a "niche opening" (Nicholls, 2014, p. 28). Next, I will describe how the MC embodies Counter-Cultural Communities of Practice (CCCoP) (Duncan-Andrade & Morrell, 2008). I will then provide a description of how Tamkin, the feminist organization, acts as a scaffold (Vygotsky, 1978). I will then discuss how MWEG facilitates the "dark knowledges" (Zipin, 2009, p. 317) of migrant workers. Lastly, I will talk about the role of Freirean thought (1970) within this NGO system which contributes to powerful counterspaces (Yosso, 2006) of empowerment.

Niche Opening

The accomplishment of the activist and migrant communities working together to provide a cultural and educational space lies in a few key elements. The first is that the activist community operates as a "niche opening" (Nicholls, 2014) which is defined as a discursive space in social, legal or political networks in which a "moral ambivalence" exists and to which certain subaltern groups such as migrant workers, immigrants, and refugees have access by way of certain "attributes to push forth rights claims in spite of general hostility and closure" (p. 28). If a subaltern person possesses the advantageous attributes, whether they are social networks or cultural, social or economic capital, she or he can navigate within that niche opening. In this study, the activist community functions as the niche opening for the migrant community because of the humanitarian norms Tamkin represents, thereby creating a powerful "counterspace" (Yosso, 2006), which are "academic and social spaces that foster [student] learning" (Muñoz & Maldonado, 2011, p. 295) and served as a way "to nurture a supportive environment where their experiences were validated and viewed as important knowledge" (Yosso, 2006 as cited by Muñoz & Maldonado, 2011, p. 295). In their study, Muñoz and Maldonado (2011) identify the counterspaces of the female Mexican college students in their study as "study groups where students' social groups develop into academic support groups; centers where students receive tutoring or assistance with academic skills; or student organizations that enable students to give back to their communities" (p. 295). The counterspaces at the MC are similar, and I would add that the space becomes appropriated to exemplify not just an educational space but a counter-cultural space as well.

Counter-cultural Communities of Practice

Within the space of the niche opening, the activist and migrant community created a powerful CCCoP (Duncan-Andrade & Morrell, 2008), which are contextualized, empowering spaces for marginalized populations that explicitly fit the cultural, educational, and social needs of that population.

The mission of the MC and its ideological positionality encapsulate a common feminist-activist vision, as demonstrated by its focal participants, specifically Fakira, who represents the ideology of the feminist collective Tamkin, and MC coordinator Suba, who is acutely aware of the human rights atrocities committed against migrant workers as a former domestic worker herself. In the MC's functionality, its social cohesiveness is evident in the ongoing cooperation between Suba, Fakira, other Lebanese activists, volunteer teachers, migrant community leaders, and the migrant workers who use the space; and, the production of services such as educational opportunities, (in conjunction with other grassroots movements, initiatives, and NGO groups), shared resources, and knowledges contribute to a common vision among these cooperating organizations.

The praxical implications of the NGO synergies are explained in Duncan-Andrade and Morrell's (2008) idea regarding CCCoP, which is defined as recognizing "the existence of a dominant set of institutional norms and practices and intentionally sets itself up to counter those norms and practices" in order to develop "a critical and engaged citizenry with a democratic sensibility that critiques and acts against all forms of inequality" (p. 11). There are several indicators that reflect the counter-cultural aspect of the MC; for instance, its very existence reifies a critical, transformational and oppositional ideology held by social justice and civil rights groups that runs in direct opposition to the dominant beliefs held by many Lebanese people.

While the CCCoP framework stems from research conducted in urban high schools in the United States, this idea is easily recognizable in (and transferable to) the MC, in that both target groups (Black, Latinx, and Native American populations in the United States and African and Southeast Asian women in Beirut) encounter structural and systemic inequalities and racism in their everyday lived experiences in contested social spaces. This critical pedagogical framework as enacted by volunteer teachers and students in a dialogic manner seeks to activate an oppositional and critical consciousness within migrant students, transforming the classroom space into an empowering, constructivist, and activist space.

The "counter-cultural" characteristic of the CCCoP model is evocative of Vygotskian[5] thought as a lens for studying the issues of subaltern education, and in particular the mediated learning that occurs in the relationship between culturally organized activities and cognition. In this study, the volunteer teachers I interviewed recognized that "cognition is embedded in the social and cultural worlds" of the learner, which highlights the importance of "contextual factors to the cognitive process" (Moll, 1990, p. ix) as evidenced by a curriculum that speaks to their lived experiences. Teachers recognize the criticality in contextualizing the lived experiences of their students in the classroom space, especially since their lives are fraught with almost daily direct and indirect interactions with blatant racism, xenophobia, segregation, and in some cases, physical and sexual abuse. Migrant workers laboring in the Middle East/SWANA and Gulf region belong to marginalized, subaltern groups. They experience much stress and trauma not only in their home countries, but in the country in which they labor. As I have detailed throughout this book, migrant domestic workers often encounter sexual assault by employers, physical abuse, mental and emotional distress; a policing of their every movement; withholding their wages; in essence, human trafficking. According to Zipin (2009), such traumatic events call for a "pedagogical and ethical commitment" (Moll, 2014, p. 142) to contextualize the "dark funds of knowledge" (Zipin, 2009) subaltern groups have accumulated. And, those in positions to empower at the organizational level (e.g., coordinators and migrant leaders) and educational level (e.g., teachers) at the MC recognize the importance of culturally contextualizing their space, as evidenced by the myriad cultural relics hanging on the MC walls and the availability of a kitchen space to cook the foods of their homelands, which is often not permitted in the homes of their employers.

ZPD and Scaffolding as an Organizational Method for NGO Management

Vygotsky's contributions[6] to the advancement and understanding of learning processes are rooted in his sociocultural model. According to Rosa and Montero (1990), "[Vygotsky's] starting point was the consideration that the higher psychological processes have a cultural origin. In order to develop this principle, he elaborated a theory of how the developing individual acquired these processes from his or her culture" (p. 79). From a critical pedagogical standpoint, within the space of the classroom, the critical educator places emphasis on the students' lived experiences, which typically encompass the cultural, economic, political, and ideological facets that affect cognitive development (Kanpol, 1997). For the critical educator, Vygotskian ideas, such as the sociohistorical model and the zone of proximal development, inform their classroom practices, serves as an instructional mechanism, and shapes curriculum; the teacher strives to "encourage students to see themselves and how they became themselves from the perspective of other people. In this context we gain the benefit of self-knowledge and thus the ability to change ourselves in say, emancipatory ways..." (Kanpol, 1997, p. 68).

A key notion of Vygotskian thought is that "human beings and their social worlds are inseparable. They are embedded in each other; thus, human thinking is irreducible to individual properties or traits" (González, et al., 2005, p. 261). Vygotsky emphasized the importance of external artifacts (such as signs and symbols) facilitating the learning process. Probably his most salient work within the field of education is the concept known as the zone of proximal development (ZPD or, "the zone"). According to Moll (1990),

> ...Vygotsky developed the zone, in part, as a critique, and as an alternative to static, individual testing, namely IQ testing. He claimed that static measures assess mental functioning that has already matured, fossilized, to use Vygotsky's term (1978); maturing or developing mental functions must be fostered and assessed through collaborative, not independent or isolated activities. (p. 3)

In a classroom context, the holistic nature of the zone as a phenomenon and scaffolding as a teaching practice facilitates learning by way of the lived experience of the student and via a connectedness with the educator in a "safe" space for that learning to occur. The concept of the zone is also utilized for capturing "the relationship in schooling between... 'everyday' and 'scientific' concepts" in that they are reciprocal in nature and mediate each other (González, et al., 2005, p. 261).

While scaffolding is typically utilized for classroom instruction, its application is visible in the functionality of the management of the NGO system in this study. Recall that Fakira, the general coordinator of Tamkin, meets often with Suba, the coordinator of the MC. As coordinator, her duties include the management of the Center, the day-to-day duties such as being present for patrons' questions and to help with computer use, and the administrative duties, such as making sure bills are paid on time. Fakira gives Suba a wide girth in terms of how she chooses to run the Center, and Fakira is always available to assist her with questions. They meet daily so Suba has a support system in Fakira's participation, who acts as a scaffold instead of a manager or authority figure. The way these NGOs and collectives operate is demonstrative of Vygotsky's notion of whole activities. According to Moll (1990),

> Vygotsky proposed partitioning the whole into what he called units... In contrast to atomistic elements, units designated a product of analysis that contained all the basic characteristics of the whole. The unit, then, is an irreducible part of the whole....Vygotsky rejected artificial divisions and abstractions and insisted on what we would call a holistic approach: The unit of study must be psychological activity in all its complexity, not in isolation. (p. 6)

An aspect of the dialectic is present in the functionality of this symbiotic NGO system and in the activist and migrant community, at the macro, meso and micro levels. Each unit is necessary for the functionality of the whole: The MC, Tamkin, and the MWEG all work in tandem and symbiotically to inform a classroom space where messages of anti-racism, feminism, and human rights create transformative learning for students, all mediated by the niche opening of this NGO system (see Figure 7.2).

Recent disastrous events on the global stage suggest that "The world is in urgent need of reinterpretation" (Kincheloe, 2008, p. 46), much like after World War I. This study's contribution to the theorizing of practices of subaltern groups hopes to heed the call for a paradigm shift in development studies and practice by utilizing an educational and anthropological lens and contribute a critical subaltern praxis to the educational domain within the NGO sector (and other places of teaching and learning). According to

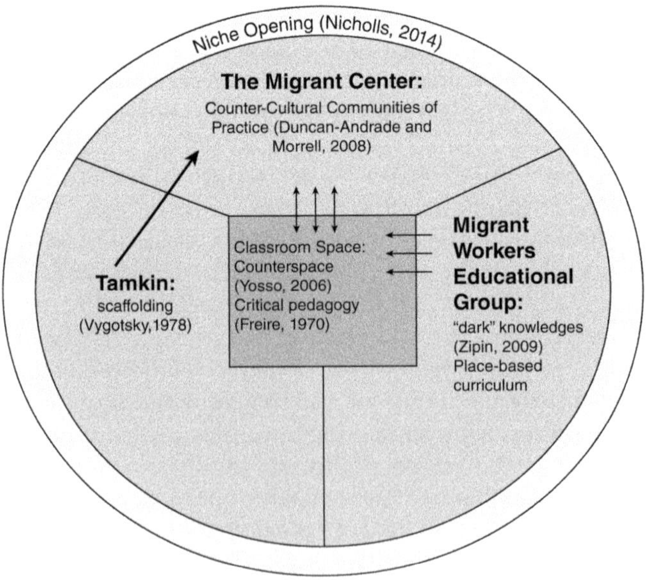

Figure 7.2 Critical subaltern practice model

Duncan-Andrade and Morrell (2008), a classroom that situates "the core principles of critical pedagogy" and couples this with "empirical data from theoretically informed practice" constructs a grounded theory that bridges the disconnect between theory and practice (p. 49), which is the aim of this project.

Discussion and Implications of a Critical Subaltern Pedagogy and Practice

This study brings to the field of education and development studies an understanding of how marginalized groups, particularly migrant domestic workers who partake in transnational movement, navigate systems of oppression. Subaltern ways of knowing resonate from this process through education, community building, and partnership with advocates and activists. Here I will discuss the implications of a critical subaltern pedagogy and practice in this NGO system and issues for further study.

Technology and Activism of Migrant Domestic Workers

Since the advent of the internet, the use of social media among suppressed groups is not new; Iran's youth, who have endured the oppression of a garrison state for the past 30 years, started using blogs in the early 2000's in an attempt to circumvent the tyrannical state system and as a way to share and create knowledge online (Alavi, 2005). Also noteworthy is the use of social media in Iran to contest the alleged fraudulent presidential elections between Mir Hossein Mousavi and Mahmoud Ahmadinejad in summer 2009 (Shirky, 2011) and the 2011 Arab Uprisings in Egypt (Papic & Noonan, 2011). Migrant domestic workers have also harnessed the power of social media in Lebanon using Facebook and YouTube as a tool for activism to appropriate their voices of resistance against human rights atrocities.

The ancillary function of a critical subaltern pedagogy and practice linking social media, education, and community activism illuminates the use of new media within oppressed communities. We learned how Ethiopian migrant workers helped compose a YouTube video with written messages in English, Arabic, and their native language of Amharic protesting Alem Dechasa's death, and we learned how individual migrant workers and Lebanese activists use Facebook as a means for economic gain and to protest abusive treatment.

These examples depict the ubiquitous and ever-present nature of the internet and social media when it is accessible to oppressed groups, in this case, migrant domestic workers. Most people in Western, developed countries have 24/7 internet access by virtue of home internet access and/or public access at schools, coffee shops, fast food restaurants, and libraries;

however, for most migrant workers in Lebanon, who work upwards of 12–15 hours per day; whose physical movements are surveilled 24 hours a day, 7 days a week; whose meager paychecks cannot afford the expensive coffee drinks at coffee shops; and, even if these limitations did not exist, migrant workers are frequently not allowed into coffee shops, their access to the internet is extremely limited. However, by way of the MC, migrant workers have access to computers with internet connection. This activist space performs as a facilitatory function for access to social media platforms. Therefore, the physical space of the MC acts as the niche opening into cyberspace. When that opening presents itself, the potential for activism is unlimited.

Implications of a Critical Subaltern Pedagogy and Practice in U.S. Context

Subaltern groups are in need of educational services that better "fit" and contextualize their lived experiences. This study's contribution to the theorizing of practices of subaltern groups in nonformal educational settings in a global context heeds the call for a paradigm shift in development studies. I posit a critical subaltern pedagogy and practice within the NGO educational sector and other places of teaching and learning that serve refugee and migrant populations. An immediate example in the U.S. context is the arrival of refugees and their children from Afghanistan fleeing the Taliban in fall 2021. As of this writing, Afghan refugees are beginning entry into the United States (Hesson, 2021). As they begin the resettlement process in U.S. cities throughout the country, children will enter school systems which require teachers who can engage in critical and constructivist ways to enact a pedagogy and practice specific to marginalized border-crossers.

As the public education systems begin the work of addressing the educational needs of these children, it is imperative that educators are trained in critical subaltern pedagogy and practice. Teaching & Teacher Education (TTE) programs in our U.S. higher education institutions need to include teacher training courses that focus specifically on the education of subaltern groups. Such a curriculum would include three main components. First, a TTE program would include an area studies component to provide context of subaltern groups' lived experiences; second, a thorough grounding in critical pedagogy (Freire, 1970, 1985; Giroux, 1985, 2006), critical race theory (Ladson-Billings, 1995, 1998; hooks, 1990, 2014), critical spatial analysis (Soja, 1996, 2008, 2010), and postcolonial studies (Spivak, 1988; Said, 1978; Fanon, 1963) would be provided. Third, a component to learn about a critical subaltern practice is essential: how to create place-based curriculum; how to contextualize dark knowledges and create niche openings; how to enact scaffolding among student groups, between students and teachers, and between communities and their schools; and, how to create counterspaces to build a powerful critical and social consciousness within not only our subaltern students, but all students.

Future Research in Critical Subaltern Pedagogy and Practice

In order to understand how a critical subaltern pedagogy and practice would function in a U.S. classroom, further ethnographic studies that implement a critical subaltern praxis would be beneficial; it would require training teachers in the Funds of Knowledge (González et al., 2005) tradition of research in addition to training in post-traumatic stress of students in classroom contexts. Those trained teachers would implement such a praxis by way of home visits, taking detailed field notes related to the informal teaching and learning that occurs in the home space between family members. Afterward, teachers would engage in active reflection with their fellow teachers. These home-based funds of knowledge inform culturally relevant and place-based curricula.

According to Duncan-Andrade and Morrell (2008), a classroom that situates "the core principles of critical pedagogy" and couples this with "empirical data from theoretically informed practice" constructs a grounded theory that bridges the disconnect between theory and practice (p. 49), which is the aim of this project.

Notes

1 Matters of choice between resisting and resigning oneself to dominant power structures are dependent on context; for instance, if a worker's employer forcibly confines her and abuses her emotionally, psychologically, sexually, and physically, her choice to resist may be met with untimely death at the hands of the employer. One domestic worker may have the luxury of choice to resist or resign, while another's physical movements are so severely limited, matters of choice do not exist.
2 For more information on "voluntourism" see Zakaria (2014).
3 Educational opportunities for subaltern groups often depend on age, immigration status, and resettlement country. In the United States, all children regardless of immigration status have access to a free public education, kindergarten through 12th grade, and children younger than kindergarten age can often qualify for Head Start, a U.S.-government funded preschool program. Adults with legal refugee status can register for basic education courses at local community colleges, and/or NGOs like International Refugee Committee offer English as a Foreign Language courses for free.
4 While this study focuses on the education of adults in NGO spaces when conceptualizing a subaltern pedagogical theory and practice, that does not mean a subaltern praxis is not relevant for children of refugees and migrant workers in U.S. public schools; on the contrary, such praxical implications are expedient in the schools located in the border regions and other U.S. schools, especially in light of the recent influx of Central American (majority)

unaccompanied children fleeing the violence in their homelands and seeking asylum in the United States. A subaltern praxis would incorporate the "dark funds of knowledge" (Zipin, 2009), or the deeper knowledges that some students have accumulated in their lifeworlds. However, children of undocumented immigrants in the United States pose a special case in that many of these children are not aware of their undocumented status until they attempt to enroll in college, apply for financial aid, obtain a driver's license, or apply for a job, all of which require a U.S. social security number and birth certificate (Gonzales, 2011). It is important that the academy as a whole and critical practitioners and scholars in particular continue to monitor the trajectory of these students who come to learn of their "illegality" as adolescents. For more on this topic, see Gonzales (2011), Galindo (2012), Nicholls (2014), Perez et al. (2009), Muñoz and Maldonado (2012).

5 Lev Vygotsky, a Russian philosopher, theorist, and psychologist, departed from the decontextualized, individualistic psychology of his contemporaries (such as developmental psychologist Jean Piaget) and instead placed emphasis on the necessity of situating the individual within his/her social, cultural, and historical context; in so doing, he recognized the importance of the sociocultural model and contextualization on cognitive development.

6 Critical pedagogues such as Paulo Freire recognize the value of Vygotsky's work within critical pedagogy's epistemological base. In *We Make the Road by Walking: Conversations on Education and Social Change* (1990), Horton and Freire discuss their admiration for scholars such as Frantz Fanon and Albert Memmi, and they say this about Vygotsky: "The third one who 'influenced' me without knowing it was the famous Russian psychologist Lev Vygotsky, who wrote a beautiful, fantastic book, *Thought and Language*. When I read him for the first time, I became frightened and happy because of the things I was reading" (p. 36). This excerpt illustrates that thephilosophical traditions and influences that inform critical pedagogy are interdisciplinary in nature, resulting in a rich and nuanced ontological and epistemological base.

References

Abu-Lughod, L. (1990). The romance of resistance: Tracing transformations of power through Bedouin women. *American Ethnologist*, *17*(1), 41–55.

Abu-Lughod, L. (2002). Do Muslim women really need saving? Anthropological reflections on cultural relativism and its others. *American Anthropologist*, *104*(3), 783–790. DOI: 10.1525/aa.2002.104.3.783

Alavi, N. (2005). *We are Iran: The Persian blogs*. Boca Raton, FL: Catapult.

Aronowitz, S., & Giroux, H. A. (1993). *Education still under siege*. London: Bergin and Garvey. DOI: 10.4324/9780203222034

Bernal, D. D. (2006). Learning and living pedagogies of the home. In D. D. Bernal, C. A. Elenes, F. E. Godinez, and S. Villenas (Eds.), *Chicana/Latina education in everyday life* (pp. 197–213). Albany, NY: State University of New York Press.

Bhabha, H. (1994). *The location of culture*. New York, NY: Routledge. DOI: 10.4324/9780203820551

Butler, C. (2012). *Henri Lefebvre: Spatial politics, everyday life and the right to the city*. London: Routledge-Cavendish.

Canipe, C., & Rosenberg, M. (2021). U.S. immigration border apprehensions. Retrieved from https://graphics.reuters.com/USA-IMMIGRATION/BORDER/xklpyoalapg/index.html

Charmaz, K. (2006). *Constructing grounded theory: A practical guide through qualitative analysis*. London: Sage Publishers.

Damon, A. (2013, February 11). *Not all colors welcomed in Lebanon's cultural tapestry. CNN*. Retrieved from http://edition.cnn.com/2013/02/10/world/meast/lebanon-racism-migrants-sting/?hpt=hp_c2

Du Bois, W. E. B. (1903). *The souls of black folk*. Chicago, IL: A.C. McClurg and Co.

Duncan-Andrade, J. M. R., & Morrell, E. (2008). *The art of critical pedagogy: Possibilities for moving from theory to practice*. New York, NY: Peter Lang Publishing. DOI: 10.3726/b12771

Escobar, A. (2000). Beyond the search for a paradigm? Post-development and beyond. *Development*, *43*(4), 11–14.

Fanon, F. (1963). *The wretched of the earth*. New York, NY: Grove Press.

Figures at a glance. (2020). Retrieved from https://www.unhcr.org/en-us/figures-at-a-glance.html

Freire, P. (1970). *Pedagogy of the oppressed*. New York, NY: Herder and Herder.

Freire, P. (1985). Reading the world and reading the word: An interview with Paulo Freire. *Language Arts*, *62*(1), 15–21.

Galindo, R. (2012). Undocumented & unafraid: The DREAM Act 5 and the public disclosure of undocumented status as a political Act. *The Urban Review*, *44*(5), 589–611. DOI: 10.1007/s11256-012-0219-0

Geisler, C., & Currens, B. (2017). Impediments to inland resettlement under conditions of accelerated sea level rise. *Land Use Policy*, *66*, 322–330. DOI: 10.1016/j.landusepol.2017.03.029

Giroux, H. (1985). Introduction. In P. Freire (Ed.), *The politics of education: Culture, power, and liberation* (pp. xi–xxvii). Westport, CT: Greenwood Publishing Group. DOI: 10.1007/978-1-349-17771-4

Giroux, H. A. (2006). *The Giroux reader*. New York, NY: Routledge. https://doi.org/10.4324/9781315634487

Giroux, H. (2010). Lessons from Paulo Freire. *Chronicle of Higher Education*, *57*(9), B15–B16.

González, N. (2005). Beyond culture: The hybridity of funds of knowledge. In N. González, L. C. Moll, & C. Amanti (Eds.), *Funds of knowledge: Theorizing practices in households, communities, and classrooms* (pp. 29–46). Mahwah, NJ: Lawrence Erlbaum and Associates. DOI: 10.4324/9781410613462-7

González, N. (2006). Testimonios of border identities: "Una mujer acomedida donde quiera cabe". In D. D. Bernal, C. A. Elenes, F. E. Godinez, & S. Villenas (Eds.), *Chicana/Latina education in everyday life* (pp. 197–213). Albany, NY: State University of New York Press.

Gonzales, R. G. (2011). Learning to be illegal: Undocumented youth and shifting legal contexts in the transition to adulthood. *American Sociological Review*, *76*(4), 602–619. DOI: 10.1177/0003122411411901

González, N., Moll, L. C., & Amanti, C. (Eds.). (2005). *Funds of knowledge: Theorizing practices in households, communities, and classrooms*. Mahwah, NJ: Lawrence Erlbaum and Associates. DOI: 10.4324/9781410613462

Hesson, T. (2021, August 26). Explainer: Who are the Afghan refugees coming to the U.S. and what happens when they arrive? Retrieved from https://www.reuters.com/ Retrieved from https://www.reuters.com/world/who-are-afghan-refugees-coming-us-what-happens-when-they-arrive-2021-08-26/

hooks, b. (1990). Postmodern blackness. In *Yearning: Race, gender, and cultural politics*. Boston, MA: South End Press. DOI: 10.4324/9781315743110-9

hooks, b. (1994). *Teaching to Transgress: Education as the Practice of Freedom*. New York: Routledge.

hooks, b (2014). *Teaching to transgress: Education as the practice of freedom*. New York, NY: Routledge.

Horton, M., & Freire, P. (1990). *We make the road by walking: Conversations on education and social change*. Philadelphia, PA: Temple University Press.

Jamali, D., & Keshishian, T. (2009). Uneasy alliances: Lessons learned from partnerships between businesses and NGOs in the context of CSR. *Journal of Business Ethics*, *84*(2), 277–295. DOI: 10.1007/s10551-008-9708-1

Jureidini, R. (2011). *An exploratory study of psychoanalytic and social factors in the abuse of migrant domestic workers by female employers in Lebanon*. Beirut: Kafa (enough) Violence & Exploitation Organization.

Kanpol, B. (1997). *Issues and trends in critical pedagogy*. New York, NY: Hampton Press.

Kapoor, I. (2004). Hyper-self-reflexive development? Spivak on representing the Third World "Other". *Third World Quarterly*, *25*(4), 627–647. DOI: 10.1080/01436590410001678898

Kincheloe, J. L. (2008). *The critical pedagogy primer*. New York, NY: Peter Lang Publishing. DOI: 10.3726/978-1-4539-1455-7

Ladson-Billings, G. (1995). Toward a theory of culturally relevant pedagogy. *American Educational Research Journal*, *32*(3), 465–491.

Ladson-Billings, G. (1998). Just what is critical race theory and what's it doing in a nice field like education? *International Journal of Qualitative Studies in Education*, *11*(1), 7–24.

Mohanty, C. T. (2003). "Under Western eyes" revisited: Feminist solidarity through anticapitalist struggles. *Signs*, *28*(2), 499–535.

Moll, L. C. (1990). *Vygotsky and education: Instructional implications and applications of sociohistorical psychology*. Cambridge: Cambridge University Press. DOI: 10.1017/cbo9781139173674

Moll, L. C. (2014). *L.S. Vygotsky and education*. New York, NY: Routledge. DOI: 10.4324/9780203156773

Moore, S. F. (1987). Explaining the present: Theoretical dilemmas in processual ethnography. *American Ethnologist*, *14*(4), 727–736. DOI: 10.1525/ae.1987.14.4.02a00080

Muñoz, S. M., & Maldonado, M. M. (2011). Counterstories of college persistence by undocumented Mexicana students: Navigating race, class, gender, and legal status. *International Journal of Qualitative Studies in Education*, *25*(3), 293–315. DOI: 10.1080/09518398.2010.529850

Nayak, A. (2008). On the way to theory: A processual approach. *Organization Studies*, *29*(2), 173–190. DOI: 10.1177/0170840607082227

Nicholls, W. J. (2014). From political opportunities to niche-openings: The dilemmas of mobilizing for immigrant rights in inhospitable environments. *Theory and Society*, *43*(1), 23–49. https://doi.org/10.1007/s11186-013-9208-x

Papic, M., & Noonan, S. (2011). Social media as a tool for protest. *Stratfor Global Intelligence*, *3*, 1–7.

Perez, W., Espinoza, R., Ramos, K., Coronado, H. M., & Cortes, R. (2009). Academic resilience among undocumented Latino students. *Hispanic Journal of Behavioral Sciences*, *31*(2), 149–181. DOI: 10.1177/0739986309333020

Pollock, D. C., & Van Reken., R. E. (2009). *Third culture kids: Growing up among worlds*. Boston, MA: Nicholas Brealey Publishing.

Reid, K. (2019). Iraq conflict: Facts, FAQs, and how to help. Retrieved from https://www.worldvision.org/refugees-news-stories/iraq-conflict-facts

Rosa, A., & Montero, I. (1990). The historical context of Vygotsky's work: A sociohistorical approach. In L. C. Moll (Ed.), *Vygotsky and education* (pp. 59–88). Cambridge: Cambridge University Press. DOI: 10.1017/cbo9781139173674.004

Saavedra, C. M., & Nymark, E. D. (2008). Borderland-Medtizaje feminism: Critical and indigenous methodologies. In N. K. Denzin, Y. S. Lincoln, & L. T. Smith (Eds.), *Handbook of critical and indigenous methodologies* (pp. 255–276). Los Angeles, CA: SAGE Publications.

Saavedra, C. M., & Pérez, M. S. (2017). Chicana/Latina feminist critical qualitative inquiry: Meditations on global solidarity, spirituality, and the land. *International Review of Qualitative Research*, *10*(4), 450–467. DOI: 10.1525/irqr.2017.10.4.450

Said, E. (1978). *Orientalism: Western conceptions of the orient*. Routledge and Kegan Paul Ltd.

Sharma, A. (2008). *Logics of Empowerment: Development, gender, and governance in neoliberal India*. Minneapolis: University of Minnesota Press.

Sherpa, C. (2014). *Countering the hegemony of "hegemony" in social science: A Marxist critique of "subaltern" pedagogy in Indian academia*. International Conference on Educational Transformation and Transformative Education: Possibilities and Alternatives to the Educational Crisis. Abstract retrieved from http://sau.ac.in/~mlta/soc/abstracts.html

Shirky, C. (2011). The political power of social media: Technology, the public sphere, and political change. *Foreign Affairs*, 28–41.

Soja, E. W. (1996). *Thirdspace: Journeys to Los Angeles and other real-and-imagined places*. Malden, MA: Blackwell Publishers.

Soja, E. W. (2008). Thirdspace: Toward a new consciousness of space and spatiality. In K. Ikas & G. Wagner (Eds.), *Communicating in the third space* (pp. 63–75). New York, NY: Routledge. DOI: 10.4324/9780203891162-10

Soja, E. W. (2010). *Seeking spatial justice*. Minneapolis, MN: University of Minnesota Press. DOI: 10.5749/minnesota/9780816666676.003.0005

Spivak, G. C. (1988). Can the subaltern speak? In C. Nelson & L. Grossberg (Eds.), *Marxism and the interpretation of culture* (pp. 271–314). Champaign, IL: University of Illinois Press. DOI: 10.1007/978-1-349-19059-1

United Nations High Commissioner for Refugees. (2022). Operational data portal: Ukraine refugee situation. Retrieved from https://data2.unhcr.org/en/situations/ukraine

Villaverde, L. (2008). *Feminist theories and education*. New York, NY: Peter Lang Publishing.

Vygotsky, L. S. (1978). *Mind in society: The development of higher psychological processes*. Cambridge, MA: Harvard University Press. DOI: 10.2307/j.ctvjf9vz4

Vygotsky, L. S. (2012). *Thought and language*. Cambridge: MIT Press.

Yegenoglu, M. (1998). *Colonial fantasies: Towards a feminist reading of Orientalism*. Cambridge: Cambridge University Press.

Yosso, T. J. (2006). *Critical race counterstories along the Chicana/Chicano educational pipeline*. New York, NY: Routledge.

Yosso, T. J. (2013). *Critical race counterstories along the Chicana/Chicano educational pipeline*. New York, NY: Routledge. DOI: 10.4324/9780203624821

Zakaria, R. (2014, April 21). The White tourist's burden. *Al Jazeera America*. Retrieved from http://america.aljazeera.com/

Zipin, L. (2009). Dark funds of knowledge, deep funds of pedagogy: Exploring boundaries between lifeworlds and schools. *Discourse: Studies in the Cultural Politics of Education*, *30*(3), 317–331. DOI: 10.1080/01596300903037044

Index

For Product Safety Concerns and Information please contact our EU representative GPSR@taylorandfrancis.com
Taylor & Francis Verlag GmbH, Kaufingerstraße 24, 80331 München, Germany

www.ingramcontent.com/pod-product-compliance
Ingram Content Group UK Ltd.
Pitfield, Milton Keynes, MK11 3LW, UK
UKHW022354190926
475702UK00015B/2285
* 9 7 8 0 3 6 7 7 6 3 4 8 0 *